Guide to Criticism on
Don Quijote (1790-1893)

Juan de la Cuesta
Hispanic Monographs

Series: *Documentación cervantina* Nº 6

An Analytical and Bibliographical Guide to Criticism on *Don Quijote* (1790-1893)

by

DANA B. DRAKE

Virginia Polytechnic Institute and State University

and

DOMINICK L. FINELLO

Rider College

Juan de la Cuesta
Newark, Delaware

Copyright © 1987 by Juan de la Cuesta—Hispanic Monographs
270 Indian Road
Newark, Delware 19711

MANUFACTURED IN THE UNITED STATES OF AMERICA
Printed on paper with a pH of 7.0.

ISBN: 0-936388-27-7

CONTENTS

*For Sterling A. Stoudemire, Hensley C. Woodbridge,
John J. Allen, and Anita Malebranche.*

D. D.

For Janet, Carmine, and Frances Finello.

D. F.

Preface

THIS WORK IS THE first comprehensive critical and bibliographical guide to nineteenth-century research on *Don Quijote* published since Leopoldo Rius' *Bibliografía crítica de las obras de Miguel de Cervantes Saavedra, 1895-1904.* Our goal has been to present a clear, complete, and objective picture of the fortunes of the *Quijote* in that century. To this end we offer in the introduction to this book an analysis of nineteenth-century commentary, with emphasis on the long-neglected Spanish criticism of the era. This is followed by a list of principal sources employed in the preparation of our study. The main body of the book contains bibliographical entries with substantial summaries of books, articles, pamphlets, reviews, and notes of significant import to *Quijote* criticism. Biographies, editions of the *Quijote*, bibliographical catalogues, *homenajes*, and miscellaneous items are also included if they have proven to contain noteworthy commentary on the *Quijote*. At the end of this volume appear indexes to aid in its use.

Rius' work continues to have the highest value to scholars investigating Cervantine criticism from its beginnings to the end of the nineteenth century. However, Rius does not bring materials of a purely analytical nature into sharp focus, because he does not isolate them from items of a strictly historical, biographical, or textual sort. In our study we have gleaned from the larger body of nineteenth-century research specifically analytical material. We have reconstructed and synthesized this diverse and voluminous bibliographical corpus in our initial essay and then summarized in detailed fashion nearly all of its 504 sources so that the reader may have a complete idea of each critic's interpretation. Rius, we note, anthologized them, an approach that, despite its worthiness, is not adequate for presenting fully the views of some of these early Cervantists.

In this main body of our study we have included all major publications of Spain, the rest of Europe, and America, and to round out the picture, we have added many brief but interesting items. We have not attempted to record every allusion to the *Quijote* registered during the nineteenth century. That would be an impossible task and would not serve our purpose of drawing an accurate yet unincumbered picture of this body of criticism as a whole.

In the course of our research we discovered many sources, especially outside Spain, which were apparently unknown to Rius or to other scholars. Hence the reader will find a vastly expanded study of European and American critiques. This non-Spanish section of the book is arranged chronologically by country (except Latin America, which is under one heading). We felt that this geographical separation and chronological grouping would be most practical, since interested scholars might wish to examine particular national attitudes and perspectives and follow them over an extended period of time.

We have handled virtually every source directly and in most cases in the first edition. However, at times we consulted a second or later edition. Furthermore, as we indicate in the text, it was occasionally necessary for us to rely upon second-hand information when an item could not be located.

The time span 1790-1893 was selected because Paolo Cherchi's *Capitoli di critica cervantina (1605-1789)* brings us up to 1790, and Dana Drake's recent bibliographies, begun in 1974, resume where the present work leaves off, at the end of 1893. We originally intended to adhere strictly to the opening and closing dates, 1790-1893 inclusive, but in a few instances we added earlier or later items, which we believe necessary for the understanding of the material presented in this book.

In some respects this was an enormous undertaking, and we called upon colleagues who generously gave of their time to read the manuscript or to assist in locating materials. We are especially indebted to John J. Allen, R. R. Anderson, Robin Bromley, and W. Pierre Jacoebée. We gratefully acknowledge the services of the Hispanic Society of America and the Carol Newman Library at Virginia Polytechnic Institute and State University. Finally, to the National Endowment for the Humanities, Rider College, and Virginia Polytechnic Institute go our thanks for grants supporting this project.

DANA B. DRAKE
Blacksburg, Virginia

DOMINICK FINELLO
Brooklyn, New York

Nineteenth-Century
Interpretations of the *Quijote*:
A Synthesis

ET US BEGIN OUR story of the critical and artistic success of the *Quijote* in the nineteenth century with the historical perspective that selected earlier opinions of the novel from Spain and the rest of Europe provide. Because *Quijote* criticism in this pre-nineteenth-century phase, examined fully in Paolo Cherchi's admirable book (14), is sometimes naïve and inconclusive and other times sparse, it is difficult to characterize. In France, however, prejudices against the Spaniards evidently influenced early evaluations of Cervantes' novel. Although the *Quijote* had generated a measure of enthusiasm and was appreciated by such writers as Jean de La Fontaine and Charles de Saint-Evremond, many censured it. In an age of intense rationalism, in which reason was seen as the underlying impulse of truth and beauty and as the key to resolving society's ills, French critics tended to search for a moral in literature, or for that which was useful. They saw the *Quijote* therefore as primarily a satire written to attack Spanish obscurantism, the Inquisition, and Scholasticism. In addition, French proponents of both the "Ancients" and "Moderns," taking a narrow view of the concepts of verisimilitude and decorum as their standard, found the events and characters of the *Quijote* lacking in truth. Charles Sorel, J. Chapelain, and Pierre Perrault, for instance, were disturbed by the work's "baseness" and

1

improbability. Late seventeenth-and early eighteenth-century critics also found it difficult to appreciate the intrinsic value of the *Quijote*. René Rapin, quoting a Spaniard, concluded in 1672 that the novel was fundamentally an attack on the Duke of Lerma and a parody of Spain and its chivalric customs, an idea which has enjoyed much popularity among critics everywhere throughout the centuries; and in 1688, an anonymous writer determined that the hero of the *Quijote* was a caricature of Ignatius of Loyola, a belief accepted by Voltaire in the following century. Even when positive, French criticism revealed an anti-Spanish bias: some scholars adhered to the dictum of Montesquieu that the *Quijote* was the only "good" literary work produced by the Spaniards. In view of this, it becomes clear that early French critics did not fully understand the *Quijote*'s universality or literary merit. In fact, no comprehensive interpretation of the *Quijote* was produced in France until the nineteenth century.

In England, critics as eminent as William Temple concurred with their French counterpart René Rapin. In 1690, Temple accused the author of the *Quijote* of being a cause of the ruin of Spain and of subjecting romantic love and honor to ridicule. George Carleton, in his *Memoirs of an English Officer* (1728), agreed with him, and like Rapin and Temple, attributed this judgment to a Spaniard. However, later English reactions to the *Quijote* serve as a contrast to those of the French. Initially, Peter Motteux, in his English translation of 1700, had found the novel a mirror of humanity, not an attempt to satirize Spain, and asserted that in all men there was something of Don Quijote. In fact, the English came to revere Cervantes' hero fairly early. Stuart Tave observes that while there were only one or two hints during the early eighteenth century that Don Quijote was anything other than "a figure of mockery, or, at best, a symbol of wrong-headedness" (48), that belief changed dramatically as the century moved on. Alexander Pope, in a letter to George Lyttleton in 1739, stated that a mutual friend was "so very a child in true simplicity of heart, that I love him, as he loves Don Quixote, for being the most moral and reasoning man in the world," a lofty description of Don Quijote that would be repeated often in the following century. Some ten years after Pope, Samuel Johnson pointed out that most readers loved, identified with, and even pitied Cervantes' hero. "When we pity him," said Johnson, "we reflect on our own disappointments, and when we laugh, our hearts inform us that he is not more ridiculous than ourselves, except that he tells us what we have only thought." In this same period, Henry Fielding created various lovably quixotic characters, such as Parson Adams, while his sister, Sarah, claimed that it was wrong to single out the comic element in Cervantes' novel, since in Don Quijote's madness and extraordinary good sense there was a beautiful representation of human nature. In the following year, Tobias Smollett, seeking to determine the target of Cervantes' satire, claimed that he attacked the absurdities of the books of chivalry but did not impugn the spirit of knight-errantry itself. Toward the end of the century, in 1785, Clara Reeve tersely expressed a fundamental paradox in understanding Cervantes' masterpiece: the reader felt obliged to respect the *Quijote* and the books it condemned at the same time. Finding the protagonist more noble with all his idiosyncrasies than the ordinary man absorbed in his worthless self, Reeve raised a problem that romantic writers would later resolve with a new definition of tragedy, which characterized the mad Knight as a champion of lofty ideals that were scorned but never destroyed by the vulgar and prosaic world. Unlike the French, the British discovered much of the genius of Cervantes' art long before the nineteenth century. They were among the first outside Spain to display enthusiasm and admiration for Cervantes and his *Quijote* and to realize that the work was more complex than the simple satire many had thought it to be.

In Germany, critics applied French rationalistic ideas to the *Quijote* during the first part of the eighteenth century, regarding it as an assault on excesses in literature and on the Spanish taste for bizarre adventures. J. C. Gottsched saw the *Quijote* as a deathblow to knight-errantry, and C. M. Wieland thought the work an attack on unbridled imagination. In 1741, however, Johann Bodmer moved toward the sympathetic English view of the *Quijote,* declaring that one could find an element of wonder in Cervantes' personification of wisdom and folly. With Bodmer, too, Don Quijote became a universal figure, not a Spaniard. Later in the century, J. G. Herder's observations prognosticated four central tenets of the early nineteenth-century romantics: (1) that Sancho is the living model of the people, and his everyday sayings contain their wisdom; (2) that the *Quijote* is the comic epic upon which modern romance is based; (3) that the *Quijote* is a patriotic novel and the expression of the spirit of the Spanish people; and (4) that the reader should empathize with the misunderstood hero. According to Herder, Sancho emerges as the true hero of the novel, while Don Quijote, a man with beautiful qualities, is too severely mistreated. Thus Herder joins other commentators who first observed the theme of cruelty underscored by many critics outside Spain since the eighteenth century.

The often sporadic criticism from Italy was largely negative and anti-Spanish. G. Casanova conceded that the *Quijote* was an admirable work, but also maintained (c. 1767) that its goal was futile, that its episodes lacked variety, and that its general form was monotonous. A writer, Casanova asserted, should not reproduce what time will erase, and Cervantes' satire continually directed itself at an absurdity that could not survive him. A notable exception to the anti-Spanish commentary among Italian critics was that of Carlo Denina, but his remarks were limited to the brief statement that the *Quijote* was an "original work" (1786). Otherwise, according to Cherchi, Italians generally lacked interest in Cervantes until the appearance of the post-romantics C. De Lollis, G. Toffanin, B. Croce, P. Savj-López, and M. Casella.

In Spain, besides a few brief comments on the *Quijote* by Cervantes' contemporaries and near-contemporaries, the first real plaudits did not appear until 1672, when Nicolás Antonio wrote of the novel's popularity. Before that, a critique by Mateo de la Bastida in 1668 had constituted the first systematic analysis of the *Quijote* in Spain. Bastida claimed a place for it in world literature by comparing it with the Apuleius' *Golden Ass*. Interestingly enough, both Antonio and Bastida emphasized the importance of the *Quijote* as an attack on the novels of chivalry, which suggests the continuity of the conviction that the *Quijote* was primarily a satire of those books and the people who read them. Not all Spaniards, however, were favorably impressed by Cervantes' humor. Many believed that he disliked Spanish customs and that his novel led to the decline of Spanish values—an idea we have seen reported by writers like Temple and Carleton. Then in 1738, Lord Carteret published for Queen Caroline of England what was to become an early landmark in Cervantine criticism. This was an edition of the *Quijote* containing Gregorio de Mayans y Siscar's *Vida de Miguel de Cervantes Saavedra* (published a year earlier in Spain). Mayans, like Motteux, perceived the universality of the Don Quijote figure and praised Cervantes for his inventiveness and excellent style. He also devoted attention to alleged defects in the novel, especially the lack of verisimilitude in some of its episodes. Mayans' comments on the *Quijote* as a satire of human habits and customs, while not wholly original, proved beneficial for subsequent scholarly investigations of Cervantes' novel.

In mid-eighteenth-century Spain an interesting polemic arose between conservative defenders of Spanish institutions and reformers who wanted to bring Spain into the orbit of the European community. The conservatives condemned Cervantes' apparent attack on Spanish chivalric customs in the figure of his mad Knight, while their opponents, sensitive to the delicacy and purity of Cervantes' artistic invention, believed that he created original Spanish types and thereby buoyed esteem for the Spanish character and spirit. For instance, in 1772 José Cadalso, among the reformers, took issue with Montesquieu's view that Spain's only "good" book was the *Quijote* and maintained, first, that Cervantes' novel was by no means Spain's only worthy book, and second, that his criticisms were selective, only debunking certain books of chivalry along with specific works of drama. In his *Cartas marruecas* of 1774, Cadalso distinguished the literal meaning of the *Quijote* from its real meaning, finding a "conjunto de materias profundas e interesantes" beneath the extravagant acts of a madman. Cadalso's specific preoccupation arose from the general concern over the problem of Spain. Right-wing critics of the time perceived the *Quijote* as a parody of the absurdity of chivalry books, and so-called radical or left-wing critics saw in it a deeper, symbolic meaning connected with the destiny of Spain. These two tendencies intermittently took center stage in the Spanish criticism of this century and a good part of the next, as we shall see especially in the Benjumea era discussed below.

Before the prejudices of conservative critics against the *Quijote* could be eliminated, the novel had to be reevaluated and its high literary and historical merit had to be recognized. This was accomplished by Vicente de los Ríos in his introduction to the Royal Academy edition of the *Quijote* of 1780. Ríos emphasized both the originality and universality of Cervantes' novel and praised its unity and variety in his analysis of the protagonists' dual nature: Don Quijote's sanity alongside his madness and Sancho's ingenuousness alongside his maliciousness. Like other neoclassicists, Ríos lauded Cervantes for the moral value of his story, that of deriding the custom of reading chivalry books. He did not agree, however, with those who believed that Cervantes sought to destroy chivalry; he found instead that the *Quijote* merely attacked rashness. Nor did Ríos believe that Cervantes was satirizing only Spain, for chivalry flourished in every European country. Like Mayans before him, Ríos pointed out defects in the *Quijote*, but with more restraint, inferring from its geographical and chronological mistakes that the author wrote hastily and did not bother to proofread his manuscript. Ríos thus anticipated the common practice among nineteenth-century critics of finding fault with inaccuracies in Cervantes' text.

We may now make a few general statements about criticism of the *Quijote* prior to 1790. First, critics of the pre-nineteenth-century period tended to view the *Quijote*—and all imaginative literature—from a rigidly rational and moral standpoint, which helps us to understand why eighteenth-century neoclassicists thought the *Quijote* a supremely satirical work, highly critical of social behavior. Suspicious of sentimentality, they saw the *Quijote* as a satire against a specific historical phenomenon; thus critics like Ríos, for example, could not see why Don Quijote might inspire generosity in every man, an idea well established in England and Germany in the latter part of the eighteenth century. The second concerns the attitude toward the figure of Don Quijote, which began to grow in stature during the early eighteenth century in England and later in Germany until it emerged from its comic stereotype. At the same time, critics in France persisted in using the *Quijote* to argue in favor of their rationalistic positions and to demonstrate the cultural backwardness of Spain. And the view that Cervantes attacked Spain was, in fact, widely accepted, even in the author's own country, for well over a century. Therefore, the issue of Spain's contribution to European culture—What did Spain stand for? Was Don Quijote a symbol of Spain?—would surface only in later criticism. Finally, one should observe that a pessimistic strain developed early in *Quijote* criticism, chiefly manifested in the belief that the *Quijote* mocked the chivalric spirit and the heroic ideal by depicting its protagonist as essentially a foolish figure. We shall see how these tenets were adopted, expanded, or rejected by neoclassical and romantic critics in the years to follow.

NINETEENTH-CENTURY SPANISH CRITICISM

The late eighteenth-century critic's task was to establish the *Quijote* as a world classic and to make the Spaniard aware of that fact. This was facilitated by one of the first serious attempts at editing the *Quijote*—that of Reverend John Bowle, who published an edition of the novel in Salisbury, England in 1781. With its copious notes, prologue, and ample indexes, Bowle's edition considerably eased the labor of scholars in Spain who undertook the immense responsibility of working with the *Quijote*'s textual problems. Critical appraisal of the text by Spaniards began with Vicente de los Ríos, in the Royal Academy edition of 1780 (as we said), and Juan Antonio Pellicer in 1797 (58). Their work was continued by Agustín García Arrieta in 1827 and Joaquín Bastús y Carrera in 1832 (69), and culminated in Diego Clemencín's monumental *Comentario* and edition of the *Quijote*, dating from 1833 to 1839 (70), an investigation of the novel that not only raised issues which would be addressed throughout the nineteenth century, but also revealed the preoccupations of previous critics.

Language and style of the *Quijote* formed one of the nuclei of *Quijote* criticism from its genesis to the end of the nineteenth century. The attempt to recognize the *Quijote*'s language as pure (*castizo*) Castilian, which contributed so much to the richness of the Spanish idiom and indeed expressed the full spectrum of the Spaniard's philosophy, was the principal focus of this particular issue. Nevertheless, although most critics eagerly applauded the discovery of the treasures of Cervantes' language after more than 150 years of nonrecognition, there were a few skeptics. In 1805, García Arrieta (61) pointed out occasional lapses in Cervantes' style and attributed them to the novelist's inexactness and oversights. That Cervantes may have been a careless writer also troubled Clemencín; however, when Juan Eugenio Hartzenbusch disputed that accusation in his 1863 edition of the *Quijote* (110), there arose a rather lively debate about what some called Cervantes' negligence and trifling mistakes and what others insisted were more likely printers' errors. Some who disliked the *Quijote* even used Cervantes' "faulty" language as a subterfuge hiding their real reason for attacking the novel—moral outrage over Cervantes' apparent ridicule of the Spanish nobility. A case in point is Valentín de Foronda's *Observaciones sobre algunos puntos de la obra de Don Quijote*, 1807 (64), featuring a personal attack against Cervantes based on an exposé of his grammatical errors and "low" language. This was most ironic because Foronda recommended that the *Quijote* be studied by those wishing to learn to write proper Spanish.

As one might imagine, a torrent of opinion defended the excellence of Cervantes' prose. It was Antonio de Capmany in the 1780s (53) who recognized the extreme richness of Cervantes' formal discourse and wisdom and who complimented his sententious language. He lauded Cervantes' decorum, variety, and naturalness and asserted that because it possessed clarity and truth, his language could be understood by anyone, while Manuel José Quintana (59) believed that mistakes in the text of the *Quijote* demonstrated the author's freedom and ease. Writing in the journal *Revista de España, de las Indias y del Extranjero* (83), F. P. Anaya summed up succinctly the arguments of other early enthusiasts: Vicente de los Ríos found the *Quijote* most appropriate for those wishing to familiarize themselves with the Spanish language, and others said Cervantes was the much-needed master stylist who proved how beautifully thoughts could be expressed in Spanish at a time when the language was still in flux. Indeed, "purity," "simplicity," and "beauty" were the three terms most frequently employed to describe Cervantes' language by early commentators as they proclaimed the *Quijote* the standard model for Castilian prose.

The publication in 1791 of Sancho's proverbs in two manuals [(56), (57)] marks another important strain of *Quijote* commentary—the collections of Sancho's conversations with Don Quijote and the latter's advice to his Squire and the world at large that became gospels for both civil government and personal demeanor. Stating that young and old alike would find a profound philosophy of life in the novel, García Arrieta (66) published a list of maxims on various subjects treated in the *Quijote*, most of a moral nature. Similarly, in 1839 and 1842, Mariano de Rementería y Fica and Luis Igartuburu, respectively, wrote lists and dictionaries on the wisdom of Cervantes [(76), (81)].

An issue that commanded more attention than Cervantes' lan-guage or maxims was that of chivalry and its moral implications along with the satire of the partisans of that genre and the general decline of Spanish society, if not all of European civilization, exhibited by the decay of chivalric customs. Pellicer sensed that the principal aim of the *Quijote* was to check the deleterious effects of books of chivalry on their readers by making a mockery of the *Amadís* and its progeny. But the solutions to this riddle of the *Quijote* were not so simple, for some felt that parodies like it often tended to be frivolous. Quintana responded to this charge by declaring that no book that corrected men's customs could be considered a frivolity. The *Quijote* portrayed not simply a madman, but an *ingenious* one, who had the sense to destroy his own foolish schemes, thereby becoming a profoundly moral character. However, no single man, continued Quintana, no matter how generous, could put himself above the laws of his fellow men, and such scornful behavior, commonplace in books of chivalry, had to be rejected. Since these neoclassical scholars were steeped in the tradition of classical satire, moral judgments founded on Cervantes' ridicule of the books became the cornerstone of their thinking. Cervantes, they believed, descended from the ancient line of Juvenal.

Another preoccupation of these early nineteenth-century critics, as we said, involved the establishment of a rigorously corrected and annotated text of the *Quijote*. This was an arduous task because the earliest editions of Part I, 1605-1608, were terribly inconsistent and fraught with errors, some committed by printers and some by Cervantes himself. This prompted critics to try to identify the culprit, a problem that still plagues scholars today. Whatever the eventual upshot of this perennial debate, all remain indebted to the investigator who did so much to draw attention to Cervantes' poor editing—Diego Clemencín.

Clemencín represented to an extent the neoclassical school in that he abided by its requirements of unity, variety, and verisimilitude, concepts which the Canónigo used to launch an attack against books of chivalry in the final chapters of the 1605 *Quijote*. Such principles help partly, but not entirely, to explain Clemencín's brilliant success as an editor and scholar. His observations in the prologue to his *Comentario*, the tenor of which was tempered compared to the sometimes extravagantly laudatory interpretations of his contemporaries, suggest that the *Quijote* was a modern novel, a new genre with few established rules. Clemencín's goal was to study the literary and cultural influences on Cervantes' text. He began the critique by stating that the *Quijote* figured among the most moral of books, an idea consistent with the thinking of the early nineteenth century, and he claimed that Cervantes wrote the *Quijote* to reform the literary habits of those who avidly read books of chivalry. Clemencín also justly derided those who thought that Cervantes wrote the *Quijote* only to elicit laughter. In fact, the seriousness of Cervantes' satire was not fully appreciated until Clemencín and his generation took a long, hard look at Cervantes' novel.

Clemencín objected to the studies of Mayans, Ríos, and Pellicer, which, he believed, offered too little information about the literary and historical backgrounds of the novel and lacked an intricate analysis of the *Quijote*'s literary anthropology. We might add parenthetically that Clemencín had company in his critical task. V. Joaquín Bastús y Carrera (69) anticipated him with annotations published in the Royal Academy's 1832 edition. The chronology indicates that Bastús did not know of Clemencín's enormous project. Thus, he becomes the forerunner of Clemencín in his call for an elaborate examination of the customs of chivalry, such as jousting and knighting ceremonies, and in his search for the sources of the episodes of the *Quijote* in the books of chivalry themselves, achievements for which Bastús has not been given the credit he deserves. Clemencín's notes, however, are broader in scope, revealing an encyclopedic knowledge of the literature and history of the Ancients and the European and Spanish Middle Ages and Renaissance. While they are detailed to a fault and sometimes even trivial, they remain on the whole authoritative to our day.

The majority of these notes deal with linguistic usage and literary sources, arising especially from books of chivalry. Like others, Clemencín censured many words and expressions in the *Quijote* so effectively that his assumptions about the inaccuracies in specific passages endured until Francisco Rodríguez Marín answered him with his 1911 edition of the *Quijote*, arguing that Clemencín applied standards that were too rigorous. A description of a few of these notes, however, demonstrates not only their variety, but also how methodically Clemencín approached the *Quijote*. First, he carefully researches the identity of the place where Cervantes supposedly composed the novel (I, 1, note 1) and supplies information concerning the custom of the *velada de las armas* (I, 3, note 8). He then offers some insights into the little known fiction of the Spanish Golden Age (I, 6, note 43), explains why windmills are necessary in La Mancha (I, 8, note 1), and analyzes the Arthurian tradition in literature, explaining why Don Quijote uses the dead crow legend while discussing his profession with Vivaldo (I, 13, notes 10, 11, and 12). Next, he evaluates the poetry (I, 14, note 21), concluding that Cervantes had "escaso talento poético" in the "Grisóstomo-Marcela" interlude, and scrutinizes the character of Marcela, finding her speech "impertinente, afectado y ridículo" and her self-defense "ladina y habladora" (I, 14, note 21). Returning to poetry (I, 23, note 32), Clemencín describes what might be expected of the aesthetic skills of the knight-errant so that the reader can better understand why Don Quijote appreciated Cardenio's sonnets. Finally, in a passage recalling the Canónigo (I, 47, note 34), Clemencín criticizes the literature of chivalry: "Nos ceñiremos a dar algunas muestras en general del desconcierto con que los cronistas de los caballeros fingieron los disparates que tan justamente llama desaforados el Canónigo de Toledo." Clemencín, it appears, did not think that the Priest or the Canónigo were proposing that the novel of chivalry be saved. This, of course, calls to mind the perennial quarrel over Cervantes' real opinion of the books of chivalry: Did he like them?, or did he wish to destroy them? Most of Clemencín's contemporaries believed that the *Quijote* banished them forever from the face of the earth. One important exception, however, was Vicente Salvá (78), who was convinced that Cervantes did not wish to offer a blanket condemnation of the chivalric novel, but rather to purge it of its incredible events and situations, an attitude developed by critics who wrote later in the century.

Clemencín remains an authority, if perhaps only because he endeavored to explain allusions, motifs, and ideas unknown to practically any critic of his time; and needless to say, there was substantial reaction to him, some of it positive and some negative. Alberto Lista, in his *juicio crítico* (160) of the *Comentario* in 1833 (its final version appeared in *La Ilustración Española y Americana* in 1872), declared Clemencín's notes a unique contribution to Cervantine scholarship and a vast improvement over the attempts of Pellicer and Bowle. On the other hand, Juan Eugenio Hartzenbusch (82) and Juan Calderón (94) were quick to point out that Clemencín overstated the problems of Cervantes' grammatical errors and textual misprints. Later, others used Clemencín's *Comentario* as a sounding board for further controversy and varying interpretations of Cervantes' masterpiece, and with these debates we find Cervantine criticism maturing as it moved toward mid-century.

The number of scholars studying the *Quijote* during Clemencín's time was not great, but in the period immediately following, roughly between the early 1840s and the late 1850s, that number grew significantly; and among the signs of escalating interest in the novel stood conspicuously the famous *Buscapié* hoax (86) along with the heated outcry it provoked. The renowned critic and scholar Adolfo de Castro authored this "long, lost" pamphlet, which he contended, Cervantes published shortly after the first part of the *Quijote*. Castro explained that while the document had not been reprinted in the interim, it was known "by tradition," until uncovered at a book auction in Cádiz sometime in the late 1840s. The *Buscapié*, according to Castro, did not really serve as a "key" to hidden allusions in the *Quijote*, but rather vindicated the novel in the face of unjust censure. Castro's work consists of a conversation between the author of the *Quijote* and a *bachiller*, in which the *bachiller* argues that the hero of the novel is a foolish knight-errant, while the author defends it on the grounds that it provides good entertainment in a pleasing style. Castro added footnotes to the text to explain that, despite the claim of the earlier eighteenth-century legend of Antonio de Ruidíaz, the *Quijote* was not a *roman à clef* attacking certain persons, and in the 1851 edition of the *Buscapié* (three editions were published between 1848 and 1851), he included information about its translation into various languages, creating the illusion of its authenticity.

Critics responded quickly to expose the literary crime, seeking public acclaim for their ability to prove that the *Buscapié* was a deception, and probably a disgrace, too, since Castro commanded much respect as a scholar. C. A. de la Barrera (88) traced the history of the *Buscapié* legend to its eighteenth-century origin to show how Castro's work was a fraud, and B. J. Gallardo (93) wrote an especially blunt attack, going so far as to recommend that the ruse be examined by dogs. In another piece, written under the pseudonym "El Bachiller Bo-vaina" (92), Gallardo listed several convincing arguments for the unlikelihood of Cervantes' authorship of the pamphlet: the *Quijote* enjoyed much popularity and needed no defense; no record of the *Buscapié's* composition or publication existed; no scholar had ever mentioned it among Cervantes' works; and the style did not resemble that of Cervantes or anyone else of his period.

The fact that critics rushed to intensify this scandal clearly manifested their passionate concern for any issue dealing with the *Quijote*, while at the same time problems addressed earlier by the neoclassicists continued to be debated. But at this mid-nineteenth century mark the perspective on them had broadened. Meanwhile, chivalry remained the locus of the critical controversy over literary taste and moral values, because, as many saw it, Cervantes was trying to ferret out of Spanish society the bad habits bred by this medieval institution. This did not mean, however, that Don Quijote, as a symbol of chivalry, represented bad taste. According to most critics, by portraying a mad hero Cervantes aimed to show how one could ward off the effects of reading too many harmful books; Don Quijote's conversion, his abandoning *Amadís* et al., was his salvation. Some even believed that he was a visionary searching for an ideal way of life [see Gil de Zárate (80)]; and in plain words Fernando de Castro asserted that Don Quijote was actually a model for all utopians (96). Moreover, Vicente Salvá, as we have seen, claimed that Cervantes did not primarily wish to deal chivalry a final blow. Instead, and in conformance with the dictates of the Canónigo, Cervantes wanted to purge the literary genre of its improbable elements because he held the values of chivalry in high regard. If placed in the proper light, Salvá contended, the knight-errant would come to be admired, not laughed at. This comment of Salvá's is especially revealing in light of the twentieth-century notion that Cervantes sought to defend moral values while reproving the artistic form that chivalry took in the sixteenth century. Salvá felt that Cervantes attempted to extract the hidden truth from chivalry's unimaginable events in order to give it a degree of sanity and artistic purpose. Similarly, Eugenio de Ochoa (85) believed that the novelistic genre, which for a long time had suffered from the low esteem of the neoclassicists, needed someone like Cervantes to bestow upon it the kind of meaning and substance that would make it pleasing to those who still had faith in the heroic ideal. While these romantic views gained a few partisans in Spain, they did not thoroughly alter mid-century criticism. However, they did expose a fundamental problem about chivalry: although the chivalry of the sixteenth century presented false and exaggerated values, and although it was, according to Agustín Durán (89), an artificial phenomenon imported into Spain from France and England and essentially non-native, it could influence strongly the study of Spain's heroic past when divested of its superficiality.

Early nineteenth-century Spanish investigators of the *Quijote* pre-occupied themselves with its language and style and the satire of chivalric customs. They also made some modest achievements in editing the text and developing Cervantes' biography. Then, the years 1860 until the end of the century witnessed another period of extraordinary growth. Cervantine criticism thrust forward with dynamic personalities—Nicolás Díaz de Benjumea and José María Asensio y Toledo among them—, academic journals, a profusion of *homenajes* inside and outside Spain, the gathering of documents for collections of Cervantine bibliography, and, of course, a variety of new and often controversial interpretations of the *Quijote*. And while the partially successful romanticism of the earlier part of the century in Europe had a mild impact on some critics in Spain, others continued with the practices of the neoclassical school with textual criticism and the study of language. Furthermore, interpretations of the work tended to be either absolute, admitting no ambiguity in the meaning of the novel, or open-ended, recognizing the novel's multiple perspectives.

Nicolás Díaz de Benjumea, a self-styled romantic, poet, and polemicist, was one of the leading figures in Cervantine criticism of this period. He was of the conviction that Cervantes' hero represented a "new" chivalry, which, once purged of its crudeness and barbarism, would lead to a liberal society. This somewhat political approach of Benjumea's (termed "philosophical," "symbolic," "esoteric," and "occult") created a stir among Cervantists of the time. A good part of this method had to do with the application of events in Cervantes' life against the broader background of sixteenth-century Spanish history to the overall understanding of the *Quijote* and to its various episodes. Benjumea published his ideas initially in the journal *La América* in 1859 and then proceeded to write short pamphlets and entire books beginning in the year 1861 with *La estafeta de Urganda* (100). In them he sought to prove that by discovering deep, dark secrets of the author's background, one could find the key to the hidden meaning of the *Quijote*, which he viewed as a recondite or "occult" novel. Benjumea claimed, as did the early Ruidíaz legend of the *Buscapié*, that Cervantes' novel was replete with allusions to his contemporaries; in other words, it portrayed real people who figured prominently in Cervantes' personal fortunes and misfortunes. Sansón Carrasco, for example, embodied Juan Blanco de Paz, Cervantes' avowed enemy and agent of the Inquisition; Dulcinea wisdom, and so forth. Benjumea thus worked on both a literal and figurative plane. Accordingly, reading the *Quijote* as a satire of chivalry oversimplified the interpretation of a very complex work of art, which the commentaries of Pellicer, Clemencín, and the like hardly began to elucidate. Benjumea also argued that one had to consider the effect that the Inquisition, the courts of Philip II and III, and other institutions had on Cervantes, and realize that the reason for his having created a mad protagonist was that a madman had the special privilege of uttering truths that ordinary people would not dare to speak. Therefore, concluded Benjumea, the novel embraced primarily symbolic meanings whose genesis was the author's life of disillusionment; neither ridicule nor literary parody were Cervantes' chief aims, as many had thought.

While Benjumea was not always accurate, one can see the beginnings of certain twentieth-century theories about the *Quijote* in his work. It also bears a likeness to eighteenth-century criticism, because, like the neoclassicists, Benjumea enjoyed singing the praises of Cervantes and his masterpiece. Additionally, one must remember that Benjumea's inquiries went beyond finding clever analogies between real and fictional people, for he made his contemporaries aware of the important function of Cervantes' "historical" or "real" presence in his novel: From a historico-social point of view, Cervantes, through his protagonist, sought to reform chivalry, not to mock it, and in the process made Don Quijote a revolutionary hero rather than merely an object of derision inherited from an antiquated literary genre. Furthermore, while critics like Pellicer (whom Benjumea bitterly attacked for not offering anything more than a few tiny morsels to the margins of the text) thought Don Quijote mad, Benjumea added a new dimension to the analysis of his character—melancholy. Thus, for him, the Knight's battles were symbolic manifestations of the struggles of the spirit (much like those of poets and philosophers) and his reward was wisdom (Dulcinea). Breaking away from his predecessors who, he believed, had read Cervantes' life and exploits in too literal a fashion and who consequently could not have given them proper weight, Benjumea emphasized the idea that the *Quijote* arose from the heart and soul of its author, contending that this intimately autobiographical conception of the work gave rise to to the supremely tragic theme of failure in it. Moreover, Benjumea found that the satirical element in the *Quijote*, which had been underscored by so many critics long before him, was actually a grave matter that touched the human heart in an allegory of man's folly. Benjumea then asserted (221) that the *Quijote* transcended even its own artistic purpose to become the "Biblia humana," and reiterated his belief that the *Quijote* was not written to undermine books of chivalry, but instead to serve as a smokescreen for an attack on blind faith and the orthodoxy of the Spain of the

Inquisition. He also averred (207) that the 1615 *Quijote* eclipsed the first part because its adventures are more noble and idealistic and less plastic and because there Don Quijote portrays the critic, preacher, and moralist rather than the grappling knight-errant. Therefore, whatever the excesses of Benjumea's determinations, he dismissed absolutist approaches and alerted his contemporaries to the fact that the *Quijote* could evoke scores of possible interpretations. He made it clear that Cervantes' scoffing at chivalry was not the only explanation for Don Quijote's artful contrivances. The *Quijote*, he showed us, incorporates many truths about human nature.

Like Clemencín's before him, Benjumea's commentaries invited a plethora of reactions, including those of Hartzenbusch, Valera, Máinez, Asensio, and Pardo de Figueroa. It is therefore fitting that the opinions of these and other well-known critics be viewed against the background of Benjumea's formidable effort. Juan Eugenio Hartzenbusch's proclamation in the Argamasilla de Alba edition of the *Quijote*, 1863 (110), that Cervantes' great novel has the power to create other men in the Don Quijote mold, is a romantic vision of the Cervantine hero that can be associated generally with Benjumea's notion of struggle. Ramón León Máinez defended Benjumea's views and methods more directly. After a rather vehement attack by José María Asensio y Toledo against the *Estafeta de Urganda* and *Correo de Alquife* (123), Máinez published his *Cartas literarias sobre Cervantes y el Quijote por el Bachiller Cervántico* (125), supporting the *sentido oculto* propounded by Benjumea and declaring that he deserved praise, not condemnation, for making critics aware of the truths that until his time lay undiscovered in the *Quijote*. In a later review of Benjumea's work (193), Máinez crowned him as the one member of his generation who explored new horizons for the Spaniards' understanding of their greatest literary achievement: no longer could Spain afford its fixation with Don Quijote as a foolish madman and Cervantes' novel as merely a satire of a literary genre. Because of Benjumea, continued Máinez, the *Quijote* would reign as a book of the new Spain, a book about men who strive to free themselves of ancient authority through the protest of an independent spirit. Similarly, Máinez later wrote (194) that not only Cervantes but also "a new age of ideas" put to rest the influence of a decaying system of chivalry.

Controversy was something to which Ramón León Máinez was accustomed. As the founder and chief editor of the first journal devoted solely to Cervantine scholarship, he often used its pages as a springboard for polemics. The *Crónica de los Cervantistas* (151), published in Cádiz between 1871 and 1879, presented the opinions of nearly all the prominent (and not so prominent) Cervantists of the time. As the logical product of an era in which interpretations of the *Quijote* were rapidly abounding, the *Crónica* became the forum for debate on any scholarly controversy, whether important, petty, radical, or otherwise. The "occult" approach to the *Quijote*, Cervantes as theologian, surmises as to where he lived and composed the novel, and attacks on Benjumea were the kinds of issues aired in the *Crónica*. It also regularly featured bibliography (editions and translations of Cervantes' works) and biographical documents and was the only specialized journal on Cervantes that survived as long as it did. It published critics like Manuel Cervantes Peredo (150), who persisted in the belief that the *Quijote* was a satire of the social "hallucination" of chivalry and the exaggeration of the enduring chivalric ideal, as well as Mariano Pardo de Figueroa, who invented correspondence between Dr. Thebussem and M. Droap, two fictional experts in Cervantine scholarship, to advance his own ideas about Cervantes and the *Quijote*. Pardo's letters and notes [(126), (136)] indicate that he was something of a dilettante and meddler in the controversies among Cervantists. He supported Benjumea and was especially impressed by his invention of a system of recondite symbolism in the *Quijote* that produced anagrams like that of the *bachiller* López de Alcobendas (*Quijote*, I, 19), which, when rearranged, spells "es lo de Blanco de Paz," Cervantes' so-called odious enemy. Pardo's publications, nonetheless, must concern us because they register the events in the Cervantine world during the 1860s and 1870s. He recorded, in conversations between Thebussem and Droap, news of books, tributes, and other sundry matters, and his studies often enlivened the pages of the *Crónica de los Cervantistas*. Further, his activities involved textual and philological investigation of the *Quijote*. His critique of the Hartzenbusch edition (181), for instance, testified to the revival of text criticism during the latter part of the century.

Romanticism, as we said, was influential but not prevalent during this period, while the neoclassicism of the earlier part of the nineteenth century still had its proponents. Chief among them was José María Asensio y Toledo, founder of the *Sociedad de Bibliófilos Andaluces*. A gifted and prolific writer, editor, and bibliographer, Asensio often dramatically opposed Benjumea, thereby injecting a measure of common sense into Cervantine criticism at a time when divergent views made the study of the *Quijote* somewhat chaotic. Although Asensio did not produce a systematic study of Cervantes' novel, he did comment generously on all aspects of the polemics of these final decades of the century. In a short piece called "Comentario de comentarios, que es como si dijéramos Cuento de Cuentos: Carta a Mr. Mariano Droap" (123), he rejected Benjumea's conclusions outright, claiming not only that they were absurd and far-fetched, but also that they offered little in the way of original interpretation of the *Quijote*; additionally, he criticized Benjumea for having derived his ideas from misleading foreign commentators. In *Cervantes y sus obras* (139), Asensio said that studies which had implied that Cervantes meant to attack the Spanish Inquisition, the monarchy, or figures in high places were unfounded. Cervantes, according to Asensio, had too much respect for Spain to write a veiled diatribe against institutions and men that were products of its culture, and therefore Benjumea failed to understand Cervantes' purpose in writing the *Quijote*. For Asensio the *Quijote* was a moralistic novel that dissected social and individual evils through an amusing story. But the message of the *Quijote* could not be limited to this neoclassical view of social satire dependent on literary parody. The *Quijote* had universal appeal for this critic because it portrayed two of the most original characters the literary world had ever seen, suggesting the symbolic polarities of sublime aspiration and crude realism. Asensio's form of conservatism therefore did not confine him to earlier neoclassical ideas. He was a sensitive critic who understood the *Quijote* as most modern critics do. In an excellent little piece, "Cervantes, inventor" (174), for example, he spoke of Cervantes as a *modern* writer who created characters who would remain forever within us; "even the beasts they rode attract us," he declared. Asensio also affirmed that Cervantes discovered the modern novel in the ruins of the books of chivalry, adding that the numerous imitations of his works throughout Europe prove that Cervantes gave modern literature its primary impulse. Although Asensio's opinions often clashed with the radical thinkers of his age, he was, in retrospect, one of its true standard-bearers.

Another way in which Asensio built his reputation as a Cervantist was through his bibliographical activity. No other single figure of the century (with the possible exception of Leopoldo Rius) did as much spadework for his generation—and those who followed—by gathering sources crucial to the study of the *Quijote*. Asensio carefully scrutinized early editions of the novel (130), and on several occasions catalogued some very rare secondary sources dating from the 1600s to the 1800s [(155), (230), (240); see Miguel Santiago Rodríguez, *Catálogo de la biblioteca cervantina de D. José María Asensio y Toledo*, Madrid, 1948 (43)]. The works by Asensio listed in our bibliography contain literally hundreds of items of major importance to scholars. It should be noted as well that this crucial activity of collecting primary and secondary sources for the study of Cervantes did not elude Asensio's contemporaries, for published both independently and in the *Crónica de los Cervantistas* were various catalogues of seventeenth- eighteenth- and nineteenth-century editions of the *Quijote* along with enormous lists of critical commentary and documents for Cervantes' biography. Among critics who saw fit to record this information for the good of posterity one finds Leopoldo Rius (42), Jeronimo Morán (107), José Bartolomé Gallardo (109), Manuel Cerdá (157), and Franciso López Fabra (162).

The whirlwind of activity in the last four decades of the nineteenth century brought with it critics who paved the way for major new interpretations of the *Quijote* and its relationship to world literature and literary study in general. Francisco Tubino, who participated in the Benjumea controversy [see *El Quijote y La estafeta de Urganda* (108)], claimed that Cervantes upheld the notion of a good book of chivalry because he believed in the chivalric spirit. But, Tubino adds, by doing away with faulty chivalric conceptions of his era, Cervantes also dismantled the Spanish nobility as he knew it. This idea, reminiscent of the neoclassicists, advances criticism toward the twentieth century. Tubino noted, in addition, that there were two kinds of *Quijote* critics— intelligent readers who appreciated the beauty of the book's words and their meaning and those who read into the text ideas that simply were mistaken or nonexistent. Benjumea, along with Puigblanch, Salvá, and Creuzé de Lesser, may be associated with the latter, according to Tubino, because they constantly emphasized the *Quijote's* many historical allusions and insisted that Cervantes was anticlerical and anti-Spanish. Speaking out against such opinions in his *Cervantes y el Quijote* (168), Tubino asserted that Cervantes was not a socialist or a theologian but a man very much of his times who created new avenues for moral thought, despite his having failed in exiling the decadent chivalric habits of the nobility. Although Tubino made a plea for an intrinsic approach to the *Quijote*, it appears that he was influenced by

Benjumea's determination that Cervantes' biography had much to do with the composition of his novel, a novel which ought to be studied, Tubino said, from an ethical standpoint as well as an aesthetic one.

Juan Valera wrote prolifically on the *Quijote* [(114), (115), (116)] and strongly contested the methods used by Benjumea. He was particularly disturbed by the esoteric claims that Benjumea and his followers made about the novel and countered with the following argument: Cervantes was a plebeian who tended to circulate in places like the *Percheles de Málaga* and thus could not have been a Raimundo Lulio or an Albertus Magnus. Furthermore, Valera maintained that there was not the slightest trace of the occult, mystic, or recondite in the *Quijote*, and to insist on that kind of cold allegory was to diminish the artistic integrity of the work: Cervantes was a passionate man who lifted the real world of his hero to a poetic plane. With the vigor of his imagination he painted with uncanny fidelity the totality of real life. He did not create with the calculating eye of the scientist, he had no hidden secrets or magic formulas, only the genius to be able to make poetic the prosaic human reality of Spain in the dynamic and imposing form of a novel with epic proportions. To indulge in finding contemporary models for Cervantes' fictional characters served little purpose and stifled the critic's ability to understand the artist's creative act and function. Hence, for Valera, the *Quijote* was a beautiful story whose simple pretext was the satire of books of chivalry, a satire which developed into something far more profound once beyond the initial chapters of the novel.

In part, Valera was responding to the appearance of a large number of studies on Cervantes (see below) that claimed that he was an expert in various branches of science (navigation, medicine, etc.). Valera summarily dismissed such ideas as useless and time-consuming and argued, like others who followed, for a vision of the *Quijote* as a universal or archetypal novel. José Fernández Espino (152) took a similar stance. Rejecting the assumption that the *Quijote* was a satire of chivalry books, Espino called it a *comédie humaine* that concerned a man with boundless imagination, energy, and wit, attracting the sympathy of his readers. Don Quijote, for these critics, was the expression of human generosity, who, with his madness, brought, paradoxically, a modicum of sanity to life.

In the 1870s and 1880s, Manuel de la Revilla [(185), (217)] argued for a pre-Benjumean interpretation of the *Quijote*. Attempting to

convince his fellow critics to put to rest the excesses of their generation, especially of those who espoused the occult approach convinced
that the *Quijote* was a political allegory, Revilla pointed out that
Cervantes' original intention was to ridicule the foibles of chivalry
books and that only indirectly did he attack the Spanish nobility. To be
sure, Revilla said, Cervantes was repudiating an outmoded and out-
landish literary genre; he did not realize when he composed his
masterpiece that it would come to have transcendental value. Therefore, Revilla concluded, only with time and hindsight can one discover
the significance of a work of genius.

The *Quijote* for Revilla was a novel of profound human experience,
the experience of searching for ideals, and although in this quest for
the impossible Don Quijote appeared ridiculous, ironically he was not.
As it turned out, Revilla would admit to only one pretext for
Cervantes' novel: the satire of books of chivalry—his only stated
purpose. To say that Cervantes had come upon the true meaning of
the human condition was acceptable, but to believe that he wrote the
Quijote as a political allegory was, according to Revilla, sheer folly. His
arguments, though somewhat traditional, were tempered, balanced,
and convincing, and if we may extrapolate from his comments, we see
that the theme of the *Quijote* implied in them is *failure*.

By Revilla's time, Spaniards had begun to see the importance of the
Quijote to the study of world literature, not just to Spain's own
intellectual history. And it was Marcelino Menéndez Pelayo who, with
his *Historia de las ideas estéticas en España* [begun in 1883 (231)] and
subsequent studies on Spanish orthodoxy and literary history, attempted to find for Spain its proper place in the cultural landscape of
Europe. His most authoritative Cervantine studies are beyond the
chronological scope of our commentary, but some of his pre-1894
criticism is of interest to us. Don Marcelino aided in bringing Cervantine scholarship back to classical sobriety. Like Valera, he did not
believe in imposing a symbolic or esoteric system on the *Quijote*, nor did
he judge Cervantes to be a scientist who invented a theory of art.
According to this pioneering scholar, Cervantes developed his fiction
from what he observed and gave it poetic substance and clarity: a poet
perceived form qua form, without having to study the science of form.
In other words, Cervantes was an *ingenio lego* who did not create
literary precepts, since ideas in the *Quijote* resulted from common sense
and intuition, not scientific formulas:

I mean to say that the intuition that an artist has is not the intuition of scientific truths, but only the intuition of form, which is the intellectual world in which he lives. Dante and Goethe were both poets and men of science, the greatest of their respective eras. But they were not poets because of their science, nor scientists because of their poetry. Instead, they united the two distinct aptitudes which complemented each other marvelously. But Cervantes was a poet and only a poet, an *ingenio lego*, as they said in his times. His scientific ideas could not be other than those of the society in which he lived. [*Historia de las ideas estéticas en España*, 1883, vol. 2 (231)].

Krausismo, introduced into Spain in the 1860s by Julián Sanz del Río, made its mark on Cervantine criticism. A minor German philosopher and self-proclaimed successor of Emmanuel Kant, Karl C. F. Krause (1781-1832) believed that the body belonged to the realm of Nature, while the Spirit belonged to an entirely different sphere. Krause argued that since Spirit and Nature, though distinct and in one sense opposed, acted upon one another, man should search for the common ground of both to create the perfect essence, called God or the Absolute. Thus, Federico de Castro in a short essay entitled "Cervantes y la filosofía" (140), in *krausista* fashion, traced the empiricism and mysticism of the Spanish Renaissance and showed how Cervantes had reconciled these two currents. According to F. de Castro, Cervantes may have destroyed books of chivalry, but their spirituality survived their decadent literary form, as the faith-militant concept of knight-errantry proved that this way of life worked miracles. Arriving in Spain long after the German romantics had applied similar philosophical dualities to Don Quijote and Sancho, *krausismo*, with its emphasis on achieving a synthesis of the two basic human traits—spirit-nature, idealism-realism—, gave an immediate and dynamic impulse to Spanish criticism and especially to the Generation of '98, which was to employ the idealism of Don Quijote and the realism of Sancho as twin forces which could be harnessed for the rejuvenation of Spain.

A constituent part of nineteenth-century commentary on the *Quijote* was the panegyrist mode. Although its roots went back to the earlier portion of the century, it came to full fruition later with masses for Cervantes celebrated by the Royal Academy, numerous *homenajes*, and other encomia honoring him throughout Spain and in other countries. As most scholars and critics eagerly gave recognition to his genius, constant were the efforts to demonstrate through the corpus of Cervantes' works his vast knowledge of specific aspects of human endeavor. But these enthusiasts proclaimed too ardently that little had remained for Cervantes to know about humankind, crediting him with the skills of many major professions, from that of navigation [Fernández Duro (134)], law [A. Martín Gamero (141)], culinary arts [Fernández Duro (159)], economics [Piernas y Hurtado (182)], administration [Hermúa (213)], travel [Foronda y Aguilera (222)], medicine [Olmedilla y Puig (244)], and diplomacy [Carreras (251)] to theology and psychiatry. The publications of these critics bear some of the dreariest pages written on Cervantes, for motivated mostly by emotion, they offer little to the understanding of the *Quijote*. However, one commentator from this group whose essays did shed light on Cervantes' work, José M. Piernas y Hurtado, writing on the economics of the *Quijote*, believed, and not without reason, that Sancho's personality could be understood in terms of his drive for and interest in money. This critic also saw the *Quijote* as a critique of the *hidalguía* and examined its habits and the causes of its decline as a social class. Piernas' study is an intelligent one, especially since it offers interesting information about Don Quijote's social origins. Unfortunately, it stands virtually alone among the commentaries that yielded to what A. Martínez Duimovich (248) called "cervántico-manía." Happily, he and others contravened to offset this literary craze, as did José María Asensio's important address to the *Academia Sevillana*, "Cervantes, inventor," discussed above, challenging zealous Cervantists to search themselves for the real sources of Cervantes' genius. Américo Castro's *El pensamiento de Cervantes* (1925), picturing Cervantes as a man who was by no means unlearned, but a writer well-versed in the literary currents and aesthetic theories of his age, did much to redress this extreme, rescuing Cervantes from both the zealots as well as from earlier detractors, who viewed the novelist as a man of little learning.

One of the controversies associated with "cervántico-manía" was the claim that Cervantes possessed a knowledge of theology. Led by Ramón León Máinez and José María Sbarbi y Osuna, the two major opponents in this dispute, the debate appeared somewhat less absurd than the ones concerning Cervantes as navigator and the like. However, the war of words over Cervantes' theology exposed the flaws inherent in monolithic and esoteric criticism. Verbal exchanges between Máinez and Sbarbi took place between 1870 and 1872, with Máinez relying on the pages of the *Crónica de los Cervantistas* [October 7,

1871 (154)] to refute Sbarbi's claim that Cervantes was a theologian. According to Sbarbi (144), Cervantes, as an intelligent writer of his day, had to know theology, and Don Quijote was similarly obliged as a knight-errant to learn something about the science. In the May 29, 1872 issue of the *Crónica*, Sbarbi conceded that Cervantes' knowledge of theology did not reach "perfection" (166); however, added Sbarbi, as a student of religion Cervantes must have understood the discipline quite well. Sbarbi opined that Cervantes could have preached as well as his protagonist, as Don Quijote himself was capable of writing a sermon.

Another protracted dispute dealt with the question of Cervantes as psychiatrist, an issue of some importance since madness figures prominently in the *Quijote*. This polemic was spearheaded by Emilio Pi y Molist, a psychiatrist who published a lengthy study on the subject in 1886 (245), probably at the suggestion of Hernández Morejón's work of 1836 (74). Molist analyzed the causes of Don Quijote's madness, which were excessive reading, idleness, and isolation. He then described the treatment necessary for his cure, a common prescription in Molist's times: quiet the madman but do not contradict or punish him. Molist thus paved the way for viewing psychopathology as a dominant feature of the *Quijote* and monomania as a major component of the hero's personality, as well as for believing that Cervantes was far in advance of the medical theories of his times. These ideas were roundly disputed the following year, however, when Luis Carreras published several essays in *Diluvio* (Barcelona), which were translated into French with modifications and additions by C.-B. Dumaine in Paris, 1896 (247). Both author and translator especially rejected the diagnosis of monomania and insisted on characterizing Don Quijote's illness as an "illusion." Pointing to the Knight's melancholy after his final defeat and to the fact that he wanted to die sane, they argued that such moments of sanity were obviously rare in madmen. Although some critics went overboard in their presumption that Cervantes was a doctor, the dialogue among physicians brought to light some of the questions pertinent to the analysis of Cervantes' protagonist.

Language never ceased to be a focal point of the study of the *Quijote*, and in this period statements abounded on the beauty and excellence of Cervantes' prose. Fernando de Castro (132) proclaimed Cervantes the father of the Castilian language. Others believed that his Spanish was too pure to be translated, and Asensio's and Sbarbi's disagreement over the translatability of the *Quijote* [(167), (171)] spawned a whole new generation praising the work, including Sbarbi's own collection of sayings and proverbs. Furthermore, as explorations of Cervantes' language had uncovered so many truths about the Spanish character and temperament for nineteenth-century readers, critics began to condemn Spaniards for their lack of interest in Spain's rich heritage and in the *Quijote*'s stature as a world classic, and then, as Benito Pérez Galdós did several times in 1868 [(127), (128), (129)], to call upon their countrymen to pay homage to Cervantes. Thus the critics of this period increased patriotic fervor in favor of Cervantes. Esteban Azaña's publication (211), which records tributes paid to Cervantes (like the erection of statues of Cervantes in Alcalá de Henares and throughout Spain) and cites ceremonies held in his honor during the 1870s, runs to fifty-eight pages. These and other celebrations, many of them quite solemn and which constitute a story too long to tell here, are summed up by Rius in the third volume of his bibliography [(42), pp. 472-508]. A similar earnestness is shown by Leopoldo Alas ("Clarín"), who believed that a steady diet of reading the *Quijote* was essential for its comprehension (239), although he also lamented the fact that in Spain, surprisingly, no great thinker had ever studied the *Quijote* in depth.

A final habit of Cervantists of the era that evolved in part from the panegyrist mode was the publication of lengthy biographies of Cervantes [Morán (107), Máinez (194), Benjumea (207)]. These investigations, like the earlier ones by Navarrete et al., were critically examined by Luis Vidart in a series of articles published between 1886 and 1889 [(246), (259), (260)]. In them he called his fellow Spaniards "semidoctos" for their failure to appreciate Cervantes beyond his importance to Spain. Vidart's attitude signaled a maturation of Spanish literary criticism, manifested in a sense of awareness of what needed to be done to reach a full understanding of Cervantes' work, and it marked the end of a trajectory in Spain that began with attempts to fashion thinking on the *Quijote* in terms of rhetoric, style, and satire. These efforts then became a reflection of the Spaniard's growing knowledge of himself as he developed his understanding of a book that so deeply penetrated the heart of his national character. Vidart then moved beyond when he called the novel a work of negation (others called it failure), a poem of modern life in which man must come to terms with the amorphous world in which he lives [see "Cervantes, poeta épico" (203)]. To do so, Vidart said that man must reject the past and build on the crumbling foundation of his own folly. In other words, Cervantes' novel and his critics had to move on to the uneasy twentieth century.

CRITICISM OUTSIDE SPAIN

Let us now move on to *Quijote* criticism outside Spain, beginning with the German romantics. Writing in the last decade of the eighteenth century and the initial decades of the nineteenth, the German romantics were among the first scholars and literary critics to be fully aware of the importance of the *Quijote* as a modern novel. Even prior to the romantics, J. G. Herder discovered the significant strides Cervantes had made in the development of narrative fiction. He took particular note of Sancho Panza as the living model of the people and of the *Quijote* as the first European comic epic to bear the seeds of a modern genre, two ideas that would occupy crucial positions in the romantic canon. Toward the end of the eighteenth century, Friedrich Schiller (337) anticipated the romantic revolution against neoclassicism by treating Cervantes' hero as a catalyst in an inert world, who, with dreams of grandeur, imposed goodness on the society around him. For Schiller the *Quijote* represented the tragic clash of the real with the ideal on a grand scale, a view that had substantial influence on thinking during and beyond the nineteenth century. Indeed, German critics who followed him would be principally responsible for making the *Quijote* a universally renowned classic.

Another important finding of the time was the realistic portrayal in Cervantes' novel of Spain's customs and attitudes, especially as it was advanced in the work of J. G. Herder and Wilhelm von Humboldt. This idea received further support from Friedrich Schlegel, one of the most important spokesmen for the romantic movement (362). Schlegel believed, among other things, that all literature was national in character and the *Quijote* an expression of Spain in epic proportions. He also counted the *Quijote* among the world's great classics in the mold of Shakespeare and Homer, and said that although the novel was a universal work it was also a very Spanish work, one of which Spaniards could be justly proud as it delved into their life and character.

The interpretation of the *Quijote* as anti-heroic (or anti-chivalric) was accepted in Germany, although it was not engendered by German romantics but first recorded by English and Spanish scholars of the seventeenth century. Among the nineteenth-century German critics who adopted this view one finds Franz Grillparzer (384), a disciple of Byron, and Friedrich Nietzsche (398). Grillparzer in his 1839-1842 literary studies called attention to Byron's belief that Cervantes laughed Spanish chivalry out of existence. In a letter dated December 8, 1875, Nietzsche said that after reading the *Quijote* during a summer vacation, all his personal sorrows seemed small; the *Quijote* for him was a bitter tale. Earlier, Heinrich Heine (381) had gone so far as to say that the *Quijote* attacked all human enthusiasm.

Residual tensions from the anti-heroic claim brought forth the contention that Cervantes was the first novelist to penetrate man's psyche. In other words, critics writing about the *Quijote* as an "anti-chivalric" or "anti-heroic" novel were frequently reminded of its profoundly human aspect, which went beyond superficial laughter. For instance, Friedrich Bouterwek, finding the *Quijote* much more than a parody, pointed out the originality of Cervantes' novelistic form and the vividness of his character portrayal (355), while F. Schlegel [(362), (363)] and Ludwig Tieck (372) demonstrated how Cervantes brought the everyday to a literary level. According to Tieck (354), parody elevated itself to genuine poetry; that is, Cervantes, in the *Quijote*, seeing how far poetry and life had become separated in the *Amadis*, invented out of love of poetry and the marvelous a most daring joke, and as a result, parody and poetry joined hands in the happy meeting ground Cervantes provided.

The German romantics' idea that the two protagonists of the *Quijote* were symbols of opposing forces—idealism and materialism, body and soul, the poetic or generous and the prosaic or egotistic—typifies their *Quijote* criticism. Following Schiller's lead, they, and principally Schelling and Tieck, contended that Don Quijote was a noble figure in conflict with an unworthy society [(353), (372)]. In 1781, Schiller drew a picture of Don Quijote as a complex man of enthusiasm, frenzy, limitless energy, and grand schemes, who could not find his own niche in the world and whom the reader loved and hated simultaneously. He also maintained that Cervantes' protagonist sought power in order to disobey man's laws and to clash with the established order. Clearly, the German romantics found little in the *Quijote* to laugh about (though others did) and much to admire. As they read Don Quijote's mission in terms of the antagonism between the

forces of the ideal and real worlds, and as they believed him fundamentally a symbolic figure embodying the strife between the collective
and the individual, they generally viewed the events of the novel as a
painful struggle—an idea that has profoundly influenced generations
of thinkers and critics, including Unamuno and the *noventayochistas*, as
well as many present-day Cervantists.

One immediate consequence of the German romantics' investigation into the heroic and anti-heroic nature of the *Quijote* was the
attention it drew to the related problem of Cervantes' humor. On the
one hand, Tieck (372) praised the way Cervantes lifted the humorous
to epic heights, while Jean Paul Richter (358) lauded the tolerance his
humor engendered. But Gerhard Amyntor (409) did not like the comic
aspect of Cervantes' novel; he, like many outside Spain, saw too much
cruelty in the farcical events and situations in the *Quijote*. In fact,
humor in the novel was for the Germans at the service of some
"higher" human value. Thus, it came as no surprise that A. W. Schlegel
(345) could say that Cervantes wanted to destroy the absurd world of
the books of chivalry.

In Germany, as in other European countries, one may also find a
conflict between critics who regarded the *Quijote* as realistic portraiture
and those who thought the Knight and Squire universal representations or symbols. And yet, while the allegorical approach dominated
German thinking in the nineteenth century, attempts were made to
reconcile these two opposing ideas. In addition, it is important to
remember that while some German thinkers seemed pessimistic as
they converted the Knight into a noble madman and a martyr for
liberty, crushed by the real (prosaic) world, they at the same time
became largely responsible for the movement in modern criticism that
extolled the Don Quijote figure. Finally, German critics from Herder
and Schiller to the end of the century were highly active not only in
studying basic questions about the *Quijote*, but also in developing novel
approaches to the problems presented by its style, structure, and
intent. Some of these ideas will be discussed further in our commentary (as they have been already in the case of Spain) because they
illuminate critical methods of scholars throughout Europe.

With the rising prestige of the *Quijote* in the nineteenth century,
there was a growing inclination in European criticism to examine its
influence on world literature. F. Schlegel compared Cervantes' novel
with Goethe's *Wilhelm Meister*, for instance, and other Germans compared it with Grimmelshausen's *Simplicissimus* and with the works

of Hoffmann, Beaumont and Fletcher, and Lessing, all of which shed light on the direction in which the *Quijote* had led writers in Europe outside Spain.

Although, as we indicated earlier, the French did not at first appreciate the profoundly human aspect and universality of the *Quijote* before the nineteenth century, they began to read the novel with new zeal as the century progressed and to admire Don Quijote's mirth, folly, and sincerity. Jean Pierre Claris de Florian's comments in his 1799 translation (266) indicate some residual neoclassical concern for morality that would endure into the century. Emile Chasles (311) found the *Quijote* to be a harsh judgment of Spain and a critique of false ideas, such as the ethereal and inflated rhetoric of platonic love along with chivalric mania; Charles Furne (301) understood the book to be a resentment against the people and institutions of the era; and Emile Montégut (323) went so far as to imply that the *Quijote* was the story of sixteenth-century Spain told with silent rage. Nevertheless, while Florian believed that the *Quijote* was a deeply moral book, he was equally impressed by its ability to inspire laughter and love. This penchant of the French for accepting both Cervantes' comic and serious moods is also apparent in Louis Simon Auger's 1825 essay (272) in which he declared that there were two worlds in the novel—the imaginary and the real. Auger realized that this dualism could appear natural only in Cervantes, while it would have been awkward in the hands of most other writers. E. Littré in his 1837 comments on the well-known French translation of Louis Viardot, 1836 (277), said that Cervantes owed a debt to the book of chivalry for his satire. Littré, however, was quick to point out that after the initial chapters Cervantes abandoned his plan of chivalric parody, at which point he became the consummate psychologist in whose creation one found the alliance of reason and "hallucination": chivalry may have seemed ridiculous, but its values had traditionally upheld honor, virtue, and faith—hardly traits to be scorned (278). Like Auger, this commentator maintained that the rational and the absurd could coexist only in a book like the *Quijote*.

French critics were also stimulated by the romantic and allegorical ideas of the Germans. In his influential commentary on the literature of southern Europe in 1813 (270), J. C. L. Simonde de Sismondi, for one, popularized theories that the *Quijote* set the imagination against the petty details of everyday life and depicted the struggle of the noble, heroic, and virtuous man in a vulgar world. These and other views prevalent among the romantics had additional proponents in François René de Chateaubriand, Alfred de Vigny, E. F. A. Rosseeuw, Théophile Gautier, Edouard Mennechet, Victor Hugo, Edmond Scherer, and others. Chateaubriand, in 1821 (290), discovered a cruel gaiety in the *Quijote* because the hero's painful self-awareness led to his downfall, while Vigny (282), writing in 1840, considered the *Quijote* a story of misplaced enthusiasm. Following an earlier interpretation, E. F. A. Rosseeuw, 1838 (281), characterized Cervantes as an ungrateful Spaniard because he dealt a blow to the poetry and miracles of chivalric Spain. This exaltation of the chivalric spirit was also one of the major themes of Gautier's commentaries [(283), (302), 1843 and 1858, respectively]. For him Don Quijote was the symbol of the poetic spirit who spurned the real world, and in his attempts to fight for justice, the Knight was defeated by the onslaught of material forces; one could not expect a character like Don Quijote to survive in that world. Mennechet described Don Quijote in terms of generosity and goodness, 1846-48 (285), and Hugo, 1864 (304), exalted the *Quijote* as a philosophical poem composed by a champion of intelligence, who knew intuitively and rationally the human heart. Finally, Edmond Scherer, 1882 (325), loved Don Quijote because he embodied a paradoxical, yet beautiful, blend of wisdom and madness.

Sismondi also dwelled on the pessimistic tone of the *Quijote*, noting a strong underlying mood of melancholy in the book, and several French thinkers pursued the idea. Léon Gautier and Rosseeuw asserted that Cervantes destroyed the chivalric ideal, and Jules Barbey d'Aurévilly (332) bitterly insisted that Cervantes' novel was a mockery of the most beautiful customs that ever existed and provoked many a tear. Although these pessimistic readings had been fashionable since the time of Temple and Carleton, when the prevailing idea was that Don Quijote symbolized the decadent and ridiculous notions of sixteenth-century chivalric Spain, the romantic critics, by refusing to see him as a fundamentally comic personage, intensified this view and came to perceive the novel as a tragedy. But it should be observed that the romantic-allegorical approach to the *Quijote*, which gained support among critics during the middle of the century in Europe, met with some opposition in France. Prosper Mérimée in 1826 (273), found this interpretation interesting but not Cervantes' explicit intention: Cervantes' characters were real, not symbolic, because, unlike Voltaire, the author of the *Quijote* had resigned himself to living in the world as he found it. C. A. Sainte-Beuve (307) saw few mysteries and hidden meanings in the *Quijote*, and Antoine de Latour (306) carried the anti-Benjumea banner into France, roundly criticizing the Spanish commentator for believing that the *Quijote* was a transformed biography of its author and a cryptic condemnation of Juan Blanco de Paz. These two critics were more interested in the work's character delineation and language, which, they noted, expressed clearly and directly the truth about human nature. Their work typified the kind of admiration for truth, transparency, and realism in the *Quijote* and its characters that became a hallmark of much French criticism of the nineteenth century.

Indeed, the long-held conviction that the *Quijote* was a parody of chivalry suffered many severe blows at the hands of French critics. Adolphe de Puibusque (284) concluded that Cervantes did not attack the institution of chivalry but merely the extravangances of the novels of chivalry; and Charles Magnin (287) asserted that the author wanted only to contrast false enthusiasm with true heroism and that the *Quijote* was essentially an attack on fantastic, foreign literature. Edouard Mennechet (285) went so far as to claim that Cervantes, by placing noble virtue in his hero, was actually paying tribute to chivalry; and Léon de Monge (331) bitterly attacked Léon Gautier (309), saying that the *Quijote* was simply the revenge of Christianity and common sense on a contagious folly. Louis Viardot, in the introduction to his translation, noted that Cervantes' initial attack on chivalry was short-lived because the author quickly grew fond of his protagonist, and as he did so, Don Quijote aroused both sympathy and belief on the part of the reader. Finally, Emile Montégut (323) found in the *Quijote* a strange mixture of the heroic and the commonplace. Writing during the 1880s, after the infusion of romantic ideas had begun to level off, Montégut believed that the book was a truly sad one because Don Quijote had to disavow what he loved. The hero, he said, was a man always in conflict because his mind told him one thing and his emotions another; folly and madness had never sufficed to fully characterize Don Quijote: it was better to say that Don Quijote loved what he did, whether folly or not. These notions, influenced by romanticism, were partially responsible for, and led ultimately to, some rather profound character studies of Don Quijote in France, as evidenced by the work of Montégut and others.

The exercise of comparing the *Quijote* with world classics was also prevalent in France during this period. Prior to the nineteenth century a few comparative studies demonstrated the similarities between the *Quijote* and earlier works such as the *Golden Ass* and *Orlando furioso*. Then, with Cervantes' increasing prestige, many began to examine his influence on modern European writers. In France, H. Hignard (330) studied the influence of the *Quijote* on Dickens' *Pickwick Papers*; G. Larroumet (324) compared the *Quijote* with Marivaux's *Pharsamon*; an anonymous critic (299) insisted that Cervantes influenced Goethe's *Goetz von Berlichingen*; and Ch. M. de Feletz (267) probed the artistic kinship of Cervantes with Lesage and Fielding.

During the final two decades of the nineteenth century, French critics established the *Quijote* once and for all as a work that revealed the true irony of man's condition and a work that served as a paradigm for realism in the modern novel. In 1880, J. Demogeot (322) declared that the *Quijote* was not a tale about a man who ventured naively into the world, but a story of a genuine human being whose experiences rang true because his creator came to love him. Demogeot was obviously impressed by the tableau of life-like characters depicted in the work, as was Mérimée earlier in the century. Emile Gebhart, 1884 (328), called the *Quijote* the first literary manifesto of irony in Spain, since no one there before Cervantes had ever exposed the superficialities and incredible fantasies of chivalric literature. Because of its ironic vision, conflict, and paradox, Gebhart affirmed that the *Quijote* was the "most European" of novels. We can now see why the history of French criticism of the *Quijote* in the nineteenth century, unlike the eighteenth, was a felicitous one, displaying admiration for the work's beautiful harmonization of disillusion, folly, reason, and love, and honoring its crucial place in the world of letters. As Frenchmen tried to penetrate the enigmas of the *Quijote*, criticism of the latter part of the nineteenth century was able at last to advance many good reasons for the novel's universal wisdom and appeal.

Before the nineteenth century, England produced two key scholarly contributions to Cervantine criticism: the Bowle edition of the *Quijote* of 1781 and the earlier, elaborate 1738 edition with Mayans' treatise. In the nineteenth century, with growing admiration for the *Quijote*, the English romantics fancied using Cervantes' masterwork for glorifying the human mystique. Wordsworth, Coleridge, Hazlitt, Lockhart, Byron, Lamb, and others, often under the pervasive influence of the Germans, added much to the already massive Cervantine bibliography. William Wordsworth (416) initiated the trend with his figure of a beautiful but crazed Moorish Don Quijote appearing to a dreaming poet friend in *The Prelude*, written in 1805 (V, 28-139). Samuel Taylor Coleridge, 1836 (436), lauded Don Quijote's impassioned struggle to conceive of a world that could believe in chivalry books and to convince people of their reality by using reason to overcome disbelief in literature. John Dunlop, writing in 1814 (418), paid homage to Cervantes for creating such wonderfully fantastic ideas and imposing them on the world at large in his novel. Following the romantic belief in the imaginative and chivalric ideal, William Hazlitt contended in 1819 (423) that, despite the battered Knight's defeats, chivalry shone with undiminished lustre. Imagination was an instinct, according to Hazlitt, which strengthened Don Quijote's genius, and the whole of the Cervantine masterpiece aspired toward an imaginary good. Hazlitt also demonstrated how, in various ways, Cervantes contributed to the art of the modern novel: First and foremost, his characters were as Nature's own originals; second, like Fielding, Cervantes gave us familiar characters from everyday life with whom the reader could identify, so he might gain insight into the human condition; and third, Cervantes dared to combine the pathetic and sentimental, even more than Fielding and others. Hazlitt thus was among the first to examine Cervantes' influence on modern English novelists, an influence which other romantics began to recognize. Sir Walter Scott [(425), (426)] demonstrated how Cervantes was imitated by Fielding, Smollett, and Lesage in the use of interpolated tales. Scott found similarities between the Don Quijote figure and Fielding's Parson Adams in *Joseph Andrews* and Smollett's Mr. Mackercher in *Peregrine Pickle*. Additionally, an anonymous critic in 1838 (439) compared, apparently for the first time, the Quijote-Sancho fraternization to Dickens' Pickwick and Weller; Swinburne (473) identified Don Quijote with Sterne's Uncle Toby, Thackeray's Colonel Newcome, and Charlotte Brontë's Paul Emanuel, although Leslie Stephen (469) took issue with the idea that Emanuel was in any way comparable to the Knight; and in 1871, W. Thornbury, H. J. Shorthouse, and H. E. Watts published three articles [(461), (462), (463)] on Shakespeare's knowledge of the *Quijote*.

John Lockhart, in his introduction to the 1822 edition of the Peter Motteux translation (428), succinctly summed up the romantics' admiration for the *Quijote*: (1) Cervantes did not confuse the absurdities of knight-errantry with the generosity of his protagonist; and (2) the reader respected Don Quijote despite his madness and revered the noble spirit of the Castilian gentleman in every insane action. Moreover, continued Lockhart, Don Quijote gained true genius and wisdom through experience. Thus, beginning with Lockhart and Hazlitt, critics had come a long way. Not only did they affirm Cervantes' significant influence on modern English and European novelists, but they also understood Cervantes' novel as one of profound human experience in the clash of the imagination against inert reality.

Some romantic and allegorical ideas were challenged head-on in England, however, and the belief that the *Quijote* represented the eternal struggle between the poetic and prosaic even met with wholehearted rejection. John Ormsby (480), for instance, considered such an approach ungainly. Clearly anticipating a less romantic way of thinking about the *Quijote*, Richard Ford, 1845 (444), said that the value of the work lay in its contrast of the sublime and the ridiculous, the true contradiction of Master and Squire. Though aware of the differences between Don Quijote and Sancho, Ford believed, unlike the allegorists, that this dichotomy exuded a spirit of wit throughout the novel.

Other English critics developed the pessimistic view of the *Quijote* established by Sismondi. John Ruskin (460) thought the work so sad as to be deadly, while K. H. Digby (427), driven by the novel's melancholy, concluded that Cervantes even attacked virtue. Surely one of the most pessimistic of Cervantes' critics, Lord Byron, took this idea even further in the unforgettable lines of his *Don Juan*, XIII, 8-11 (429), where he cites the "too true tale" of the *Quijote*, as proof that "all such efforts fail." According to Byron, the sadness in this saddest of all stories is compounded by the fact that it makes us laugh, and with this painfully ironic laughter, Cervantes smiled away Spain's chivalry and all the lofty but empty notions that went with it. Charles Lamb (434) was another who wrote of the *Quijote* in such a despairing and forlorn tone, declaring that laughing at Don Quijote and his Squire shielded the reader from Cervantes' true purpose; and Thomas Roscoe (440) continued in the same vein. Turning back to Sismondi's 1813 critique, Roscoe saw the *Quijote* as a work of melancholy, an attack on the perverse literature of its times. John Ruskin agreed (443), stating that the satirical bent in the interpretation of the *Quijote* only catered to minds of average intelligence; more alert readers would discover the work's full meaning in its moral beauty and universal love. Satire and its antithesis, as one can see, were the focus of much commentary in nineteenth-century England.

Others in England stressed the social, religious, and universal themes of the *Quijote*. Rawdon Brown (466) thought that Cervantes attacked the oppressive policies of the Duke of Lerma. Alexander J. Duffield, one of the most active Cervantists of the time, who often entered into critical dialogue with Spanish scholars, opined that Cervantes was an anti-Church social reformer. Taking part in the famous debate over Cervantes' supposed theological expertise with J. M. Sbarbi in the 1870s, Duffield (467) argued that it was a mistake to claim that Cervantes had the knowledge of a theologian, for by doing so, one risked diminishing his stature as an artist. Duffield also studied the numerous English translations of the *Quijote*, most of which he denounced in the *Crónica de los Cervantistas* (470) and in *Notes and Queries* (474). In 1881, he published his own translation of the *Quijote*, reproducing some of the notes of Bowle and other early editors, and in his full-length book, *Don Quijote, His Critics and Commentators* (478), he addressed such significant issues as the psychology of the Don Quijote character, claiming, as others in the late nineteenth century did, that Cervantes actually made a study of the symptoms of insanity (see C.-B. Dumaine [247]). Duffield was attacked by James Gibson (479), who faulted him for placing too much emphasis on humor in his interpretation of the Don Quijote figure. The *Quijote*, Gibson asserted, could no longer be considered a "pleasant pastime." John Ormsby, in another translation (480), reinforced the ideas of the neoclassicists of the period by shedding light on Cervantes' style, satire, and attack on "bad" literature, as well as on the romantics' "mistaken" theories about the *Quijote*.

American and British critics resembled each other in their approach to the *Quijote*. Both emphasized the novel's practical wisdom [Thomas Roscoe (440)], its wholesome wit, and its cheerful confidence in human nature [Richard Ford (444), George Ticknor (491), Henry Giles (493)]. They also praised the skillful manner in which Cervantes delineated his two protagonists and understood the mysteries of the human mind [Lowell (497), Matthews (498)]. James Russell Lowell further asserted in 1887 that Cervantes' main characters were created from real life with a sufficient amount of artistic distance so as to become stylized portraits separated from reality. Don Quijote and Sancho, said Lowell, were real not because they were drawn from actual people but because of their very abstraction: "they were not so much taken from life as informed with it." Henry Giles also praised Cervantes' inspired character depiction, noting the novelty and naturalness of Cervantes' figures and commending his consistency in their portrayal.

The English-speaking critics introduced several additional topics that would attract the attention of Cervantists after the nineteenth century. Among these were Mary Cowden Clarke's detailed discussion (449) of the dynamism of Cervantes' female characters, Ormbsy's strong suggestion (480) that the *Quijote* was originally intended as a short story, and Hazlitt's praise (423) of Cervantes' inventiveness in describing his characters strictly as individuals, which signals the mutual influence of Don Quijote and Sancho, an issue of great importance in the twentieth century.

The Anglo-American world thus took a strong liking to the *Quijote* before and during the nineteenth century. Along with an ever-increasing awareness of Cervantes' abilities to picture the inner man, these critics tended to reject the earlier anti-chivalric interpretation of the *Quijote* introduced by Temple, Carleton, and Sismondi. There emerged as well much skepticism regarding the romantic and allegorical interpretations associated with these anti-chivalric notions.

As America was embroiled in its struggle for independence and unification throughout the nineteenth century, its criticism was neither as plentiful nor as sophisticated as others until the end of the century, though one could find scattered reaction to Cervantes' work and to the critical controversies in Europe [J. Dennie (487), E. Wigglesworth (488), and the anonymous article "Cervantes and his Writings" (489)]. In 1837, William H. Prescott (490) wrote to praise British scholarship, claiming that the *Quijote* was a moral lesson in correcting the social ills brought about by the reading of books of chivalry, he clearly revealed his alliance with the didactic sphere of criticism. In his 1879 history of Spanish literature, on the other hand, the outstanding American Hispanist George Ticknor (491) found the *Quijote* in no manner limited to an attempt to debunk books of chivalry. He also thought the humor of the *Quijote* extraordinary in the light of Cervantes' calamitous personal experiences. The wit, wisdom, and idealism of the *Quijote* also impressed American critics like H. Giles (493) and E. Thompson (494). Mark Twain (495) declared that the *Quijote* not only attacked books of chivalry but the institution of chivalry itself and its values, which, according to Twain, had been falsely idealized by Sir Walter Scott. Still, James Russell Lowell's critique of 1887, mentioned above, remains one of the most substantive, provocative, and revealing early American interpretations. Like Irving and Ticknor before him, Lowell was intimately acquainted with Spanish letters and figured among the most gifted American Hispanists of the past century. He saw Don Quijote as a noble, heroic, pathetic, imaginative, and sometimes ridiculous figure, one of the most perfect characters in all of fiction, so psychologically true and so full of marvelously whimsical inconsistencies. Lowell also felt that Cervantes' satire was pervasive but never obtrusive and that, in sum, the *Quijote* featured good-humored criticism of the doctrinaire reformers of its time. Lowell's commentary was obviously one of the most inspired in a time and place where *Quijote* criticism did not abound. Nineteenth-century Americans, like their British antecedents, profoundly admired Cervantes' novel, an attitude which endured in the twentieth century, particularly in the studies lauding the geniality, transparency, and originality of Cervantes' figures.

The influence of the *Quijote* in Russia was spawned by translations early in the nineteenth century, and Cervantine criticism emerged there in the 1840s with Vissarion Belinski (499), long after other Europeans and North Americans agreed on the noble nature of Cervantes' hero. The legendary commentaries of Turgenev and Dostoyevsky especially indicate how attractive the *Quijote* was to the Russians, but a few Russian critics, namely A. Lvov, 1862 (501), and N. I. Storozhenko, 1885 (507), did not accept the dignity of Don Quijote, seeing him instead as an irrational figure concerned principally with his own fame.

Since religious orthodoxy had been imposed in Russia at the time, a major problem for Russian critics involved portraying a saintly character in a convincing way for a modern audience. Belinski and V. G. Korolenko, 1890 (509), pictured Cervantes' hero as an eternal type, a man of faith and imagination. Ivan Turgenev's 1860 study of Don Quijote and Hamlet (500) devised the two figures according to two fundamental aspects of human nature: fidelity and doubt. Don Quijote, ever faithful to his goal, never wavered from his path to idealism; Hamlet, on the other hand, constantly submitted himself to introspective analysis and therefore always doubted himself. According to Turgenev, Don Quijote had faith in something eternal; despite his irrationality, he had ideals, as one would expect from a knight-errant. Recalling Clemencín and other neoclassicists, Turgenev believed Don Quijote essentially a moral figure. He also used him as a model of a revolutionary, although he thought his character, like that of all idealists, was limited by too narrow a vision of the world. V. Karelin, 1866 (502), another who associated social conditions with the literature of chivalry, attributed the latter to a diseased society, all of which brought about Don Quijote's madness.

Late in the century, Fyodor Dostoyevsky wrote some of the most laudatory words on the *Quijote* that have ever been recorded. No literary work, according to Dostoyevsky, was more powerful or more profound. Cervantists everywhere had probably come to the same conclusion in one form or another, but none so inspiringly and so poignantly as Dostoyevsky, especially in this story from *Diary of a Writer*, 1876-81 (504): If the world were to come to an end and man were asked how he would describe the way he understood life, he would exhibit a copy of the *Quijote* and say, "Such is my inference from life—can you condemn me for it?" For Dostoyevsky the *Quijote* was a work of bitter irony that revealed man's tendency toward self-deception and self-knowledge at the same time. Only once every several hundred years, he declared, does a book like this one come along. Dostoyevsky's observations on the *Quijote* have become well-known to modern critics.

As the language of the *Quijote* is so close to the language of colonial Latin America, it comes as no surprise that critics and scholars there studied Cervantes' work with much enthusiasm. Andrés Bello's classic Spanish grammar, written for Latin Americans in 1845 (529), lists numerous words and expressions from the *Quijote*. Yet another side of Latin American commentary showed some inclination toward the politics of liberation in the novel. But these political interpretations of the *Quijote* did not emerge until the last two decades of the nineteenth century, with well-documented commentaries on the anti-despotic spirit of the *Quijote* of Martínez Silva, 1879 (539), and Adolfo Saldías, 1893 (551). Others in Latin America downplayed the socio-political meaning of Cervantes' work. While Sergio Arboleda, 1879 (538), conceded that the *Quijote* accurately reflected the author's times, he insisted that its greatness lay in its originality, its epic breadth and depth, and its lofty opinion of human dignity, not only in its political values. Other critics, like Juan Montalvo, 1882 (540), and Enrique José

Varona, 1883 (541), adopted the romantic interpretation that the *Quijote* represented all of mankind in its two protagonists: the high and the low, the spirit and the senses, the imaginative and the realistic. Miguel Antonio Caro in 1874 (533) supported this allegorical interpretation in part, stating that Cervantes did not present the poetic and the prosaic in their purest forms, but rather combined them in characters who have both virtues and vices: he added madness to the spiritual-poetic and discretion to the material-prosaic. Amenodoro Urdaneta, author of one of the most important pieces of literary criticism on the *Quijote*, 1877 (536), accepted Don Quijote's madness as one of the salient features of his character and declared the work a profound commentary on human history, because it dealt with ordinary people and at the same time reached the depths of the human heart. Several critics also turned their attention to the importance of the autobiographical elements in the work. Arboleda, for example, emphasized the noble character of the author (who, he said, was reincarnated in his hero) rather than the unfortunate events and circumstances of Cervantes' life.

This sampling shows a universally positive tone in Latin American criticism vis-à-vis the *Quijote*, and in line with this favorable reception, toward the end of the century, poetry competitions commemorating Cervantes abounded and eventually became an integral part of an upbeat Cervantine tradition there [(534), (537)].

In Italy, *Quijote* criticism, developed by Francesco de Sanctis, Rodolfo Renier, Enrico Nencioni, Angelo Gubernatis, Michele Scherillo, and Arturo Farinelli, tended to treat the novel's comic aspects. In his famed *Storia della letteratura italiana*, 1870 (515), De Sanctis claimed that Cervantes' Quijote was even more of a parody of chivalry than Ariosto's *Orlando furioso* and that the comic element in chivalry stands out more because of the presence of the realistic elements in the Cervantine masterpiece. Similarly, Renier, in his *Ariosto e Cervantes*, 1878 (516), rejecting the symbolic interpretations of the work, declared that the contrast of the real and ideal and the resultant comedy set the predominant tone in the *Quijote*. Nencioni (517), on the other hand, claimed that Don Quijote was an admired but anachronistic madman. This critic concerned himself with the medical causes of Don Quijote's monomania, as did others in Europe during the latter part of the nineteenth century. Angelo Gubernatis, writing in 1883 (518), described the *Quijote* as a humorous rendition of the Icarus theme, although, as he saw it, the fault of Don Quijote's mission lay in the fact that it was rooted in the past. It is difficult, however, to fully measure Italy's contributions to *Quijote* criticism—either in depth or quantity—during this period, because it did not reach the plateau at which we find this criticism in other countries.

Nineteenth-century thinkers and critics confronted for the first time many of the issues crucial to a modern reading of the *Quijote*. First, they rescued the work from obscurity and began to treat it as a world classic, a reward they felt it so richly deserved. Broadly examining the intent of the author, they rejected the notion that it had limited interest as a fundamentally Spanish work depicting Spanish types and attacking Spanish institutions. Critics had begun to whittle away at this narrow approach after the seventeenth century; in fact, the first breakthrough in recognizing the novel's universality came in 1700 with Motteux's translation. Later, the *Quijote*'s universal appeal became the prime concern of German romantics, especially as they searched for moral values in the work, which they saw as an allegory of man. The ideas of these German allegorists arrived late in Spain, but at the end of the nineteenth century, with the thrust of the *krausista* movement, the belief in the symbolic power of the Knight and Squire as regenerative forces in Spain grew in intensity and profoundly influenced turn-of-the-century thinkers.

Thus the romantic approach to the *Quijote*, carefully treated in Anthony Close's recent book (15), and fundamental to Cervantine criticism in Europe and the Americas throughout the nineteenth century, is a phenomenon for which that century has become famous. Those critics pictured Don Quijote and Sancho as symbolic characters representing the poetic and prosaic, the imaginative and the concrete, and the heroic and the selfish. They also viewed Don Quijote as a noble figure who must struggle with a workaday world hardly cognizant of the spiritual, an idea which emerged along with increased admiration for him among writers like Pope, Johnson, and Reeve. Later, Schiller converted Don Quijote into a tragic figure, preparing the way for the romantic interpretation. Opposed to these allegorists were critics who insisted that the value of the novel lay in Cervantes' realistic depiction of people and customs of his times. Herder and Humboldt were of this persuasion, and they were later followed by Valera and Mérimée. However, while a major debate of the nineteenth century did arise between these two groups, critics like Friedrich Schlegel made efforts to fashion an analysis that would account for both the universal as well as the particular in Cervantes' masterpiece.

The *Quijote* as a bitterly ironic tale and a novel that uncovered the paradox of mankind was an important interpretation opened up by thinkers like Dostoyevsky and a few others. Cervantes' ironic approach to matters, treating comic incidents seriously and serious incidents humorously, caused critics to conclude that the *Quijote* was an enigma. Many pondered the author's dual attitude toward idealism, bravery, and honor, and numerous attempts were made to explain its double meaning. Indeed, conflicting sentiments on Cervantes' part concerning his hero's illusions and credibility became the one of the major themes of twentieth-century criticism from Ortega onward.

Pre-twentieth-century thought also contributed to this idea of paradox by showing that it was the *Quijote* that first began to break down Spain's ancient heroic ideal. Valera rejected the simplistic interpretation of chivalric satire and Luis Vidart reflected on the novel's ambiguous tone, its concern with the amorphous nature of man's existence, while various French, German, British, and American critics mused on its irony. This irony, so important for our understanding of the *Quijote* today, seems to have stemmed from the pre-nineteenth-century belief that the *Quijote* spelled the destruction of Spain's chivalry and heroism. Critics such as Clemencín and Salvá then perpetuated this idea and left it for others to build upon, and it was this central principle of chivalric satire that critics in the twentieth century pursued in their attempts to solve the riddles of the *Quijote*. Emile Gebhart summed the problem up well in 1884 with the observation that chivalric literature in the sixteenth century had never suffered an ironic jolt until Cervantes in his *Quijote* manifested the ambiguity which others in Spain refused to impose on that hallowed tradition.

Critics of the nineteenth century devoted themselves to additional challenging questions of Cervantes' literary satire, for they realized that the objective of the author of the *Quijote* was to dismantle a perverse literary genre and the evil reading habits it had bred. Unquestionably, one of the *Quijote*'s major themes was the value of what people read, since Cervantes had his characters frequently stop to ponder the merits of the books they liked or heard that others liked. Little wonder that what Cervantes considered a good book became a central issue for all who studied his work in the nineteenth century.

However, even in the earliest interpretations of Cervantes' novel scholars attempted to find some authorial intention other than the one Cervantes had explicitly mentioned in the text. Thus researchers in the nineteenth century became profoundly interested in extrinsic influences on the *Quijote*. Seventeenth- and eighteenth-century French commentators thought the *Quijote* a parody of Spanish institutions, a work of reason opposed to the unreasonable in society. This approach gained new life in the early nineteenth century with Sismondi and Puigblanch, who saw Spain as a land crushed under the heel of the Inquisition. As the nineteenth century moved along, and especially after the revolutions of 1848, critics of a political bent began to believe that the author and his hero-knight were true fighters for liberty. In Spain, Benjumea's books and commentaries supported this conviction, and from there, the socio-political tendency in criticism spread to Latin America, where it became popular later in the century.

Nineteenth-century investigators discovered the merit of Cervantes' language; in fact, they are in part responsible for the awe in which we hold it today. In addition, they called attention to Cervantes' profound knowledge of the Spanish character as revealed both in the words he used and the proverbs he employed. In this regard, then, one must remember that a good portion of the nineteenth-century legacy has to do with reverence for Cervantes' wit and the naturalness of his prose, as well as fascination for his penetrating character studies. And to wind up matters, Valera, Revilla, and others, like French critics before them, hit upon a key interpretation of the *Quijote* late in the century: although mad, Don Quijote brought a measure of sanity to life because he gained the sympathy of his readers. It thus became easy for nineteenth-century critics to believe in the Knight and Squire because of the transparency and truth of their motives and actions.

With the ever-rising prestige of the *Quijote* came a plethora of commentaries in the nineteenth century about its influence on later writers, another major criterion for judging the value of a literary work. Although only sporadic in Spain, such studies abounded in France, Germany, and England. And clearly, with these studies, which affirmed that the *Quijote* was a world classic, a supreme parody and allegory of man, and a model of Castilian prose (not to mention its accurate picture of sixteenth-century Spain), nineteenth-century critics left a solid framework upon which the twentieth century could build.

Principal Works Consulted

The following list of principal works consulted is not meant to be exhaustive. As the list would suggest, source material for nineteenth-century *Quijote* criticism is abundant and presents the subject in incredibly detailed variety. While we have examined virtually all bibliographical materials, both major and minor, we have elected to record hereunder only those works which have been the most useful in locating the richest storehouses of information on early *Quijote* criticism.

1. Baldensperger, Fernand, and Werner P. Friederich. *Bibliography of Comparative Literature*. New York: Russell & Russell, 1960. [Issued in 1950 as *University of North Carolina Studies in Comparative Literature*, No. 1.]
2. Barbera, Raymond E. *Cervantes: A Critical Trajectory*. Boston: The Mirage Press, 1971.
3. Bardon, Maurice. *Don Quichotte en France au XVIIe et au XVIIIe siècle, 1605-1815*. Paris: Honoré Champion, 1931.
4. Bardon, Maurice. "*Don Quichotte* en France: L'interprétation romantique." *Les Lettres Romanes* 3 (1949): 263-82; 4 (1950): 95-117.
5. Bardon, Maurice. "*Don Quichotte* et le roman réaliste français: Stendhal, Balzac, Flaubert." *Revue de Littérature Comparée* 16 (1936): 63-81.
6. Bergel, Lienhard. "Cervantes in Germany." In *Cervantes Across the Centuries*. Edited by Angel Flores and M. J. Benardete. New York: Gordian Press, 1969, pp. 315-52.
7. Bertrand, J.-J. A. *Cervantès et le romantisme allemand*. Paris: Félix Alcan, 1914.
8. Bertrand, J.-J. A. "Génesis de la concepción romántica de *Don Quijote* en Francia." *Anales Cervantinos* 3 (1953): 1-41; 4 (1954): 41-76; 5 (1955-1956): 79-142.
9. Betz, Louis Paul. *La Littérature comparée: Essai bibliographique*. Second edition. New York: AMS Press, 1969.

10. Brimeur, J. "Supplément français à la *Bibliographie* de Rius." *Revue Hispanique* 15 (1906): 819-42.

11. Brüggemann, Werner. *Cervantes und die Figur des Don Quijote in Kunstanschauung und Dichtung der deutschen Romantik.* Münster/Westfalen: Aschendorff, 1958.

12. Burton, A. P. "Cervantes the Man Seen through English Eyes in the Seventeenth and Eighteenth Centuries." *Bulletin of Hispanic Studies* 45 (1968): 1-15.

13. Carilla, Emilio. *Cervantes y América.* Buenos Aires: Imp. de la Universidad de Buenos Aires, 1951.

14. Cherchi, Paolo. *Capitoli di critica cervantina (1605-1789).* Rome: Bulzoni, 1977.

15. Close, Anthony. *The Romantic Approach to "Don Quixote."* Cambridge, England: Cambridge University Press, 1978.

16. Consiglio, Carlo. "Datos para una bibliografía italiana de Cervantes." *Revista Bibliográfica y Documental* 2 (1948): 107-18.

17. Derjavin, Const. "La crítica cervantina en Rusia." *Boletín de la Real Academia de la Historia* 94 (1929): 215-38.

18. Efron, Arthur. "Satire Denied: A Critical History of English and American *Don Quixote* Criticism." Ph.D. dissertation, University of Washington, 1964.

19. Ford, Jeremiah D. M., and Ruth Lansing. *Cervantes: A Tentative Bibliography of his Works and of the Biographical Material Concerning him.* Cambridge, Mass.: Harvard University Press, 1931.

20. Fucilla, Joseph G. "Italian Cervantiana." *Hispanic Review* 2 (1934): 235-40.

21. Fucilla, Joseph G. "Bibliografía italiana de Cervantes (Suplemento a Ford and Lansing: *Cervantes: A Tentative Bibliography*)." In *Relaciones hispanoitalianas. Revista de Filología Española*, Anejo 59 (1953): 50-62.

22. Giménez Caballero, Ernesto. *Don Quijote ante el mundo (y ante mí).* San Juan, Puerto Rico: Inter-American University Press, 1979.

23. Grismer, Raymond L. *Cervantes: A Bibliography.* Vol. I, New York: H. W. Wilson, 1946. Vol. II, Minneapolis: Burgess-Beckwith, 1963.

24. Harkey, Joseph Harry. "*Don Quixote* and American Fiction through Mark Twain." Ph.D. dissertation, University of Tennessee, 1967.

25. Heiser, M. F. "Cervantes in the United States." *Hispanic Review* 15 (1947): 409-35.

26. Icaza, Francisco A. de. *El Quijote durante tres siglos.* Madrid: Imp. de Fortanet, 1918.

27. Knowles, Edwin B. "Cervantes and English Literature." In *Cervantes Across the Centuries.* Edited by Angel Flores and M. J. Benardete. New York: Gordian Press, 1969, pp. 277-303.
28. Krauss, Werner. *Miguel de Cervantes: Leben und Werk.* Neuwied and Berlin: Luchterhand, 1966.
29. Mañach, Jorge. "Las interpretaciones del *Quijote.*" *Mercurio Peruano* 5 (1920): 443-62.
30. Meier, Harri. "Zur Entwicklung der europäischen *Quijote*-Deutung." *Romanische Forschungen* 54 (1940): 227-64.
31. Meregalli, Franco. "Cervantes nella critica romantica tedesca (stato degli studi)." *Annali della Facoltà di Lingue e Letterature Straniere di Ca' Foscari (Università degli Studi di Venezia)* 11, no. 2 (1972): 381-95.
32. Meregalli, Franco. "La critica cervantina dell'ottocento in Francia e in Spagna." *Anales Cervantinos* 15 (1976): 121-48.
33. Murillo, Luis Andrés, ed. *Don Quijote de la Mancha, III: Bibliografía fundamental.* Madrid: Editorial Castalia, 1978.
34. *The National Union Catalogue: Pre-1956 Imprints.* 754 vols. London: Mansell, 1968-1981.
35. Neumann, Max-Hellmut. "Cervantes in Deutschland." *Die Neueren Sprachen* 25 (1917): 147-62 and 193-213.
36. Neumann, Max-Hellmut. "Cervantes in Frankreich (1582 bis 1910)." *Revue Hispanique* 78 (1930): 1-309.
37. Peers, E. Allison. "Cervantes in England." *Bulletin of Spanish Studies* 24 (1947): 226-38.
38. Peers, E. Allison. "Aportación de los hispanistas extranjeros al estudio de Cervantes." *Revista de Filología Española* 32 (1948): 155-88.
39. Pérez Beato y Blanco, Manuel. *Bibliografía comentada sobre los escritos publicados en la Isla de Cuba relativos al Quijote.* Havana: Diario de la Marina, 1905.
40. Pérez Pastor, Cristóbal. *Documentos cervantinos hasta ahora inéditos, recogidos y anotados.* 2 vols. Madrid: Imp. de Fortanet, 1897-1902.
41. Real de la Riva, César. "Historia de la crítica e interpretación de la obra de Cervantes." *Revista de Filología Española* 32 (1948): 107-50.
42. Rius y de Llosellas, Leopoldo. *Bibliografía crítica de las obras de Miguel de Cervantes Saavedra.* 3 vols. Madrid: M. Murillo, 1895-1904. [Reprint, New York: Burt Franklin, 1970.]
43. Rodríguez, Miguel Santiago. *Catálogo de la biblioteca cervantina de D. José María Asensio y Toledo.* Madrid: Gráficas Ultra, 1948.

44. Schevill, Rudolph. "Three Centuries of Don Quixote." *University of California Chronicle* 15 (1913): 181-206.

45. Serís, Homero. *La colección cervantina de la Sociedad Hispánica de América.* Urbana: The University of Illinois Press, 1918.

46. Simón Díaz, José. *Manual de bibliografía de la literatura española.* Barcelona: Gustavo Gili, 1966.

47. Simón Díaz, José. *Bibliografía de la literatura hispánica*, VIII. Madrid: Consejo Superior de Investigaciones Científicas, 1970.

48. Tave, Stuart M. *The Amiable Humorist.* Chicago: University of Chicago Press, 1960.

49. Turkevich, Ludmilla Buketoff. *Cervantes in Russia.* Princeton, N. J.: Princeton University Press, 1950.

50. Turkevich, Ludmilla Buketoff. *Spanish Literature in Russia and in the Soviet Union, 1735-1964.* Metuchen, N. J.: The Scarecrow Press, 1967.

51. Uribe-Echevarría, Juan. *Cervantes en las letras hispanoamericanas, antología y crítica.* Santiago de Chile: Editorial Universidad de Chile, 1949.

52. Valle, Rafael Heliodoro, and Emilia Romero. *Bibliografía cervantina en la América española.* Mexico: Universidad Nacional Autónoma, Academia de la Lengua, 1950.

A Note On Style

Entries are normally written from the point of view of the critics cited, and the original language has been preserved whenever possible. A limited number of items, which lend themselves only to description (correspondence, collections of articles and speeches, bibliographical catalogues, etc.), are written from the annotators' point of view and are enclosed in brackets.

Where absolutely necessary, original spelling of titles of entries has been kept, but in most cases spelling has been standardized or modernized for the sake of uniformity.

Spanish Criticism

53. Capmany, Antonio de. *Sumario de la vida y escritos de Cervantes*. In *Teatro histórico-crítico de la elocuencia española*, IV. Madrid: Antonio de Sancha, 1786-1794, pp. 410-510.

The *Quijote* deserves praise for its sententious language, but it is unfortunate that Cervantes' greatness as a writer has not been recognized in Spain, for the work's purity of diction and clarity of phrase is appreciated even by untutored audiences. There is strict adherence to decorum in the *Quijote* as the language is natural throughout, and its variety and beauty are demonstrated in the following passages from both parts: the armies of sheep, the Yangüesans, the fulling-hammers, and the Knight of the Mirrors episodes; the portraits of Maritornes, Grisóstomo, and various descriptions of Don Quijote; the discourse on arms and letters and several dialogues between Don Quijote and Sancho.

54. Gatell, P. *La moral de Don Quijote deducida de la historia que de sus hazañas escribió Cide Hamete Benegeli*. Madrid: José Herrera, 1789. 72 pages. [Also published in Madrid, 1793, and Barcelona, 1832.]

How can one defend morally the actions of Don Quijote? After living to a ripe old age, he decides to become a knight-errant, which is quite strange for one who, by the age of fifty, should have become wise. He clearly loses the road to virtue as contention and deceit become his occupation. He had plans to become an adventurer, but instead proves useless to his family and country. By the time the innkeeper tells him to go home and attend to his own business, it is too late for him to repent. It is always difficult to give advice, but especially difficult to advise those who do not believe they need it. The mercy of God, however, is infinite, and at the end of his life Don Quijote has his chance to renounce his madness. Thanks to good fortune, the evil books of Don Quijote's library go into the fire, while the good ones are saved, and as he prepares to die, he realizes his mistake and rejects once and for all the books that led to his derangement.

Sancho, on the other hand, is wise in listening to the moral lessons given to him by Don Quijote before setting out to govern the Insula Barataria. He also provides a moral counterbalance for his master, at first warning him not to attack windmills. But Don Quijote does not listen and looks further for more adventures, while the humble Sancho cannot command the attention of the Knight.

Some find fame the way Don Quijote did; others do what he proposed for the glory of their native land. When Don Quijote becomes Alonso Quijano el Bueno, he can truly think of righting the wrongs of society, and his faith can actually correct the actions of men for the good of their country.

55. Garcés, Gregorio. *Fundamento del vigor y elegancia de la lengua castellana.* 2 vols. Madrid: Imp. de la Viuda de Ibarra, 1791, I, pp. i-xxiii.

Cervantes' language in the *Quijote* should be praised as "ameno" and "cabal." There is reason for comparing his humor with that of Plautus and his urbanity with that of Terence. Cervantes should be regarded as a writer who uplifted the Spanish tongue to such a point of propriety and festive grace that the works of classical antiquity are hardly superior to it. Cervantes' style is faultless and pure, its cadence harmonious, and all the matters of Don Quijote's history are described thoroughly.

56. P. y. G., D. A. A. *Instrucciones económicas y políticas dadas por el famoso Sancho Panza... a un hijo suyo.* Madrid: Imp. Real, 1791. 64 pages. [Also a 1790 edition. Reprinted by Sbarbi in vol. 5, pp. 1-39 of *Refranero general español,* Madrid, 1876.]

Sancho's proverbs, which have enriched the Castilian language, were once used in a conversation with one of his offspring and describe the responsibilities of a governor. These sayings deal with presumption, gossip, humility, careful speech, learning a trade, and being a good Christian.

57. Ramírez y Blanco, Alejandro. *Respuestas de Sanchico Panza a dos cartas que le remitió su padre desde la Insula Barataria....* Alcalá de Henares: Isidro López, 1791. 37 pages. [Reprinted by Sbarbi in vol. 5, pp. 41-66 of *Refranero general español,* Madrid, 1876.]

In this parody, Sancho replies to his son regarding the art of governing in his usual semiserious tone. He, of course, makes liberal use of proverbs. Topics deal with behavior: not taking bribes, not trusting one's luck too far, not being impetuous, etc.

58. Pellicer, Juan Antonio. "Discurso preliminar" to *Don Quijote de la Mancha.* Madrid: Gabriel de Sancha, 1797, I, pp. i-liv.

Cervantes' principal purpose in writing the *Quijote* was to put an end to the influence that books of chivalry had on readers of that genre. Consequently, the *Quijote* is a satire, a kind of *Amadís* made ridiculous, or a parody of a serious book. The *Quijote* is also a didactic work, since it criticizes men's customs in order to teach, and is closer to the work of Apuleius than it is to those of other classical authors, like Homer, because it deals with transformations (or metamorphoses) and humorous situations.

The origins of the *Quijote* lie in the chivalry book, and later these books become the target of Cervantes' satire. Thus it is important to define exactly what is meant by *novela de caballerías*.

[Pellicer attempts to establish a corrected edition of the work. He employs the 1608 edition, not the 1605 original, for Part I and the *princeps* for Part II, and makes substantial emendations in both texts. Notes range from grammatical to literary and historical. He rejects the "plan cronológico" of Vicente de los Ríos and publishes a life of Cervantes along with newly discovered documents that include the suspicious murder of Gaspar de Ezpeleta by a member of the Cervantes household and other documents relating to the birth and death of Cervantes' relatives.]

59. Quintana, Manuel José. "Miguel de Cervantes." In *Obras completas. Biblioteca de Autores Españoles*, XIX. Reprint, Madrid: Real Academia Española, 1946, pp. 85-105. [From the 1797-1798 edition of *Don Quijote*, Madrid: Imp. Real. Original edition of *Obras* is 1827.]

[The original version, "Noticia sobre la vida y obras de Cervantes," was prepared when Quintana was very young and was written prior to the works of Pellicer and M. Fernández de Navarrete. Furthermore, the version found in the *Obras* is an extensively revised version of the original essay.]

Cervantes' power of fantasy and his novelistic execution are praiseworthy. He is ingenious in the way he makes his hero ridiculous as well as virtuous and discreet without offending the unity of character. The variety found in the masterpiece is also to be commended. However, the *doctos* who eviscerate the beauty of the *Quijote* seek to adjust it to rules and models that have no relationship to it. Genius and wit are not subject to rules and models. Nature presented Don Quijote to Cervantes, his imagination took control of the figure, and instinct did the rest.

In spite of what critics say, the *Quijote* is not frivolous or insipid. How can a frivolous book have corrected an era?; and how can a book of invention and discretion be insipid? One must also censure as puerile those who criticize Cervantes' grammar. True, the *Quijote* has its faults: its language is careless at times, the style is occasionally repetitious, and there are slips and anachronisms. But these facts merely indicate the ease and abandon with which Cervantes composed his narrative.

Voltaire was wrong to compare the *Quijote* with Ariosto's *Orlando furioso*, since the mad heroes are quite different and the *Orlando* is a chivalric novel. Cervantes' masterpiece had no model, and it has had few true imitations.

60. Munárriz, José Luis. "Lección XX: Examen crítico del estilo de Cervantes." In *Lecciones sobre la retórica y las bellas artes, por Hugo Blair: Las tradujo del inglés Don José Luis Munárriz*, II. Third edition. Madrid: Ibarra, 1817, pp. 198-248. [First Spanish version, 1798-1801. Based in part on Hugh Blair's *Lectures on Rhetoric and Belles Lettres*, 1783.]

While Cervantes is at times guilty of carelessness and on other occasions overly cautious to the point of affectation, his style is so elegant and estimable that imperfections are insignificant.

The *Quijote* contributed to the extinction of the books of chivalry; the ingenious "invención" of Cervantes' novel as well as its morality should be emphasized and the studies of Cervantes' work by V. de los Ríos and A. Capmany should be considered important analyses of Cervantes' language and style.

61. García Arrieta, Agustín. *Principios filosóficos de la literatura: obra escrita en francés por M. Batteux, profesor real, de la academia francesa, y de la de inscripciones y bellas letras: traducida al castellano, ilustrada y completada con varios suplementos, y los correspondientes apéndices sobre la literatura española*. Madrid: Imp. de Sancha, 1805, pp. 151-223.

Cervantes' novel deserves praise for its originality, but it is wrong to compare it with an epic poem as V. de los Ríos did. Cervantes' work has many merits: naturalness, mirth, satire, as well as the veracity of sketches, a variety of episodic adventures, and above all, skill at teaching while it delights.

Cervantes has events in the *Quijote* make the hero laughable and at the same time make him seem valiant. Only Cervantes could have invented a style so ingenious that Don Quijote could be ridiculous in reality and plausible in imagination, amusing readers in a double way. Cervantes also ingeniously brings an end to the adventures of his mad hidalgo: defeated as a knight-errant, Don Quijote gives his word not to continue his profession, and thus his madness ends as a result of the very madness that required him to fulfill faithfully his original promise.

Both the Knight and the Squire have dual characters. Don Quijote is discreet yet mad on the subject of chivalry; Sancho is clever by nature yet simple in upbringing. As a result, Cervantes is able to vary his characters in so many ways without disfiguring them.

Praise is owed to other aspects of Cervantes' narrative style, including the careful manner in which the novelist prepares events, arranges episodes, creates suspense, and interpolates additional adventures. His style is natural and appropriate to the material of his story, simple and familiar without violating decorum, and highly amusing without being absurd. Nevertheless, there are shortcomings: occasional carelessness and overpolished phrases, affectation, and occasional inappropriate use of antiquated words.

The moral purpose of the *Quijote* merits attention. The novel condemns those who feel that they are above the law and interfere with others—faults in society attributable to the anarchy praised in chivalry books. But it would be wrong to infer that Cervantes ridiculed knight-errantry only in Spain, for the chivalric spirit was common to all of Europe.

One would be even more mistaken to conclude that Cervantes destroys the idea of honor and extinguishes the martial spirit in the hearts of Spaniards. Cervantes knew that true valor came from reason, justice, and moderation and that chivalric novels destroyed the true concepts of honor and bravery by twisting them into impulse and reprehensible rashness. Such books contained only an extremely superficial concept of honor; moreover, they presented lascivious episodes harmful to men and women alike. However, the author of the *Quijote* was not content with merely condemning vice; he also sought to improve men by praising virtue, decency, good faith, compassion, and generosity.

62. Pérez, Nicolás [El Setabiense]. *El Anti-Quijote*. Madrid: Justo Sánchez, 1805. 272 pages.

There are many imperfections in the *Quijote*, particularly the confusion about the era in which the hero lived, variations of the name of Sancho's wife, inconsistent portrayal of Sancho's character, impossible chronology of the plot, errors regarding geography, and other historical mistakes.

[Pérez originally intended to publish six volumes of criticism of the *Quijote*, but only one appeared.]

63. Eximeno y Pujades, Antonio. *Apología de Miguel de Cervantes sobre los yerros que se le han notado*. Madrid: Imp. de la Administración del Real Arbitrio, 1806. 139 pages.

Cervantes must be defended against the attacks of editors (principally V. de los Ríos) concerning the verisimilitude of Dorotea, Luscinda, Zoraida, and the Clavileño episode. Furthermore, there is no good reason to criticize the so-called chronological inconsistency of the time lapse between Parts I and II, because that may be justified by readers who accept fiction without concerning themselves with the falsehoods sanctioned by the dictates of history.

64. Foronda, Valentín de [T. E.]. *Observaciones sobre algunos puntos de la obra de Don Quijote.* London: 1807. 74 pages. [See Baig Baños, Aurelio, *Un folleto raro cervantófilo,* Madrid: Imp. del Asilo de Huérfanos del S. C. de Jesús, 1913.]

Although the *Quijote* is a model that should be used to learn how to write good Spanish, there are several problems with Cervantes' language that ought to be noted before one agrees to the excellence of his style. Grammatical defects, gallicisms, harsh-sounding expressions, and even base language are among them. Here are two examples of sound combinations in his prose to which a reader may object: "Hasta que cuando él quisiese aquel hecho se publicase," and "Sin tener ni descubrir donde aquella noche se recogiesen."

65. Puigblanch, Antonio [Natanael Jomtob]. *La Inquisición sin máscara.* Cádiz: N. Niel, 1811, pp. 201-210. [Reprinted by B. Ruiz, Lima: Imp. de los Huérfanos, 1813, and in English as *The Inquisition Unmasked,* London: Baldwin, Craddock, and Joy, 1816.]

A tribunal so monstrous as the Inquisition could not escape the penetrating eye of the immortal author of *Don Quijote,* nor was it possible for him to abstain from holding it up to ridicule. Thus do we find Cervantes impugning this establishment, not in a slight and hasty manner, but at considerable length and in his usual tone, as a comparison between Cervantes' description of the tribunal and a real one demonstrates. As this was undoubtedly the most interesting, though at the same time the most dangerous of all objects of his criticism, Cervantes was induced to reserve it for the last of his labors, where it might serve as a kind of conclusion. The following episodes in the 1615 *Quijote* are parodies of the Inquisition: the enchanted head adventure (chapter 62), the second visit with the Duke (chapters 68-69), and Sancho's return to his village with the inquisitional trappings thrown over Dapple and the mitre used in the pretended funeral of Altisidora attached to Dapple's head (chapter 73).

66. García Arrieta, Agustín. *El espíritu de Miguel de Cervantes, o la filosofía de este grande ingenio presentada en máximas....* Madrid: Viuda de Vallín, 1814. 228 pages. [Reprinted in 1885 and again, as *Filosofía del Quijote,* in 1933).

[An alphabetized collection of some of the wisest sayings about the civil government of man, knowledge about his world, and principles of justice found scattered throughout Cervantes' writings. Themes include everything from *afrenta* to *zapatero.* This is suggested reading for all and especially for young readers, since it may serve as a manual on life.]

67. Marchena, Josef. "Discurso Preliminar" to *Lecciones de filosofía moral y elocuencia*. 2 vols. Bordeaux: Beaume, 1820, I, pp. xlvii-lvii. [Dated 1819.]

   The *Quijote* is without doubt the first of our modern novels and is founded upon the hero's mania for resurrecting knight-errantry. The protagonist is an angry man enraptured by visions of beauty and ideal virtue. It is clear that as the novel progresses, his "madness" moderates. In fact in Part II he is not always mad. But what never changes in Don Quijote is the essential goodness of his soul, his love for justice, his generosity, virtue, altruism, and compassion.

68. Navarrete, Martín Fernández de. *Vida de Miguel de Cervantes Saavedra*. Barcelona: Viuda e Hijos de Gorchs, 1834, pp. 191-253. [First published in 1819.]

   When Cervantes saw that readers did not understand the purpose of the *Quijote* he composed the *Buscapié* (Ruidíaz legend) to explain the allusions. While the novel may not be a satire of Charles V, the Duke of Lerma, or Spain as a whole, Cervantes did intend to critize Spanish customs as a secondary goal of the *Quijote*.

   The commentaries of Pellicer, V. de los Ríos, Voltaire, and Faria y Sousa should be ignored whenever they insist that Cervantes had imitated earlier works of fiction.

   The 1615 *Quijote* is especially skillful in its variety, discretion, and relationship of episodes to the main action, and is a satire of higher things, such as incompetence in government.

69. Bastús y Carrera, V. Joaquín. *Nuevas anotaciones al Ingenioso hidalgo Don Quijote de la Mancha*. Barcelona: Viuda e Hijos de Gorchs, 1834. 100 pages. [First published in the Real Academia edition of the *Quijote*, Barcelona, 1832.]

   [These notes supplement those of Mayans, Ríos, Pellicer, Navarrete, and Bowle. They focus on the customs of knight-errantry, the heroism and the majesty of the joust, and the gentility and passion of the people who take part in these games. Bastús offers, moreover, a succinct analysis of books of chivalry cited by Cervantes and explains knighting ceremonies, battles and jousts, the code of jurisprudence, and the use of various pieces of armor. He also attempts to find the sources of Don Quijote's adventures in the chivalry book.]

70. Clemencín, Diego. "Prólogo" to *Don Quijote de la Mancha*. 6 vols. Madrid: D. E. Aguado, 1833-39, I, pp. v-xxxix.

   The *Quijote* is the most moral book produced by the human mind and written to reform and ridicule the literary customs of those who read the absurd chivalry books; it was not written just to make people laugh.

Although Mayans y Siscar published an excellent edition in 1738, as did Vicente de los Ríos in 1780, in the name of analysis they really wrote praise. Furthermore, while Sir John Bowle's notes in the 1781 edition concerning references to Italian and Latin authors and books of chivalry along with explanations of difficult and obscure language did much to enrich Spanish criticism, his enthusiasm for the work did not affect the Spaniard. For instance, although Pellicer borrowed from Bowle, his observations in his 1797 edition are so desultory that one really cannot call his work a commentary, and while the Royal Academy in its 1819 edition published annotations, its notes are too short and do not offer enough information. A classic work, the *Quijote* deserves critical study and commentary by a Spaniard.

Literature of chivalry had its origins in the dark ages when, because there were no laws to protect the humble, knights-errant thrived. But in Spain the books about chivalry were written much later, in the fifteenth and sixteenth centuries. Filled with repetitive events and incorrect historical data, they were books about the impossible read with aplomb by young people who imitated their foolishness. Since they became harmful and encouraged bad morals, Spanish intellectuals like Vives and Melchor Cano condemned them and petitioned the king several times to ban them from Spain. But even people in high places read them, Santa Teresa even wrote one, courtiers celebrated their adventures, and Philip II masqueraded as a knight-errant in 1549 at Binche. War made them even more popular, and although to counteract their arousal of military spirit some people turned to the pastoral book for enjoyment of a more peaceful sort, important writers in Spain still continued to publish many books of chivalry throughout the sixteenth century. Unlike these writers and the general public, however, Cervantes painted the knight as a ridiculous figure. He invented his hero from his own imagination and formed a new genre that did not have established rules. One may compare Cervantes to Homer in that he imitated no one and no one could imitate him, reminding us that the greatest works of art, like those of antiquity, are composed by inventive, creative geniuses and that the precepts of a philosopher (e.g. Aristotle) follow those of an artist (e.g. Homer).

Like works such as *Guzmán de Alfarache, Marcos de Obregón*, and *La pícara Justina*, the *Quijote* has no single principal action or strict unity. Cervantes did not meditate profoundly over the action or compose with a preconceived plan. Instead, he worked with his instincts, filling the book with various incidents and episodes and inimitable dialogues between Don Quijote and Sancho. He made the marvelous deeds of chivalry look ridiculous with Don Quijote's enchantment, the Clavileño journey, the resurrection of Altisidora, the cave of Montesinos, and the enchantment of Dulcinea, and achieved his moral aim—that of destroying the books of chivalry.

If in his simplistic plot Cervantes had paid closer attention to details and taken greater care with language, the novel would have reached heights of perfection. But as it is, all of the incidents of Part I are concluded there, and there is nothing to arouse one's curiosity to read Part II. Some of the novel's incidents are not connected at all to its main action and, in fact, public censure of them led Cervantes to retreat in Part II. Furthermore, errors of chronology in the *Quijote* are inexcusable and its anachronisms destroy truth and verisimilitude. How could Cervantes make reference to contemporary events of the reigns of Philip II and III and at the same time claim that the manuscript of the book was older, written in Arabic, and found among the ruins of an old building?

Cervantes' treatment of the characters, on the other hand, is thoroughly admirable. The discreet Dorotea, the ingenuous Doña Rodríguez, and the Duke and Duchess, for instance, are very agreeable for their variety and delineation, while Don Quijote is a character who remains noble throughout—honorable, kind, judicious, and wise, at the same time that his folly entertains the reader. But if folly were the Knight's only attribute, he would be a character with no interest at all. We laugh at and love him simultaneously, while we love Sancho for his inimitable gift of wit.

In conclusion, the *Quijote* is praiseworthy for its invention and varied style (which is pure with a few exceptions), although it possesses careless mistakes. A delicate satire on customs, it always has been and will be enchanting to Spaniard and foreigner alike, outliving and silencing its critics, of whom there have been many.

71. López Quijada, Jorge. *El corresponsal de los muertos: Novedades del siglo XIX.* Madrid: Imp. de Pedro Sanz, 1833. 28 pages.

Cervantes contributed to the cure of a disease that produced good things for all men. This "disease" was chivalry and its customs.

72. Rementería y Fica, Mariano de. *Honores tributados a la memoria de Miguel de Cervantes.* Madrid: Imp. de Ortega, 1834. 55 pages.

Spain not only ignores the fact that the *Quijote* is one of the world's great classics, but also refuses to indicate where its greatest author is buried, leaving him without an epitaph. Cervantes should be congratulated for his excellent and accurate account of Spanish customs and for dealing the final blow to the distasteful chivalry book. The *Quijote* is a delicate satire of the partisan of these books as he becomes aware of his ridiculous habit of reading them. The monumental work also contains all the qualities that represent great art: the mixture of the useful and beautiful, morality and didacticism, originality of invention, purity of language, ingenious conceits, and lively portraits. In sum, it is a work that can never be imitated, an honor to Spain.

73. Mor de Fuentes, José. *Elogio de Miguel de Cervantes Saavedra*. Barcelona: Viuda e Hijos de Gorchs, 1835. 44 pages.

One of the most attractive features of the *Quijote* is that Cervantes never allows his hero to appear crushed or to grow vile while he undergoes suffering and humiliation. This incites the reader to venerate Don Quijote.

Despite what others have said, Cervantes does not imitate earlier writers a great deal. He is superior to Aristophanes, Lucian, and Erasmus. Cervantes is the founder of true satire, which is a civilizing force in the social life of Europe.

While there are some slight grammatical errors in the *Quijote* and at times it is diffuse and tiring, the language and style are "fluido" and "castizo."

74. Hernández Morejón, Antonio. *Bellezas de medicina práctica descubiertas en El ingenioso caballero Don Quijote de la Mancha*. Madrid: T. Jordán, 1836. 25 pages. [French version by J. M. Guardia, *Etude médico-psychologique sur l'histoire de Don Quichotte*, Paris, 1858.]

Don Quijote's illness is monomania and his story the story of his predisposition to madness as well as the ancillary causes of derangement. Don Quijote's melancholy, wit (*agudeza*), and excessive pride lend themselves to this type of madness, while violent exercise, the change from an inactive to an active life, poor nutrition, amorous passion, lack of sleep, and exposure to the elements, as in the sojourn to the Sierra Morena, promote it. Living in isolation like Cardenio is another characteristic of madness, as is Don Quijote's belief that his strength is superhuman. In short, the novel develops according to the symptomatology of a madman: "La historia del ingenioso hidalgo está trazada según todas las reglas del arte de medicina. Los médicos leen el *Quijote* para contemplar a un genio en la parte descriptiva de las enajenaciones del alma y ver con qué ingenio presentó una de las especies más nuevas del género de la locura, y el modo con que supo hacer interesante a este loco sin hacerlo ridículo."

75. Siñeriz, Juan Francisco. "Prospecto" to *El Quijote del siglo XVIII*, I. Madrid: 1836, pp. ix-xvi.

Like Don Quijote, the hero of this imitation tries to cure the ills of society, armed with a new philosophy. He takes his moral lessons to France, America, and Asia, and as he attempts to undo the "old" philosophy with his "new" philosophy, he becomes something of a revolutionary.

76. Rementería y Fica, Mariano de. *Manual alfabético del Quijote, o colección de pensamientos de Cervantes, en su inmortal obra*. Madrid: J. Boix, 1839. 131 pages.

> [A collection of summaries of Cervantes' definitions of *adulación, afrenta, caballeros, caballos famosos, desdicha, fábulas, justicia, sueño, vulgo,* and other terms and topics.]

77. Caballero, Fermín. *Pericia geográfica de Miguel de Cervantes demostrada con la historia de Don Quijote de la Mancha*. Madrid: Sucs. de Hernández, 1918. 117 pages. [First published in Madrid: Yenes, 1840.]

> Evidence such as Cervantes' physical make-up (particularly his cranial structure), his long travels, and the content of his novel suggest that he must have been a geographer. References to local products like *bellotas gordas* and the allusion to the Campo de Montiel as the place where Don Quijote began his first sally led people to believe that Argamasilla, which is part of Montiel, was Don Quijote's birthplace.
>
> Cervantes' generous commentary on various Spanish foods and his references to characteristics of different Spanish provinces further indicate how well he knew the Spanish peninsula.

78. Salvá, Vicente. "¿Ha sido juzgado el *Quijote* según esta obra merece?" In *Apuntes para una biblioteca de escritores españoles contemporáneos,* II. Edited by Eugenio Ochoa. Paris, 1840, pp. 659-76. [Published the same year in *Liceo Valenciano*]

> The *Quijote* should be examined from both a literary and moral point of view, as the latter has to do with the important question of the effect of the *Quijote* on its readers and their social customs. It was Cervantes' aim to do away with the nonsensical books of chivalry, but in the end, he created his own book of chivalry and thereby increased their number. His aim was *not* to destroy the chivalry book but to purge it of its incredibly fantastic events and personages, according to the designs of the Canónigo in chapters forty-seven and forty-eight of Part I.
>
> Part I is better than Part II because the circumstances under which Cervantes wrote it—in a prison—were dire and called for greater sharpness. The style of the *Quijote* has few defects (words are generally appropriate and well chosen). Two editions of Part I appeared in 1605 and were published by Juan de la Cuesta and another three were published the same year in Valencia and Lisbon. Since many more followed in subsequent years, Cervantes had no need to publish the *Buscapié*.

The question of chivalry books, however, is most important. Cervantes wanted to write a good chivalry book, and Don Quijote defends the values of chivalry, especially on the grounds of justice. Furthermore, it is certain that the genre often exaggerated the honor of the caballero, but the value of honor cannot be disputed. What is more, the novels that replaced them were no better for the public: most romances were filled with impossibilities and were even immoral, and the pastorals were very much removed from reality. The chivalry book had at least one saving grace according to the Canónigo and the Priest: it allowed a sound intellect to display itself. Thus Cervantes purged absurd notions from the chivalry book. There is no denying that many of the chivalry books published in Spain were full of lies and half-truths, but when free of them, they became useful reading comparable to the classics.

79. Moreno, Pablo. "Algunas observaciones críticas sobre *Don Quixote.*" *El Museo Yucateco* 1 (1841): 251-57. [Manuscrito inédito del célebre valisoletano D. Pablo Moreno.]

Don Quijote could never be an epic hero, but there has never been a more interesting hero of a novel. The Knight appears to depict Homer's maxim that the just man becomes unjust and the wise man insane when he grows too inflamed about justice, and this is Don Quijote.

Another reason that the *Quijote* cannot be considered an epic poem is the great variety of Don Quijote's adventures; this variety develops his character to the fullest, but leads to a lack of unity of action. On one occasion, the adventure of the braying village, Don Quijote is not even brave, and this lack of exemplarity and inconsistency of character would not have been possible in an epic.

Don Quijote's character changes in Part II: While in the adventure of the enchanted bark and in the Melisendra (puppet show) episode he regresses to his earlier madness, he does not persist in such foolishness; the Duke and Duchess, for example, have to employ all their skill to convince the Knight of the truth of their pranks. Furthermore, Don Quijote's love of justice, the excellence of his soul, and his generosity all remain constant.

Sancho is a cowardly, self-seeking, malicious liar, but also a figure loved by readers because of his affection for and loyalty to his master. Sancho never aims to be funny merely to amuse the people he is with; his amusing ways arise from his having lived with rustics and from his penchant for talking. While Sancho's remarks at times border on the vulgar, this element appears less frequently in Cervantes' works than in any other Spanish satire.

80. Gil de Zárate, Antonio. "Cervantes." In *Manual de literatura*. Paris: Garnier Hnos., 1922, pp. 654-73. [First published 1842-1844.]

Prior to Cervantes there were two extremes of the novel—the ideal (chivalresque) and the base (picaresque). What accounts for the charm of the *Quijote* is its supreme imagination combined with reason. In the *Quijote*, imagination and reason join hands and march along together as good friends, as if they had made a pact to produce, with their joint effort, an incomparable book.

Nothing is lacking in the *Quijote*; there are adventures of all kinds: surprising developments from the extravagant dreams of a monomaniac to the trivial happenings of private life, beautiful verbal portraits, well-described characters molded by a man who knew the human heart, laughter, tears, various social types. In short, a panorama where all things, all men, all ideas are revealed—the fruit of a happy genius not formed exclusively by reading old books, nor imprisoned in an imitation of what others had done.

With regard to the originality and immortality of the *Quijote*, instead of growing old, it seems to acquire new beauties every day, because this work is not based on the special circumstances of a particular people but on those solid values which belong to all times and which make eternal human understanding and love.

Cervantes' novel does not ridicule valor, enthusiasm, or true love—the noblest virtues. If Spain lost part of its chivalresque character, it was not because of the *Quijote* but rather dismal institutions and sad events. On the contrary, Cervantes purified chivalry of the ugliness with which many were deforming it. Perhaps foreseeing the objections that would be raised against him, Cervantes juxtaposed chivalresque exaggeration with the exaggeration of base and prosaic sentiments in the person of Sancho Panza, thus correcting one defect with the other and showing the way by which a good knight might arrive at perfection.

It is pointless to contrast the two parts of the *Quijote*; both parts have their distinct qualities and Cervantes' style is the factor which adds delight to each new reading. Though there are occasional affectations, inaccuracies, and grammatical errors (largely due to the printers), on the whole the style is smooth, clear, and harmonious, with agreeable variety, adapting itself to varying emotions, situations, and characters.

81. Igartuburu, Luis de. *Diccionario de tropos y figuras con ejemplos de Cervantes*. Madrid: Imp. de Alegría y Charlain, 1842. 257 pages.

[A dictionary listing all rhetorical figures, whether Greek or Castilian, from the works of Cervantes. And in addition to formal rhetoric and tropes, this work includes categories concerning style, beauty, and taste (*gusto*) for the benefit of young readers of Cervantes who are dedicating themselves to the study of speech (*elocuencia*).]

82. Hartzenbusch, Juan Eugenio. "Observaciones sobre el comentario del *Quijote* por Don Diego Clemencín." In *Don Quijote*. Madrid: Gaspar y Roig, 1847 and 1851, pp. iii-xiii. [Appeared also in *El Laberinto* (Madrid), November 1 and 16, 1843.]

The *Quijote* has too often been taken lightly, and it is, therefore, important to enlighten readers about both the defects and the perfections of this great work. For instance, readers must realize that Cervantes was old when he composed the *Quijote*, and consequently what one finds at the beginning of a chapter one may not find at the end of the same. In a word, Cervantes was losing his memory.

Clemencín's commentary was an improvement over Mayans, Pellicer, and Ríos. Clemencín's notes on the books of chivalry, Cervantes' target of ridicule, are abundant and often unique, and notes on the plan and structure of the work are accurate. His grammatical study is complete and justifiable; however, Clemencín often judges Cervantes as if he were a contemporary writer. Words, expressions, and idioms used by Cervantes correctly during his own time sometimes are criticized by Clemencín.

Cervantes wrote his work at a hurried pace and could not have been so meticulous as we might expect, for one may find the same carelessness among those of Cervantes' contemporaries who wrote at a deliberate pace. The *Quijote* must be considered a work improvised by a speaker intended for oral use, not written, and Cervantes wrote in a conversational tone understood by all. Furthermore, people of humble origin often intervene in his novel so that careless mistakes in speech are actually intended by the writer, a very natural observer of humankind, who deserves more praise than censure.

Clemencín's footnotes on mythology and history are detailed to a fault, but Clemencín does not always understand Cervantes' motive for writing what he wrote or for omitting details. For example, in chapter thirteen of Part I, Cervantes says that Arthus will "reinar y cobrar." Clemencín believes these words mean the same thing and are redundant. However, one can reign in a country yet not "cobrar su cetro," except where one has already reigned. In chapter twenty-three Sancho cries because he lost his ass and Don Quijote *saw* him. Clemencín believes that Cervantes should have written "oyó" and not "vió el llanto." Tears and sighs are heard more than they are seen.

Clemencín is right when he says that the early editions of the *Quijote* are so defective that we still do not have a corrected text of this universally admired work free of printer's errors.

For the learned person reading the *Quijote*, Clemencín offers a wealth of information that one could not find anywhere else. However, if a young person who had not read the *Quijote* picked up the Clemencín edition, he would be led into believing that Cervantes' language is defective. Hence, the *Quijote* should be examined with more faith than doctrine, and Clemencín should not have interpreted the rules so strictly as he went about his work on the edition.

83. Anaya, F. P. "Cervantes considerado como escritor y en cuanto a su estilo." *Revista de España, de las Indias y del Extranjero* 2 (1845): 448-67.

Cervantes' style is excellent according to V. de los Ríos and A. de Capmany. Clemencín, however, was too strict in examining his language. Most of the linguistic lapses cited by commentators abide by the formal usage of Cervantes' time and should not be deemed mistaken language even though incorrect now. Furthermore, few writers have contributed so many expressions to everyday Castilian. The Montesinos episode is the epitome of Cervantine style, especially as it mixes classical locution with the common language of a madman in a most felicitous adventure.

84. Piferrer, Pablo. *Estudios de crítica*. Barcelona: Imp. del Diario de Barcelona a cargo de Francisco Cabañach, 1859, pp. 200-09. [First published in *Clásicos españoles*, 1846.]

Cervantes' style is so original that no one could have imitated it. It is probably superior to that of the great masters such as Fr. Luis de León and Fernando de Rojas. With it, Cervantes created a new style for modern satire. His humor is ingenious and avoids base language. In fact, he ridicules chivalry books with utmost gravity. Elegance, grace, and harmony are the three elements most characteristic of Cervantes' writing. He handled language in a natural fashion, the way no other Spanish writer could.

85. Ochoa, Eugenio de. *Tesoro de novelistas españoles antiguos y modernos*, I. Paris: Baudry, 1847, pp. i-xv.

Cervantes' banishment of the chivalry book was both good and bad. Finding the sixteenth-century novel in ill repute and far below his standards, Cervantes did with the chivalric novel what Sir Walter Scott did with the historical novel: at the same time he gave it form and substance, he helped to kill it. The reason for this was that, after the *Quijote*, the chivalric novel had relatively few partisans, though many respectable genres descended from it.

The pastoral novel, full of impertinencies, false details, affected language, and excessive sentimentalism, had little importance. On the other hand, the chivalric, with its heroic ideal, was read by many and had a great following until the time of the *Quijote*.

86. Castro y Rossi, Adolfo de. *El Buscapié de Cervantes. Obra corregida y aumentada en esta 3a edición.* Madrid: Gaspar y Roig, 1851. 84 pages. [First published in Cádiz in 1848.]

[This third edition begins with two spurious *aprobaciones*, dated 1605, which attribute the *Buscapié* to Cervantes, and a "Prólogo al lector," falsely attributed to Cervantes, which alludes to the hidden meanings in the *Quijote*.

The *Buscapié* itself consists of a dialogue between the soldier-author and a *bachiller* regarding the merits of Cervantes' *Quijote*. The *bachiller* refers to the novel as a book of foolishness and acts of madness ("necedades y locuras"). The soldier-author seeks to defend the merits of the masterpiece as a book of "dulce entretenimiento sin perjuicio de tercero, y de muy lindo estilo y donosas aventuras."

The *Quijote* is not an attack on Charles V, as Ruidíaz had indicated, though Cervantes may have criticized the excessive fondness for novels of chivalry on the part of certain Spanish rulers. However, there are attacks on various Spanish institutions, such as the Inquisition and fatuous judges, in the *Quijote*.]

87. Giménez Serrano, J. "Un paseo a la patria de Don Quijote." *Semanario Pintoresco Español* 13 (1848): 19-20, 35-37, 41-43, 109-11, and 130-33.

Going southeast from Fuente del Fresno, one comes to the site of Don Quijote's encounter with Marcela, an "ameno lugar," and then through a valley to a highway of inns where Don Quijote met with his greatest adventures. But these may not have been the actual sites of Don Quijote's adventures.

[Giménez Serrano also recounts a trip to Argamasilla, where Cervantes allegedly suffered for several months in jail and conceived the *Quijote*. In addition to telling the history of the town from the Middle Ages to the time of Cervantes, he describes the windmills and fertile gardens surrounding this town, which lies six leagues from Ciudad Real, and tries to relive the difficulties of the incarcerated novelist. Afterwards he goes to El Toboso, the old city whose ruins are still visible, and to the place where Don Quijote and Sancho saw the three peasant women (Part II, chapter 10).]

88. Barrera y Leirado, Cayetano Alberto de la. *El cachetero del Buscapié. Resumen de las pruebas de hecho y de las razones críticas que evidencian la falsedad del Buscapié de Don Adolfo de Castro y la del otro tal que se mintió en el pasado siglo.* Second edition. Santander: Sociedad de Menéndez Pelayo, 1916. 282 pages. [First published in Madrid, 1849.]

The original *Buscapié* legend began in 1759, when Francisco Miguel de

Goyeneche y Balanza allegedly showed his friend Antonio de Ruidíaz a small book called *El Buscapié*, supposedly Cervantes' own explanation for writing the *Quijote*. Vicente de los Ríos believed in the authenticity of the work; Pellicer, however, doubted its validity. In 1831-1832 the question was revived by Joaquín María de Ferrer and Agustín García Arrieta, who claimed that the widow of Fernán Núñez stated that in 1807 she had seen a copy of the *Buscapié*, belonging to her husband, who had bought it in Portugal.

Adolfo de Castro's *Buscapié* is written in a style which compares poorly to Cervantes' language. Furthermore, it is not the belief of Manuel José Quintana that Castro's work is authentic. But there may be reasons why Cervantes would have wanted to write a book like the *Buscapié*: Ramón Antequera noted the role of Argamasilla in the composition of the *Quijote*, and Aureliano Fernández examined allusions by Cervantes to his contemporaries. A suspicious memorandum by Simón Contareni (a contemporary of Cervantes), containing allusions to political figures in Cervantes' times, should also influence those who believe that the *Quijote* is partly a *novela de clave*.

89. Durán, Agustín. *Romancero general*. In *Biblioteca de Autores Españoles*, X. Madrid: Rivadeneyra, 1849, pp. xiv-xx.

The *Quijote* is a parody of corrupted chivalry books, especially those like the *Amadís*, which once swarmed in Spain. The immortal Cervantes, an admirer of the genuine knights of former times, fatally wounded the new heroes of his own time and destroyed the books of chivalry as he plunged the dagger of satire, both serious and festive, into the corrupting and corrupted heart of sixteenth-century life.

Cervantes' aim was to depict the absurd notions of the selfish upper classes, forged by despotism and the Inquisition, and to contrast them to the rational spirit of the middle classes and the prosaic spirit of the lower classes. Moreover, Don Quijote, the Priest, and Sancho embody the complex Spanish society of that era, and all the other personages can be seen as combinations and progressions of these three principal types. For that reason, and because it is not an individual satire but a complete picture of the customs of the epoch, the book does not need a *buscapié*, or key.

Cervantes did not direct his pen against the chivalry which conquered the country but against the artificial way in which that chivalry was used to buoy foreign influences. Don Quijote represents men like Count Fernán González or the Cid Campeador, though many have believed that he represented Charles V, Francis I, Philip II, or their courtly warriors. Cervantes faithfully sketched the Spaniards of his era who employed their colossal powers in the service and interest of others while thinking their own interests were being served.

The spirit of chivalry was an alien spirit in Spain, imported from the French and British, which Spanish poets and prose writers ardently propagated with their imitations in the sixteenth century. This explains the appearance of chivalric parody in Cervantes. Furthermore, Don Quijote ridicules the chivalry of the Amadises et al., who could only represent the men of the Court—men who did not bear the true stamp of the Spaniard and who enjoyed a greater vogue in foreign countries.

90. Salomón, Remigio. "Nota de las personas que intervienen en la historia de *Don Quijote*." *Semanario Pintoresco Español* 15 (1850): 129-34.

91. Salomón, Remigio. "Resumen de las principales aventuras de *Don Quijote*." *Semanario Pintoresco Español* 15 (1850): 148-51.

[These two extremely detailed lists show how rich and varied are the characters and adventures in the *Quijote*, ranging from the very first people who appear in the novel to the scribe who writes Don Quijote's will. They are published for the readers of *Semanario Pintoresco Español* who have not read the *Quijote*.]

92. Gallardo, Bartolomé José [El Bachiller Bo-vaina]. *El Buscapié del Busca-ruido de Don Adolfo de Castro. Crítico-crítica por el Bachiller Bo-vaina.* Valencia: Imp. de Mariano de Cabrerizo, 1851. 40 pages.

That Cervantes had to write a rejoinder to justify his novel is incorrect because Part I of the *Quijote* was not unpopular; indeed it was published in several editions during its first year of existence. Furthermore, Cervantes never cites the *Buscapié* among his works after the supposed date of its publication, and his contemporaries do not record the publication of such a text. Critics of the eighteenth century also fail to mention it and Pellicer (1797) said that the *Buscapié* would have been unprofitable for Cervantes. There are other good reasons to doubt the authenticity of the *Buscapié*: among them, that the original manuscript has disappeared and the majority of critics who have written on Cervantes do not believe that he was its author. Ticknor has called it a "juguete," for example, and Bartolomé José Gallardo [here the author playfully cites himself] has proven that the style of the *Buscapié* dates from a period long after Cervantes' death.

93. Gallardo, Bartolomé José [El Bachiller Bo-vaina]. *Zapatazo a Zapatilla, i a su falso Buscapié un puntillazo.* Madrid: Imp. de la Viuda de Burgos, 1851. 88 pages.

Adolfo de Castro's *Buscapié* is a hoax and the author should be characterized as "pilluelo," "parlanchín," and "sin estudios."

94. Calderón, Juan. *Cervantes vindicado en ciento y quince pasajes del texto del Ingenioso hidalgo Don Quijote de la Mancha.* Madrid: Juan Martín Alegría, 1854. 256 pages.

Cervantes should be vindicated from Clemencín's criticism of his language. For example, Clemencín's assertion that the commentary on the *Tirante* is the most obscure passage in the work is wrong. Cervantes says that "con todo eso os digo que merecía el que lo compuso, pues no hizo tantas necedades de industria...." By "con todo eso" he actually means "a pesar de eso," which clarifies the phrase.

95. Barrera y Leirado, Cayetano Alberto de la. "Conjeturas sobre el fundamento que pudo tener la idea que dió origen a la patraña de *El Buscapié.*" *Revista de Ciencias, Literatura y Artes* (Sevilla) 2 (1856): 731-41; 3 (1856): 5-22, 69-80, 207-20, and 261-72.

Unfortunate occurrences in Cervantes' life in the town of Argamasilla de Alba, where Cervantes worked as a civil servant and where he was also imprisoned, may have given rise to the fable of the *Buscapié*, which, after all, deals with people who lived in that town. For instance, the possible names of Don Quijote given in the first chapter of Part I—Quijada, Quesada, etc.—are from Argamasilla, and Cervantes' wife's family name—Salazar—may also be traced there (as well as to Dulcinea's hometown). In other words, nicknames were often used in the towns of La Mancha, and Cervantes used the same kinds of names to ridicule people of La Mancha he may not have liked. Some even say that El Toboso refers to Argamasilla.

While it is true that Cervantes' principal aim in writing the *Quijote* was to attack books of chivalry, his wish to make fun of his contemporaries did not interfere with his aesthetic and moral objectives.

96. Castro, Fernando de. *El Quijote para todos, abreviado y anotado por un entusiasta de su autor Miguel de Cervantes Saavedra.* Madrid: Imp. de José Rodríguez, 1856. 620 pages.

It is a mistake to believe that Cervantes did not write the *Quijote* to make fun of chivalry and to correct the vices of men and of Spaniards in particular. While Don Quijote is a typical hidalgo of his time and Sancho Panza represents the common man of the small towns of Spain, through them Cervantes ridicules all men. Don Quijote is the prototype of all utopians, and Sancho is the prototype of the ignorant masses, interested only in material gain, who may be situated in any European society.

The *Quijote* contains many wise sayings, and its style is on the one hand natural, clear, and correct and on the other rhetorical, sublime, and elegant. It possesses a variety of styles just as it does a variety of perspectives on man.

97. Díaz de Benjumea, Nicolás. "Significación histórica de Cervantes." *La América* (Madrid) 11 (August 8, 1859). [As excerpted in Rius, III, pp. 66-68.]

Cervantes sees the beautiful social ideal of the chivalric myth. He takes charge of the spirit and kills the flesh of chivalry; he reveals that it is not arms of steel that will combat evil, but the arms of reason and intelligence. It is social, not military, chivalry that Don Quijote is to revive.

98. Díaz de Benjumea, Nicolás. "Refutación de la creencia generalmente sostenida de que el *Quijote* fué una sátira contra los libros caballerescos." *La América* (Madrid) 11 (September 24, October 8 and 24, 1859). [As excerpted in Rius, III, pp. 68-70.]

The *Quijote* is a critique against many things, and Cervantes was aware that there were worse evils in society than books of chivalry. The author did not intend an invective against such literature, nor against ideal or real chivalry. His novel is directed against the principle of force. The *Quijote*, in effect, is the first book with both social and practical goals.

99. Díaz de Benjumea, Nicolás. "Comentarios filosóficos del *Quijote*." *La América* (Madrid) 11 (November 8 and 24, December 8 and 24, 1859). [As excerpted in Rius, III, pp. 70-73.]

Don Quijote's madness should be seen from three angles: aesthetic, psychological, and critical (transcendental). Cervantes, once he had chosen the figure Don Quijote, had to justify the unrealistic nature of his actions and undertakings; as he uses madness, all becomes natural; he does not use supernatural gods, demons, genii, or magicians. But madness is not merely a means to make the extravagant seem true: Don Quijote is a man of mature understanding, unless we consider madness a psychological phenomenon with exaggerated passion. His madness is no greater than that of any man whose spirits are lifted by noble ideals.

100. Díaz de Benjumea, Nicolás. *La estafeta de Urganda, o aviso de Cid Asam-Ouzad Benegeli, sobre el desencanto del Quijote*. London: Imp. de J. Wertheimer y Cia, 1861. 64 pages.

No one has properly understood the *Quijote*. The truth is that Cervantes prophesied the life of Don Quijote: he was a transfiguration. One needs a key to obscure words, phrases, and passages to unlock the occult meaning of this great book, which transcends time and place and is, like the Bible, a household word.

The job of the critic is to unveil the secrets of this literary work: the symbolism of its combats; the personification in a decrepit body of a knight-errant; the freshness of the imagination of his so-called dried up brain; the significance of this warrior with a weak arm as a living contradiction.

The *Quijote* is popular because it has always been considered a satire of the books of chivalry. But is it a satire of chivalry? The answer to this question is very complicated, largely because it has always been a grave error to interpret the *Quijote* in isolation from its author. It is therefore necessary to undertake the study of books of chivalry because Cervantes had the books next to him when he wrote the novel, and as a result, whatever Don Quijote did had a precedent in them. Of great importance too is a study of the effects which institutions (like the Inquisition) had on Cervantes as well as an understanding of the fact that Cervantes' misfortunes were directly related to the religious fanaticism of the Holy Office and Philip II. Thus, one can see that Avellaneda is representative of the oppression that many before Cervantes had suffered, and Cervantes' enemy, Juan Blanco de Paz, is an agent of the Inquisition.

Concerning the historical significance of the *Quijote*, the learned critics say that Cervantes had his head turned toward the Middle Ages; but Cervantes looked toward the future when he dealt with chivalry, sheep, and windmills. If Don Quijote armed himself only to attack knights of the past in the form of books, then the work would collect dust in the stacks of libraries.

The commentaries of Clemencín and Pellicer are not much different from the explanations in glosses on Roman law. That is, these commentators annotated obscure words in the margins of the work and applied the same glosses to the interpretation of the book, thus leaving the reader with nothing more than a catalogue.

Don Quijote's madness is something that medical doctors cannot and ought not explain: only poets have been able to do that. For Don Quijote's derangement can be characterized as melancholy, and the majority of great philosophers, poets, ascetics, and lovers have been melancholic. To consider his madness a means of ridiculing chivalric love is to miss the point of Cervantes' invention entirely. One reason why Cervantes creates a mad character is to give more credibility to his work: that which seems impossible is possible under the rubric of "mental aberration." The madman can utter truths that people will not believe and get away with it because they think he is simply mad.

Don Quijote is a symbolic character and as such symbolizes that which is herculean: he signifies the giant, which is a symbol that we see even in the Bible; his herculean strength is the strength of the soul. His fights with the sword are nothing more than symbolic battles. Dulcinea symbolizes wisdom: the love of the knight-errant for her is not the same as the love for the common Aldonza, but rather for truth.

Critics have a long history of interpretative mistakes, but what Clemencín did can be tempered by Hartzenbusch's *Observaciones*. Biographers, too, have been mistaken, presenting the caricature, not the true portrait of Cervantes. Another great mistake is that of insisting that Cervantes wrote the *Quijote* in a prison. The *Quijote* is not a work of the prison cell because it is a metaphor for Cervantes' entire life, a life of struggle. Cervantes' profession was that of arms, for letters were not a profession in his time, and in the discourse on arms and letters in the novel, arms are superior. Cervantes' reward for his work as a soldier was immediate—money, but the reward for writing was inferior. Moreover, the period of Cervantes' life we know best is his captivity, and this is the germ of his misfortune, not, as others have said, his marriage or his imprudence. In related documents we find in Cervantes' experience in Algiers the root causes of his bad luck. In Algiers, Cervantes was a brave soldier who tried to escape several times and helped many Christians to go free. However, when it came to Cervantes himself, Juan Blanco de Paz betrayed him by holding up his ransom. This episode has great resonances in the *Quijote*. In the adventure of the *disciplinantes*, the so-called *Bachiller* with whom Don Quijote almost comes to blows is one López de Alcobendas, whose name is an anagram for the phrase "Es lo de Blanco de Paz." The name of the Knight of the White Moon is also an allusion to Blanco (de Paz), Don Quijote's mortal enemy. And when he changes his name to the Caballero de la Triste Figura, one sees an allegory of Cervantes in conflict with Spain: "que a la luz de la información falsa y caluminosa que Blanco de Paz tomó en Argel contra Cervantes y mandó a España, quedó nuestro soldado tan desfigurado a los ojos de la Corte."

101. Fernández y González, Manuel. [El Diablo con Antiparras]. *A los profanadores del Ingenioso hidalgo Don Quijote de la Mancha*. Madrid: Imp. de Manuel Galindo, 1861. 32 pages.

A subject as empty (*vacío*) as that of attacking Cervantes' detractors must nevertheless be dealt with. Many have abused the *Quijote* in poor imitations and translations. Don Quijote was created for Cervantes alone, and for no one else.

Among the writers who have authored works related to the genuine Cervantine masterpiece, Avellaneda, A. de Castro, and Ventura de la Vega should especially be censured.

102. Giner, Francisco. "Dos folletos sobre el *Quijote*." In *Obras completas*, III: *Estudios de literatura y arte*. Madrid: La Lectura, 1919, pp. 289-302. [Dated 1861-1862.]

Benjumea is right when he says that the *Quijote* is more than a satire of books of chivalry and states that no one who is reasonably educated can believe that this is all the novel contains. The spirit of the *Quijote* can be summed up by saying "... that dramatic book, that mirror of the real world, that deep and human history of illusions, that novel elevated to an epic contains, like all great literary monuments, an internal meaning which is achieved, as Benjumea observes, 'dejando la letra, y dirigiéndose al espíritu.'" The hero's adventures are an allegory of Cervantes' tragic life. As for the critic, it is his function to extract both the autobiographical and the social elements of a great work and then to point out its originality.

Comparing Tubino with Benjumea, Tubino's work is self-contradictory, first claiming that the *Quijote* is only entertainment and then asserting that it is a progressive book with elevated intention. Benjumea views the *Quijote* as largely autobiographical.

103. Ibáñez, Teodomiro. *Don Quijote de la Mancha en el siglo XIX*. Cádiz: Imp. de la Revista Médica, 1861. 36 pages.

The reason for the enduring importance of the *Quijote* lies not in its language, nor in its critique of chivalric novels, nor in its entertainment, but in Cervantes' ability to describe humanity without affectation and in his ability to depict, as no other writer could, what is lasting and essential in the aspirations and feelings of mankind, rather than what is transitory or proceeds from historical accident. Since Cervantes did not attack chivalry but fanaticism, the vice that perverted its noble character, the *Quijote* has universal relevance. It is not merely about one epoch, it is a comedy of human life, faithfully reproducing all of its miseries and joys as well as the fruitless attempts of those who fabricate for themselves a world according to their desires.

The two constituent elements of human civilization are admirably sketched in the society that Cervantes portrays and are expressly personified in Don Quijote and his Squire. Don Quijote, like Adam, has the mad desire to know good from evil, to be like God, and to create a new rational order, where he might exercise the supreme and absolute dominion that he supposes is obtainable by virtue of his disobedience and his sin. But unlike nineteenth-century Quijotes who recognize no higher authority than themselves, Don Quijote remains noble in victory and in defeat, and we love him no matter how much he may make us laugh. His sympathetic madness inspires compassion in us. And the depiction of Sancho is further proof of Cervantes' profound knowledge of the human heart. Sancho is an archetype, not a product of one era. He represents the masses, who, though they live for the life of the body, not the mind, and seem to mock all elevated thought that they do not understand, nevertheless follow men of intelligence and become blind instruments of their enterprises, a tendency illustrated in every action of the book.

Cervantes, when he wrote the *Quijote*, did not understand fully the importance of his immortal work. But this is true of even the most privileged genius, who cannot know the purpose and transcendence of every thought with which he reveals himself to the world. But great writers are distinguished from lesser ones in that the former, singing the glories or cursing the weaknesses of humankind, deepen human nature. Thus, although they judge mankind from the point of view of their own epoch, the effect of their talent is long-lasting, and succeeding generations always find in their works the faithful reproduction of the inevitable accidents of life. On the other hand, lesser writers, because of their limited capacity and their narrow vision, get bogged down in superficial details; thus their works are accepted during their own time and die with them. No one, no matter how great, can prophesy how people will think and act in the future, and even a Miguel de Cervantes always leaves something for the activity and work of future readers, who will inevitably modify his initial conception and accommodate it to the spirit of their times.

104. Segovia e Izquierdo, Antonio María. *Cervantes, nueva utopía. Monumento nacional de eterna gloria imaginado en honra del príncipe de los ingenios.* Madrid: Imp. de Manuel Galiano, 1861. 31 pages.

[An imaginary trip in the future (August 28, 1910) to a utopian colony called "Cervantes," where there is no idleness. Guided by a local resident of the colony, the grandson of Ventura de la Vega, the author and his English companion, Johnson, visit the colony's monuments to Sancho, Cervantes, Don Quijote, and others, as well as its library, museum, and bookstore. The organization, funding, establishment, and governing board of the colony are also discussed.]

105. Campoamor, Ramón de. "La metafísica limpia, fija y da esplendor al lenguaje." In *Obras completas*, I. Madrid: F. González Rojas, 1901-1903. [Discurso de ingreso en la Real Academia Española; actual date is 1862.]

Good writers are philosophers without knowing it, for they use images to express their thoughts. Cervantes sanctifies traditional phrases even better than etymologists. In addition, he and Gómez Pereira are the true founders of modern psychology, since they are the first to attempt to certify their own existence and take that as the fixed beginning of their studies. Descartes' "I think, therefore I am " is literally anticipated by Gómez Pereira's syllogism: "Lo que conoce es; yo conozco, luego soy." And Cervantes, even before Gómez Pereira, illustrates this same philosophical principle in the cave of Montesinos, where the Knight confirms his own existence and identity of conscience by touching himself and noting his own feelings.

106. Canalejas, Francisco de Paula. "Del estudio de la historia de la filosofía española." In *Estudios críticos de filosofía, política y literatura*. Madrid: Carlos Bailly-Bailliere, 1872, pp. 184 and 193-94. [Essay dated March, 1862.]

In the works of Cervantes (and of other Spanish writers, such as Luis de Granada and Quevedo) one can find more or less reflexive, yet complete, systems of philosophy. We must discover the state of the *razón filosófica* of a writer's times before we may judge his creations. If in Cervantes and other Spanish authors philosophy does not appear as an orderly and systematic inquiry, there nevertheless are in their works traces which ought to be gathered together so that one might know the philosophical sense of their age.

107. Morán, Jerónimo. *Vida de Cervantes, con una noticia bibliográfica de las principales ediciones y traducciones del Quijote*. In *Don Quijote de la Mancha*, III. Madrid: Imprenta Nacional, 1862-1863, pp. 109-312.

Highlights of the life of Cervantes are: his ancestry traced to Alcalá; his early education and interest in poetry; a long history of his captivity; his life in Seville after the year 1590 (the first time notice is given to this period); his later imprisonment in Argamasilla; the publication of *Quijote I* and the *Buscapié*; evidence for the legitimacy of the latter; the success of the *Quijote*; Cervantes' experience at court; the publication of his later works, including the *Quijote II*; and the publication of Avellaneda's second part of the *Quijote*.

[A bibliography includes eighty-three editions of the *Quijote* (1616-1862), notes on Spanish editions, all the European editions, and a separate section for the newer editions in Spain and Europe.]

108. Tubino, Francisco María. *El Quijote y La estafeta de Urganda*. Second edition. Seville: La Andalucía, 1862. 289 pages. [First edition also 1862.]

The *Quijote* is more in need of notes on the meaning of unusual words than in need of commentaries. Finding parallels between the *Quijote* and earlier works (V. de los Ríos and Pellicer), such as the classical epic and Apuleius' *Golden Ass*, has gotten out of hand. Sismondi's pessimistic interpretation of the *Quijote* is generally wrong, though it may elevate the *Quijote* and be flattering to it. One may find the struggle of poetry and prose in the *Quijote*, and one may conclude that misguided heroism is harmful, but this was not the author's intention, nor did he scorn enthusiasm.

Geniuses have a generative and formative effect and they personify the poetic and philosophical spirit of their times; they are not "new" in their thinking. Cervantes was influenced by prior critics of books of chivalry, but he went on to replace earlier ideas with new principles in accord with the laws that govern human nature. Cervantes imitates what he combats, and the *Quijote*, from its title and fictitious historian device to the very end, has as its basis chivalric literature but also adds a certain inventiveness which arouses ridicule. In other words, there are two chivalries in every episode of the *Quijote*: the old, exaggerated form in books of chivalry and the true, noble, and sensible Christian form. Cervantes destroys the exaggerated type that was out of touch with reality and replaces it with a genuine one.

Benjumea found that critics had not adequately understood the relationship between Cervantes' life and his works and had not realized that Cervantes, in truth, loved chivalric novels and sought to follow their spirit; in other words, he proposed the opposite of what he announced.

According to Benjumea, Cervantes attacks the Inquisition, fanaticism, and his enemy, the Dominican friar Juan Blanco de Paz. Benjumea also reaches the conclusion that Paz was the author of the spurious *Quijote* of 1614, an idea earlier announced by Ceán Bermúdez, which is absolutely devoid of proof.

Benjumea believes that Don Quijote's disease is a reflection of his era and his social class and does *not* represent the exaggeration of chivalric ideas or the monomania of a good-natured man. Instead, Benjumea finds that Don Quijote is a creation of the imagination, with hidden virtue and a transcendental meaning; he is Humanity. However, Don Quijote is not Humanity; he is the true son of the Middle Ages with its elevated passions. He is the living spirit that nourishes the strange legends of chivalry, plagued with absurdities and impossibilities. Don Quijote represents the aspiration of the soul toward truth and goodness, but when transformed into deeds, this aspiration goes mournfully astray under the pressure of the moral milieu in which the hidalgo lives and of the sickness that afflicts him, which does not exist exclusively in *his* mind, but which also, in greater or lesser degrees, exists in others. Similarly, the giant, which is the representation of evil to Benjumea, is only the personification of the hostile characters found in all chivalric novels prior to Cervantes.

Benjumea's anagram, "es lo de Blanco de Paz," coming from López de Alcobendas, is ridiculous. Although Benjumea may have aroused curiosity with this and other contrivances, his claim that the *Quijote* is an esoteric or symbolic novel is faulty.

109. Gallardo, Bartolomé José [El Bachiller Bo-vaina]. "Bibliografía de los libros de caballerías." In *Ensayo de una biblioteca española de libros raros y curiosos*. Madrid: Rivadeneyra, 1863, vol. I, cols. 364-1222.

[Offers a lengthy list of editions of the *Amadís* and its sequels that are important for the study of the *Quijote*. Each entry contains a citation by a previous critic or bibliographer and information on the first edition or the manuscript and their location.]

110. Hartzenbusch, Juan Eugenio. "Prólogo" to the Argamasilla edition of *Don Quijote*. Argamasilla de Alba: Rivadeneyra, 1863, pp. ix-xliii.

According to Vicente Salvá, of the two 1605 editions published by Juan de la Cuesta (both in the hands of Cervantists), the edition that bears the date December 1, 1604 in its *fe de erratas* is the original text. Juan de la Cuesta printed a third edition of the *Quijote* in 1608. It is necessary to compare all three if one is to come up with an accurate edition, and the reason for the variants and errors is, in part, that Cervantes never proofread the first draft of his *Quijote* and then neglected to examine its galley proofs. Because he was old at the time, matters like these may not have occurred to him, and other documents he wrote show lapses in memory: he often signed his name leaving out a vowel—Savedra—, and on other occasions he wrote *habí* for *había* and *nado* for *nada*; however, the majority of errors in the *Quijote* were made by his printers, not by him. The Argamasilla edition adheres to the original text when there are variants.

Cervantes' supposed aim was to satirize chivalry books by creating a good man, an hidalgo, who lost his mind reading them, deciding to become a knight-errant. Since Cervantes knew Spain so well, from its glorious soldiers to its perverse galley slaves, he was able to give true portraits of captivating characters—noblemen as different as Cardenio, Fernando, and the Duke, and innkeepers who are also individuals: one is a *burlón*, another is greedy and vindictive, and so on. The same richness is found in the novel's events, especially in the inset pieces of Part I like the *Curioso impertinente* and the "Captive's Tale." The book is great because it has the power to seduce men into being other Quijotes, since there will always be those in the world who will strive for an unrealizable dream.

111. Pardo de Figueroa, Mariano [Dr. Thebussem]. Letter in *Cartas literarias sobre Cervantes y el Quijote por El Bachiller Cervántico*. Cádiz: Imp. de la Revista Médica, 1868. 16 pages. [First published in 1863, then in 1868 in conjunction with Máinez (entry no. 125); falsely attributed to Pardo de Figueroa (?).]

Benjumea *is* original; no one else had divined the hidden meaning of the name "López de Alcobendas" (an anagram, in Benjumea's mind, for "es lo de Blanco de Paz"). Benjumea neither twists the meaning of words nor contradicts himself when presenting the literal, moral, and allegorical meanings of such episodes as that of the Knight of the Wood.

112. Asensio y Toledo, José María. *Nuevos documentos para ilustrar la vida de Miguel de Cervantes Saavedra*. Seville: Imp. de José M. Geofrin, 1864. 67 pages.

[Contains various biographical documents and short commentaries on Cervantes' portrait and the *Académicos* of Argamasilla.]

113. Guardia, J. M. "Introducción" to the translation of *Viaje del Parnaso*. Paris: Jules Gay, 1864, pp. i-clxxvi. [As excerpted in Rius, III, pp. 97-99.]

Rabelais attacks the social structure and the clergy directly, while Cervantes, writing a century after the Reformation, uses ridicule to declare war on the corrupters of reason; he composes a manual of practical philosophy. Cervantes saw the good sense of Spaniards compromised by spiritual leaders who had lost sight of reality and continued to pursue shadows and phantasms. Cervantes is the Rabelais of Spain, a reformer and revolutionary in his own way, who sought to overthrow a worn-out system and a dismal tradition.

114. Valera, Juan. "Contestación al último comunicado del señor Benjumea." In *Estudios críticos sobre literatura, política y costumbres de nuestros días*, III. Second edition. Madrid: Francisco Alvarez, 1884, pp. 31-55. [First published in Madrid, 1864.]

The *Quijote* is not a book of mysteries and recondite ideas. In particular, Benjumea is wrong in his attempt to make the *Quijote* an allegory of Cervantes' life. It would have been foolish for Cervantes to narrate his own adventures in a charade; Don Quijote would then be Cervantes, and Sancho, a friend or servant of Cervantes, etc. It is one thing for Cervantes to give to his hero much of his own character and to describe in his novel various people whom he knew. It is another to assert that Cervantes purposefully set out to represent himself and the persons most closely related to him. Benjumea confuses a work of art with a fastidious allegory. It is useless to know who served as models for characters, for above such matters lies the inventiveness and creative power of the genius, who alters, sublimates, magnifies, beautifies, and transfigures his models, making them very different from what they are in reality. This is not done for the purpose of concealing their identity, but for creating them.

Benjumea believes that the value of literature is not its beauty but the benefit that it offers to mankind. It is true that some works are both beautiful and philosophical, and in these cases beauty is secondary. But Cervantes' true purpose was to create a beautiful story. The intention to put an end to books of chivalry (or any other aim which might be discovered in the *Quijote*) was only the occasion and pretext for the story, not its true motive.

Both the *Quijote* and *Orlando furioso* employ the same two techniques: (1) they contrast chivalric pomp with the vanity of its results; (2) they present heroic individuality, free of any outside norm. Cervantes and Ariosto fuse these two elements, but Cervantes is superior: he has his hero struggle with prosaic reality, from which there arises an order of poetic beauty lacking in *Orlando furioso*.

115. Valera, Juan. "Sobre *La estafeta de Urganda, o aviso de Cide Asam-Ouzad Benengeli, sobre el desencanto del Quijote*, escrito por Nicolás Díaz de Benjumea—Londres, 1861." In *Estudios críticos sobre literatura, política y costumbres de nuestros días*, III. Second edition. Madrid: Francisco Alvarez, 1884, pp. 17-29. [First published, Madrid, 1864.]

Cervantes' novel is a work of art, of poetry, and of entertainment; it is not a hidden treasure of knowledge. There is nothing in Cervantes' life, character, studies, or habits that indicates that he was a Paracelsus, a Raimundo Lulio, or an Albertus Magnus. Cervantes was instead a soldier, a man of the world more familiar with the *Percheles de Málaga* than with science and philosophy.

If Benjumea were able to prove in his proposed *Comentarios filosóficos* that the *Quijote* is a cipher or a logograph whose mysterious meaning is unknown, the masterpiece would lose its true charm, and we would be left with cold symbolism and a few soulless allegories, which, no matter how much science they contained, would not be worth the poetic spirit that Benjumea wishes to take away from the novel. In the *Quijote* there is not the slightest trace of the occult, the mystic, or the recondite.

Cervantes composed the most realistic and the most idealistic novel that has ever been written because he knew how to paint real life with the fidelity of a photograph, with such vigor of imagination, and because he knew how to elevate this picture to the heights of poetic sublimity with the living fire and the clear light of the artistic idea that burned in his soul. These merits are enough to make Cervantes immortal. The mission of a poet is not to teach anything scientific; the mission of the poet is to give perceivable being and form to beauty, which is like truth, an immediate emanation of God, and worth at least as much as truth, with the difference that almost always beauty is more pleasant and sweeter.

116. Valera, Juan. "Sobre *El Quijote* y sobre las diferentes maneras de comentarle y juzgarle." In *Obras completas*, III. Madrid: Aguilar, 1958, pp. 1965-86. [Discurso leído ante la Real Academia Española en junta pública el 25 de septiembre de 1864, Madrid.]

Some critics have held Cervantes' work in low esteem, while others have engaged in "desatinadas alabanzas." One should be particularly aggrieved by critics of France and England who, in their praise of Cervantes, have denigrated other Spanish writers and by the Spanish critic Mor de Fuentes for referring to Cervantes as "el ilustrador del género humano," thus implying that there were not other wise men in Spain. Others turned Cervantes into a subtle psychologist, a refined politician, or a consummate medical doctor. At the other extreme, Clemencín became unreasonably critical.

With regard to the general intent of the *Quijote*, Cervantes wrote serious parody and not the light jest of the French. While the author of the *Quijote* parodied the chivalresque spirit, he confirmed it instead of denying it, at least unconsciously. Although there is a contradiction between Cervantes' premeditated intent and his inspiration or "instinto semidivino," this contradiction is only superficial. Just because Cervantes condemned an anachronistic and false form of literature, it does not follow that he condemned chivalresque ideas.

It is not true that Don Quijote symbolizes the ideal and Sancho the real, for Cervantes was too much of a poet to make symbolic figures or pale allegories out of his heroes; he created living figures like those of Shakespeare and Homer. Nevertheless, while the characters in the *Quijote* are praiseworthy, the plot lacks unity (in spite of the efforts of Vicente de los Ríos to defend it). The individual characters are a gallery of images without any strong connection to each other, and there is no true action in the work. The true unity lies in its central idea—the idea that Don Quijote and Sancho are united by madness.

There are those who seek to determine whom the author was referring to in a given episode. This group would convert Cervantes, a generous spirit, into a defamer. With regard to the expulsion of the *moriscos* and to the Ricote episode in the 1615 *Quijote*, there is no irony in Cervantes' praise of Philip III and the expulsion. Cervantes was a man of his times, who saw both the pity and the necessity of the exile of the *moriscos*. Cervantes was no liberal; he was more of a monarchist who also believed in censorship. Yet he was not servile; like other Spaniards, he was independent and capable of attacking the Santa Hermandad. Those who consider Cervantes to be anti-religious are wrong. Cervantes even participated in the supersitition and fanaticism of his times, and the passage in which Don Quijote refers to the friars as "fementida canalla" cannot be taken seriously because Ariosto, for one, used similar words in describing that group.

Those who view Cervantes' novel as an esoteric work are very much mistaken. The *Quijote* is a novel, no more, no less, and the best of them; and Cervantes is not a discoverer of truth but a poet who created beauty that uplifted the human spirit. If there is any hidden wisdom in the novel, it is that while mocking chivalry the author is a perfect knight; while mocking the epic, the *Quijote* is the greatest prose epic written in modern times.

117. Ramírez, J. de. "Aniversario de la muerte del gran Cervantes." In *La caja de Pandora*. Madrid: L. López, 1865, pp. 275-92.

Cervantes and Shakespeare are, after Homer and Dante, the greatest writers that the world produced until Byron and Balzac. Both the English playwright and the Spanish novelist wrote in behalf of and for the benefit of humanity, and both may say with Terence: "I am a man; all that concerns man concerns me."

118. Antequera, Ramón. *Juicio analítico del Quijote, escrito en Argamasilla.* Madrid: Z. Soler, 1865. 450 pages. [1863?]

Cervantes was allegedly imprisoned in Argamasilla because of a supposed love affair with Ana Zarco de Morales by a gentleman called "El caballero Quijana." Various characters in the *Quijote* are real people from the town of Argamasilla. Among the characters are the Priest, the Barber, Sansón Carrasco, the Canon of Toledo, Dulcinea, Diego de Miranda (el Caballero del Verde Gabán), Ginés de Pasamonte, and Camacho el rico. The author of the *Quijote* was the Miguel de Cervantes born in 1558 (not 1547), and he, like Vicente de la Rosa, joined the army at twelve or thirteen.

119. Díaz de Benjumea, Nicolás. *El correo de Alquife, o segundo aviso de Cid Asam-Ouzad Benengeli, sobre el desencanto del Quijote.* Barcelona: Alou Hnos., 1866. 80 pages.

Cervantes was a man of noble and liberal beliefs in conflict with the oppressive attitudes of his times. The events of Cervantes' life have a close relationship to his writings. The figure Sansón Carrasco represents Cervantes' archenemy Juan Blanco de Paz, who betrayed Cervantes in Algiers. Dulcinea symbolizes wisdom and progress, while Casildea de Vandalia, the fictitious ladylove of the Knight of the Mirrors (Sansón Carrasco), is the personification of intolerance, repression, and the Inquisition. The detailed description of Sansón indicates that Cervantes had a particular person in mind, because he normally uses nondescript types, such as the Priest and the Barber.

A particular English Cervantist (Rawdon Brown?) claimed to have found a letter in the archives of Venice indicating that readers of the *Quijote* in Cervantes' times regarded the novel as a political satire hidden in allegory. However, this is merely a continuation of the Ruidíaz *Buscapié* legend of the eighteenth century. The *Quijote* is not a satire against public figures such as the Count of Lerma: the satire, instead, is transcendental and directed at institutions, ideas, and systems.

120. Asensio y Toledo, José María. *Dos cartas literarias.* Madrid: Imp. de Campuzano Hnos., 1867, pp. 3-14. [Letter to A. Fernández-Guerra y Orbe, dated May 19, 1867.]

[Proof that the *Quijote* was begun in a jail in Seville. Also an examination of the "Canción desesperada" and the poem "A la elección del arzobispo de Toledo."]

121. Fernández, Cayetano. *Oración fúnebre que por encargo de la Real Academia Española y en las honras de Miguel de Cervantes Saavedra y demás ingenios españoles se pronunció en la Iglesia de Monjas Trinitarias de Madrid, el 29 de Abril de 1867.* Madrid: Aguado, 1867. 43 pages.

Cervantes deserves praise for what he did in life and in art. Those who were not grateful to him should be condemned.

122. Fernández-Guerra y Orbe, Aureliano. A reply to J. M. Asensio's letter of May 19, 1867. [Published in *Dos cartas literarias*; see entry no. 120.]

The jail in Seville was the cradle of the *Quijote* for several reasons: it is known that Cervantes was imprisoned there in the fall of 1597, and the description of the jail and its inmates by various writers fits Cervantes' description of a jail in the prologue to the 1605 *Quijote*. Those who believe that the *Quijote* was engendered in a jail in Argamasilla are wrong because there was no jail in that town in the sixteenth century.

123. Asensio y Toledo, José María. "Comentario de Comentarios, que es como si dijéramos Cuento de Cuentos: Carta a Mr. Mariano Droap." In *Cartas literarias sobre el Quijote*. Cádiz: Biblioteca de la Revista Gaditana (Imp. y Lib. de la Revista Médica), 1868. 14 pages.

Benjumea's ideas are extraneous, contradictory, and unoriginal. His use of anagrams to reach the conclusion that Cervantes attacked his enemy Juan Blanco de Paz is unacceptable.

Cervantes did not attack the political and religious institutions of his times (such as the Inquisition) and Casildea de Vandalia did not represent the Inquisition, while Dulcinea symbolized civilization, in the episode of the Knight of the Wood. Such ideas are very English and derived in part from Antonio Puigblanch, who was inspired by English thinking in his *La Inquisición sin máscara*, 1811 (written under the name Natanael Jomtob).

Benjumea's belief that the escutcheon on the 1605 Juan de la Cuesta edition (inscribed *Post tenebras spero lucem*) was anti-inquisitional is wrong. Several works prior to the *Quijote* contained the same escutcheon. In addition, Benjumea's view that Cervantes did not understand his mission in writing the *Quijote* is faulty. How could Cervantes compose anti-inquisitional anagrams, as Benjumea alleges, if he did not understand his purpose?

There is no hidden meaning in the *Quijote*, as Benjumea believes, and Cervantes, instead, wrote a medico-moralistic novel against individual and social evils, which he sought to correct in an amusing story. He painted the events, characters, and passions of human life; he pictured the truth without having seen it; what he did not know, he surmised.

124. Hernández, Fabián. *Ni Cervantes es Cervantes, ni el Quijote es el Quijote.* Santander: Imp. de la Gaceta del Comercio, 1868. 48 pages.

Cervantes did not write the *Quijote* as it has come to be interpreted largely because it has been so altered by printers and commentators.

Cervantes made fun of commentators in the prologue to his masterpiece and considered his novel to be easy to understand and in no need of explication.

125. Máinez, Ramón León. "Las interpretaciones del Sr. Díaz de Benjumea: crítica de críticas." In *Cartas literarias sobre Cervantes y el Quijote por El Bachiller Cervántico*. Cádiz: Imp. de la Revista Médica, 1868, pp. 1-16.

Benjumea must be defended from the attacks of Asensio in various early letters [published later in *Cervantes y sus obras*, Seville, 1870], insisting that there is no *sentido oculto* in the *Quijote*.

Benjumea should be praised for discovering various occult meanings of the adventures in the *Quijote*, including the reference to Juan Blanco de Paz, who pursued Cervantes in Algiers and Spain; veiled allusions in the prologue; the mystery and meaning of Sansón Carrasco; and the significance of the episode of the Knight of the Mirrors.

As for Asensio, he insisted that the anagrams of Benjumea were primitive because he was envious, and he objected to Benjumea's literal, moral, allegorical, and anagogical interpretations of the *Quijote* because he did not understand them—which is surprising for an authoritative Cervantist.

Benjumea never contradicted himself or falsified any of the words of the *Quijote*! Indeed, Benjumea made the truth of the *Quijote* patent and did not deserve the criticisms of Asensio.

126. Pardo de Figueroa, Mariano [Dr. Thebussem]. *Siete cartas sobre Cervantes y el Quijote*. Cádiz: Imp. de la Revista Médica, 1868. 67 pages. [Bound with entry no. 125.]

[These letters, written between 1862 and 1868, consist of the correspondence between two imaginary critics, Mr. Droap and E. W. Thebussem, Baron of Tirmenth. They are called "epístolas droapianas" because they were supposedly written by Droap and directed to Thebussem.

The letters themselves are concerned with various significant events in the world of the Cervantist during the 1860s, while the appendixes contain reviews of significant critical works about Cervantes, some of which are also cited in the letters. The first letter (dated April, 1857) tells of the death of Dr. Thebussem Sr., who bequeathed a castle in Würzburg to the memory of Cervantes, which will become a museum and library. The letters that follow discuss the proposed founding of a "Sociedad Cervantina" that will collect all editions of the *Quijote*; a magnificent new volume of Cervantes' complete works; a monument in honor of Cervantes; the Argamasilla edition of the *Quijote* to be published in 1863; Díaz de Benjumea's latest critical writings on the *Quijote*; and several other newsworthy items published in journals and periodicals. Benjumea's work receives praise more than once. The appendixes contain details about the activity of Thebussem, information regarding new books, like A. M. Segovia's *Cervantes, nueva utopía,* and notes on some dramatic farces based on the *Quijote.*]

127. Pérez Galdós, Benito, "El aniversario de la muerte de Cervantes (1616-1868)." *La Nación,* April 23, 1868, pp. 3-4. [As reprinted by Peter B. Goldman in *Anales Galdosianos* 6 (1971): 99-102.]

The lack of attention given by Spaniards to the anniversary of Cervantes' death should be condemned largely because Cervantes, more than anyone else, symbolizes the achievement of Spain in the second half of the sixteenth century, a period of military and literary accomplishment. That century is perfectly represented in Cervantes' works, while after his death, Spanish culture moved from inventiveness and good sense toward the erratic and toward a literature guided by an obscure ideal written in a style that is a mixture of the conventional, exotic, and erudite.

No genius has been so universally recognized as has Cervantes; through him Spain is respected; his *Quijote* is the patrimony of all humanity. The sun will never set on the domains of Don Quijote and Sancho.

128. Pérez Galdós, Benito. "La patria de Cervantes." *La Nación,* April 24, 1868, p. 1. [As reprinted by Peter B. Goldman in *Anales Galdosianos* 6 (1971): 104-05.]

The lack of attention to the anniversary of Cervantes' death is a sign of intellectual prostration, ingratitude, and indifference. The *Quijote* is a work that contradicts the foreigners who deny the creative capacity and the intelligence of the Spaniards.

129. Pérez Galdós, Benito. "Revista de la Semana." *La Nación,* April 26, 1868, pp. 1-2. [As reprinted by Peter B. Goldman in *Anales Galdosianos* 6 (1971): 105.]

Lamentable is the failure to celebrate the anniversary of Cervantes' death: no plays were given in his honor, no *loas,* no panegyrics, no verses.

130. Asensio y Toledo, José María. "Observaciones sobre las ediciones primitivas del *Ingenioso hidalgo Don Quijote de la Mancha." Revista de España* 9 (1869): 367-76.

Many critics and editors did not know the Juan de la Cuesta escutcheon, which has confused the issue of the textual ancestry of the *Quijote.* By dealing with the textual variants in an episode like the Sierra Morena, one may see the differences in the early editions.

131. Canalejas, Francisco de Paula. "Discurso." In *Fiesta literaria celebrada en honor de Miguel de Cervantes Saavedra por la Academia de Conferencias y Lecturas Públicas de la Universidad de Madrid.* Imp. de G. Alhambra, 1869, pp. 23-48. [Actual date is April 23, 1869.]

From his early days to the rigors of war and captivity, Cervantes had a more difficult life than most writers and thinkers. However, his real difficulties began when he came back to Spain and launched a career in writing. He faced much ingratitude as his heroics abroad were forgotten. But this misfortune preserved the originality of his thinking and genius: It is important to remember that life is a great source for art and, therefore, that Cervantes never forgot that he was a soldier at Lepanto who believed that the new and the old worlds were a theatre for Spanish domination.

The political stage is a small thing on which to express the vastness of the *Quijote* because politics can only explain tendencies and the collective behavior in the human being. While reading the *Quijote*, one discovers honor, goodness, and the virtue of the human soul and delights in the vicissitudes of life because it is an undying source for ideas that nourish the intellect. Commentary of the *Quijote* is unending because it is always teaching something to someone.

Don Quijote and Sancho together represent the totality of a human being and one should not devise "symbolic" interpretations of this work. The *Quijote* is not a personal satire or an allegorical attack on Protestantism. It is a Catholic work. Catholicism seeks the eternal truth, and art, following religion, looks for the everlasting as well. All of this is discovered in the immortal work of Cervantes.

132. Castro, Fernando de. "Discurso." In *Fiesta literaria en honor de Miguel de Cervantes Saavedra por la Academia de Conferencias y Lecturas Públicas de la Universidad de Madrid.* Imp. de G. Alhambra, 1869, pp. 9-16. [Actual date is April 23, 1869.]

There are many eloquent writers in the Castilian language, but who could describe the golden age or the rising of the sun the way Cervantes did? The richness and invention of his style delight the imagination. Should he not be considered the father and founder of the Castilian language? Because he wrote original speeches on poetry and arms and letters, should he not be thought of as a genius and a wise observer of the human condition who gave birth to our philosophy and literature? The glory of Miguel de Cervantes is something that ennobles the great country of Spain.

133. Díaz de Benjumea, Nicolás. "Educación científica de Cervantes." *El Museo Universal* 13 (1869): 19-22 and 38-39.

There is no evidence that Cervantes studied either at the University of Alcalá or at Salamanca; his only possible university studies were under Juan López de Hoyos, and they were very brief.

134. Fernández Duro, Cesáreo. *Cervantes, marino.* Madrid: G. Estrada, 1869. 46 pages.

[Efforts made by Juan de Austria in Lepanto, Cervantes' experience in that battle, Don Quijote's speech on arms and letters, and the battles with the Turks in 1571 are related in detail.]

135. *Fiesta literaria celebrada en honor de Miguel de Cervantes Saavedra por la Academia de Conferencias y Lecturas Públicas de la Universidad de Madrid.* Imp. de G. Alhambra, 1869. 94 pages. [Actual date is April 23, 1869.]

[Contains speeches by Ros de Olano, Canalejas, and F. de Castro (see under author). Also poems by Ventura de la Vega and others.]

136. Pardo de Figueroa, Mariano [Dr. Thebussem]. *Dropiana del año 1869. Octava carta sobre Cervantes y el Quijote dirigida al honorable Doctor E. W. Thebussem por el señor M. Droap.* Madrid: M. Rivadeneyra, 1869. 127 pages.

[An analysis of critical works on the *Quijote*, principally from 1868 to 1869, including Cesáreo Fernández Duro's *Cervantes, marino* and A. M. Segovia's *Cervantes, nueva utopía.* Foreign critics, including Théophile Gautier, Charles Mazade, E. Littré, and Emile Montégut are also noted, and translations, exhibitions, and adaptations are mentioned. The appendixes consist of numerous brief letters of a critical nature.]

137. Pardo de Figueroa, Mariano [Dr. Thebussem]. "Lo verde." *La España Moderna* 6, no. 63 (March, 1894): 43-60. [From 1869: "Apéndice D" of *Dropiana del año 1869*, pp. 63-74; see entry no.136.]

Cervantes had a definite predilection for the color green. He dresses the cultivated Don Diego de Miranda in that color. Dulcinea's eyes are green. The bows with which Don Quijote ties up his helmet are of that color, as is the thread which he uses to sew up his stockings. Manuel de Faria y Souza, in his commentaries on Camoens, discussed the color green and concluded that it represented joy, festivity, and hope. The same could be said for the *Quijote*, for it is a joyous, festive, and optimistic work.

138. Ros de Olano, Antonio. "Discurso." In *Fiesta literaria en honor de Miguel de Cervantes Saavedra por la Academia de Conferencias y Lecturas Públicas de la Universidad de Madrid.* Imp. de G. Alhambra, 1869, pp. 17-22. [Actual date is April 23, 1869.]

Events in fifteenth-century Spain gave rise to the greatness that characterized the sixteenth—a period not only of conquests and discoveries but
also of the birth of its literature and national unification, and a time when
many of its great writers, Garcilaso, Ercilla, and Cervantes, were warriors as
well.

One observes the same phenomenon in the novel: Don Quijote was a
caballero and poet, whose exaggerations were pointed out by Sancho; thus
why do letters and arms complement one another when they seem so
contradictory? As the strange and exceptional are so much a part of the
human heart, this combination is not necessarily rare. It was for the love of
glory that Cervantes was a soldier, and it was through that glory that he
came to love letters. One career nurtured the other.

139. Asensio y Toledo, José María. *Cervantes y sus obras: Cartas literarias
dirigidas a varios amigos*. Seville: J. M. Geofrin, 1870. 100 pages.

Benjumea is wrong in saying that Cervantes' masterpiece is an attack
on Juan Blanco de Paz, nor is it a satire on the Inquisition. Regarding the
authorship of the spurious *Quijote*, the Blanco de Paz theory is mistaken,
but the Aliaga theory of Aureliano Fernández-Guerra y Orbe and
Cayetano Alberto de la Barrera is plausible.

Argamasilla de Alba, not Seville, was the location of the composition
of the *Quijote*. Cervantes' purpose was to attack books of chivalry, but
after creating two most original characters, he gave free rein to his
imagination. The Knight and the Squire, depicting moral and physical
man with sublime aspirations and crude materialism, are the reasons for
the *Quijote's* popularity. Cervantes' novel is not really an autobiographical
work, though the author may have remembered happy or unpleasant
moments in his life and incorporated them into his book. Benjumea's
works contain foreign ideas; they are also unoriginal, distorted, and
contradictory.

140. Castro, Federico de. *Cervantes y la filosofía española*. Seville: Girones y
Orduña, 1870. 50 pages. [Also published in *Boletín de la Universidad de
Madrid* 2 (1870): 709-17; 3 (1870): 789-805, 1101-16, and 1337-40.]

Although the great merit of the *Quijote* is that it put to rest enthusiasm
over chivalry books, their spiritual values nevertheless live on, for they
represent the conquest of the soul over matter. Cervantes was not a
mystic but did appreciate mysticism, and he was attracted by the faith-
militant nature of chivalry. Chivalry consists of miracles for those who
believe in them, and especially in Part II, Don Quijote speaks as though he
possessed total faith in this institution.

141. Gamero, Antonio Martín. *Jurisprudencia de Cervantes*. Toledo: Fando
e Hijo, 1870. 38 pages.

There is evidence that Cervantes knew jurisprudence to a substantial degree, especially in Part I, where Cervantes speaks of the hardships of the scholar and the willingness of the soldier to defend him. Sancho's wisdom as a judge in Part II (Insula Barataria) also indicates that Cervantes was an eager student of law. And finally, the advice that Don Quijote gave Sancho before he left for the isle proves that Cervantes blended humanitarianism with his profound knowledge of jurisprudence.

142. Máinez, Ramón León. *Cervantes y los críticos: Carta literaria que dedica D. Ramón León Máinez al Dr. E. W. Thebussem.* Cádiz: Tip. de la Mercantil, 1870. 24 pages.

Tomás Erauso y Zavaleta, Agustín Sánchez, and Alejandro Aguado all said that Cervantes was anti-Spanish in his depiction of his homeland and hence was not a credit to Spain. Mor de Fuentes found certain adventures in the *Quijote* to be violent and improbable. Teodomiro Ibáñez praised the *Quijote* as an ever-youthful work and lauded Cervantes' deep exploration of the human spirit and his admirable description of the characteristics and conditions of an entire epoch.

143. Monescillo, Antolín. "Oración fúnebre." *Memorias de la Real Academia Española* 2 (1870): 337-72.

Cervantes created effective portraits of unfortunate people in the *Quijote* because he was one himself. Cervantes was guided in his life by Christian precepts, underlying which is the mystic tendency in Spanish literature (Spain's mystics suffered a great deal, too). But Cervantes never lost hope because of his steadfast belief in Christianity.

144. Sbarbi y Osuna, José María. *Cervantes teólogo. Carta dirigida al Sr. D. Mariano Pardo de Figueroa, precedida de una síntesis histórico-literaria por El Sr. D. Antonio Martín Gamero.* Toledo: Cea, 1870. 26 pages.

There is ample evidence in the *Quijote* and the *Novelas ejemplares* to prove that Cervantes was well-read in theology. In fact, Cervantes' knowledge of theology is encyclopedic. The fact that the Inquisition censored the author's remark about works of charity done randomly or weakly does not detract from Cervantes' status as a theologian.

145. Antequera, Ramón. "Cervantes Saavedra y el *Quijote*." *Crónica de los Cervantistas* 1, no. 1 (October 7, 1871): 11-13; no. 2 (December 12, 1871): 49-51.

The *Quijote* is a literary monument and compendium of humanity that has outlived its detractors, beginning with Avellaneda and others who tried to discredit the work. It is important that in our time we have many critics interested in *Quijote* research. Witness the correspondence of M.

Droap and E. W. Thebussem published by Mariano Pardo de Figueroa.

The reason for hoping that humanists will come to study the *Quijote* is that it is a novel that presents the mystery of human life, the conflict between negation and affirmation, error and truth. The artist can do this better than the scientist, as Cervantes has proven.

146. Asensio y Toledo, José María. *El sentido oculto del Quijote*. Seville: Imp. y Lib. de las Sierpes, 1871. 42 pages.

The *sentido oculto* of the *Quijote*, which has to do with a masked attack on people in high places such as dukes, emperors, et al., is incorrect and tends to diminish interest in the *Quijote*. Cervantes would never have indulged in such charades because he loved Spain and its institutions too much. The idea that Cervantes is Don Quijote himself is false, because Don Quijote has an existence independent from his creator. While one may argue that a character is partly a projection of his author, this idea has been extended too far and makes the argument unbelievable.

The author of the *Quijote* was a patriot who gave us an accurate picture of Spain in a lively portrait of his society and times.

147. Barrera y Leirado, Cayetano Alberto de la. "Noticias bibliográficas de varios impresos sueltos relativos a Cervantes y sus obras." *Crónica de los Cervantistas* 1, no. 2 (December 12, 1871): 45-49; no. 3 (February 20, 1872): 92-95; no. 4 (May 29, 1872): 149-50.

[Contains significant bibliographical data from the eighteenth and nineteenth centuries.]

148. Benavides y Navarrete, Francisco de Paula. "Oración fúnebre." *Memorias de la Real Academia Española* 3 (1871): 87-105.

Through his humble faith Cervantes practiced his religion as any man would. He believed in family, country, fellow Spaniards, and patrons, and through his faith he elevated his genius and enriched his mind and talents.

149. Caballero, Fermín. "La patria de Don Quijote." *Crónica de los Cervantistas* 1, no. 2 (December 12, 1871): 64-69.

Fabián Hernández claimed that Don Quijote's hometown was Villaverde, not Argamasilla. He is incorrect and should be more careful about the geography of La Mancha.

150. Cervantes Peredo, Manuel. "El sentido oculto." *Crónica de los Cervantistas* 1, no. 2 (December 12, 1871): 69-70.

The *Quijote* is not a masked satire of the Inquisition, Charles V, the Duke of Medina-Sidonia, Rodrigo Pacheco, or Juan Blanco de Paz. If anything, the *Quijote* is a masterful satire of a social "hallucination" such as exaggerated chivalresque notions.

151. *Crónica de los Cervantistas.* Cádiz: Tip. La Mercantil, 1871-79.

[First published in October, 1871 and lasting until December, 1879, this journal, directed and founded by Ramón León Máinez, had among its contributors the most prominent Cervantists of the latter part of the nineteenth century: José María Asensio, Cayetano Alberto de la Barrera, Adolfo de Castro, Nicolás Díaz de Benjumea, Mariano Pardo de Figueroa ("Dr. Thebussem"), J. E. Hartzenbusch, Leopoldo Rius, José María Sbarbi, and Francisco Tubino.

The purpose of the journal, according to Máinez, was to offer eminent Cervantine scholars the opportunity to air their views. Thus, the journal tried to faithfully represent all Cervantists, and it was the first journal dedicated solely to Cervantes.

In addition to articles on polemical issues, the journal carried bibliographical notices, personal letters, news of conferences and celebrations held in honor of Cervantes, and newly discovered documents and other information on Cervantes' life and works. Sections of each issue were quite literally a "who's who" or "who's where" among Cervantine scholars. Thanks to the efforts of José María Asensio, studies of many significant editions of all of the works of Cervantes were also published in it.

The first important scholarship on the *Galatea* was voiced here, as were news of the special new edition of the *Quijote* that was published in Cádiz and a report of the library to be erected in Cervantes' memory in Alcalá de Henares. Much of the material focused on philosophical and literary questions regarding Cervantes' works, but a great deal of space was also given to review articles and replies to particularly negative remarks made against recently published books. The following are samples of topics covered: the issue of Cervantes' birth date; imitations of *La Galatea*; the hidden meaning of the *Quijote*; Cervantes in Toledo; Cervantes as a theologian; *La Galatea* and the pastoral novel; Cervantes and Shakespeare; Cervantes and adultery; the commentators of the *Quijote*; a voyage to the cave of Montesinos; iconography of the *Quijote*.]

152. Fernández Espino, José. *Curso histórico-crítico de la literatura española.* Seville: Imp. y Lib. de las Sierpes, 1871. 788 pages.

The real meaning of the *Quijote* has been the subject of debate for a long time largely because it is something of an attack on chivalry books and also much more. Cervantes did not really write the novel as a satire on chivalry. Instead, he created a man of great imagination and wit, one who is universal, and a human comedy that satirizes human morals at the same time that it incarnates the whole of human life. It is a book for all times, not just sixteenth-century Spain, in which Cervantes exalts the poetic nature of Don Quijote and creates sympathetic characters like the hero and Sancho, who compensate for each other's mistakes. In other words, at times it is satire, at times drama, and at times moral philosophy.

The secondary characters and episodes of Part I of the novel are especially interesting. The lively portraits of the Barber, the Priest, and the discreet Dorotea, as well as the stories of the captive and the curious impertinent, are all relevant to the novel because Cervantes is drawing a picture of the whole of humanity. The style of the second part of the *Quijote* that was published in 1614 by the cleric Alonso Fernández de Avellaneda gives away its spurious authorship because Avellaneda could never equal the effort of the original. However, the cleric's style is not terribly unpleasing: his language is "castizo," and the way he executes his plot indicates that he has some talent.

Admirable are the people and situations of Part II and its moral, satirical, and philosophical framework. Episodes like the Calvileño journey and the chapters in Barcelona are enticing. On the whole, Cervantes' achievement has lasted because of the kind of human drama it recreates.

153. Jiménez, Francisco de Paula. "Oración fúnebre." *Memorias de la Real Academia Española* 3 (1871): 242-58.

Lessons from the *Quijote* are related to the book of *Ecclesiastes* from the Old Testament, and lessons and maxims from the *Quijote* are definitive statements about the way to govern as a good prince would; the work in general presents principles of behavior that can benefit everyone.

154. Máinez, Ramón León. "Cervantes no fué teólogo." *Crónica de los Cervantistas* 1, no. 1 (October 7, 1871): 19-23.

Cervantes' knowledge of theology as a discrete science is as nonexistent as is his systematic study of law, geography, and other sciences. To be able to speak of theology was a requisite for intelligent writing in Cervantes' day, just as politics is today, and it was also part of Don Quijote's role as a knight-errant to know something about theology, among many other things. Cervantes knew his religion well as a practicing Catholic, but he was not a theologian.

155. Asensio y Toledo, José María. *Catálogo de algunos libros, folletos y artículos sueltos referentes a la vida y a las obras de Miguel de Cervantes Saavedra.* Seville: R. Tarascó y Lassa, 1872. 12 pages.

[A catalogue of 133 works dating from 1667 to 1872, some of which contain very rare material. There is appropriate bibliographical information for each entry along with critical commentary.]

156. Caballero-Infante y Zuazo, Francisco. *Discursos leídos ante la Real Academia Sevillana de Buenas Letras.* Seville: Hijos de Fe, 1872. 56 pages.

[A volume comprising speeches delivered on the anniversary of Cervantes' death, April 23, 1872, and containing a series of poems published at the end of the volume in praise of Cervantes.]

157. Cerdá, Manuel. "Catálogo de algunas ediciones de las obras de Miguel de Cervantes Saavedra." *Crónica de los Cervantistas* 1, no. 4 (May 29, 1872): 146-50; no. 5 (August 10, 1872): 176-80; 2, no. 1 (January 28, 1873): 23-29; no. 2 (April 23, 1873): 67-68; no. 3 (December 31, 1874): 121-24; no. 4 (September 19, 1875): 140-42; 3, no. 5 (March 15, 1876): 172-74; no. 6 (October 7, 1876): 220-22.

[Contains significant bibliography on editions of all of Cervantes' works from early redactions through the late 1800s.]

158. Díaz de Benjumea, Nicolás. "Epístola cervantina." *Crónica de los Cervantistas* 1, no. 5 (August 10, 1872): 157-59.

[In this short article on his reaction to events in the Cervantine world, Díaz de Benjumea congratulates Máinez for his work on the *Crónica de los Cervantistas*, reiterates his philosophical stance on the *Quijote*, reviews the contemporary polemics that he has read about in the *Crónica*, and sees his idea about the *sentido oculto* of the *Quijote* gaining ground among critics.]

159. Fernández Duro, Cesáreo. "La cocina del *Quijote.*" *La Ilustración Española y Americana* 16 (1872): 535-39, 554-55, and 566-70.

Although Cervantes was not an expert in the art of cooking, many metaphors in the *Quijote* stem from culinary terminology. Examples may be found in the Camacho's wedding episode and in many of Sancho's proverbs.

160. Lista, Alberto. "Un esc ito inédito." *La Ilustración Española y Americana* 16 (1872): 39-43, 54, and 86. [Published also as "Juicio crítico del comentario que puso al *Quijote* D. Diego Clemencín"; a partial version is in *La Gaceta* (Madrid), 1833.]

The efforts of Bowle and Pellicer are really not true commentaries, especially when compared to Clemencín's, which, with the abundance of notes that real commentary requires, demonstrates how accurate Cervantes' satire of chivalry books was. In addition to satisfying the reader's curiosity about the books of chivalry Cervantes read (and to which there was previously almost no access), these notes also reveal sources in the literature of chivalry, without which an understanding of the *Quijote* is almost impossible. Clemencín's notes are further justified because they correct previous editions, explain obscurities, difficulties, and allusions in Cervantes' language, and correct what seem to be obvious defects in the language (which Clemencín attributes to the alacrity with which Cervantes wrote the novel). Clemencín reconstructed Cervantes' language as it was in the sixteenth century not only for his own edition but for all future editions.

Clemencín's notes have great variety and may be classified according to the following categories: customs, morality, classical literature, ancient history, and books of chivalry. Each category is well-documented, demonstrating the breadth and depth of Clemencín's research. Among them are his summary and subsequent dismissal of the *Buscapié*, his description of the Lope-Cervantes literary rivalry, his explanation of the background of the war against the Turk, and his analysis of the dispute among those who claim by turns Madrid and Valladolid as the site of the Court's residence. Clemencín handles Cervantes' knowledge of language with his analysis of the novelist's grammar, everyday expressions, and popular ballads and offers at least ten examples of notes that show how one establishes certain chivalry books as the sources of specific episodes.

161. López Fabra, Francisco. "Un artículo curioso." *Crónica de los Cervantistas* 1, no. 4 (May 29, 1872): 134-36.
[A list of 278 editions of the *Quijote*, 87 done in Spain and 191 outside Spain.]

162. López Fabra, Francisco. "Listas para la indagación de las ediciones que existen de *Don Quijote de la Mancha*." *Boletín de la Reproducción Fototipográfica de la primera edición de Don Quijote de la Mancha*, Nos. 5 and 6 (April and August, 1872).
[Contains a list of 234 editions of the *Quijote* as well as a letter from "Dr. Thebussem" (Pardo de Figueroa) concerning several Dutch translations of the *Quijote*.]

163. Reinoso, Emilio B. "Los comentadores del *Quijote*." *Crónica de los Cervantistas* 1, no. 6, (October 31, 1872): 212-14.
The *Quijote* is a very explicit work that speaks for itself. One need only look at Don Quijote's conversations with Sansón Carrasco in Part II: that small children read it and all grown men understand it is proof that the words of the *Quijote* are sufficient in themselves.

164. Sánchez Almonacid, Mariano. "Discurso leído en el Ateneo de Alicante." *Crónica de los Cervantistas* 1, no. 3, (February 20, 1872): 88-92. [This is a fragment of a speech titled "Cervantes y sus obras literarias" read before the Ateneo de Alicante.]

The most important idea in the *Quijote* concerns the folly of man. It is a book that laughs at human laws and at all things that involve humanity. The book leaves no person in society untouched, and everyone can learn from the *Quijote's* maxims. Obvious allusions to real persons do not wholly explain the significance of the work: it is philosophical, moral, humorous, and sad.

165. Sánchez Almonacid, Mariano. "Cervantes y sus obras literarias." *Crónica de los Cervantistas* 1, no. 3 (February 20, 1872): 88-92.

[A general response to and review of the literary criticism of the day and such issues as character identity, Avellaneda's second part, and the contributions of some of the prominent critics of the century.]

166. Sbarbi y Osuna, José María. "Cervantes sí fué teólogo." *Crónica de los Cervantistas* 1, no. 4, (May 29, 1872): 143-45; no. 5 (August 10, 1872): 182-83; no. 6 (October 31, 1872): 217-22.

A theologian is a person who is "inteligente o docto en teología," a definition that fits Cervantes, who was a good student of that discipline. While Cervantes never had a perfect knowledge of the subject, he should be classified as a theologian. His own hero could write a sermon very well because of his adequate knowledge of theology, dogma, morality, and the Scriptures, acquired not by simple contact with society but by his studies.

167. Sbarbi y Osuna, José María. "El *Quijote* es intraducible." *La Ilustración Española y Americana* 16 (1872): 262-63. [Reprinted in Sbarbi's *Intraducibilidad del Quijote*, Madrid, 1876, pp. 13-18.]

There is particular difficulty in translating such expressions as "al buen callar llaman Sancho" and "gato...rato...bellacón," because there are no non-Spanish equivalents which reflect the rhyme or wordplay of the original. Such expressions as "duelos y quebrantos," "mozas del partido," "oíslo," and "achaque" (about which Duffield had expressed concern) do not present a major problem. To think that the *Quijote* can be translated without losing the beauty of Cervantes' words and phrases is to expect the impossible, for in that sense the *Quijote* is untranslatable.

168. Tubino, Francisco María. *Cervantes y el Quijote: Estudios críticos.* Madrid: A. Durán, 1872. 285 pages.

The critics of the *Quijote* are of two types: discreet readers who enjoy the beauty of the text and who appreciate it and understand it, and those, like Gayton, Bowle, Puigblanch, Salvá, and Creuzé de Lesser, who seek to read their own ideas into it. The latter have contributed a number of extraneous (and strange) interpretations, ranging from Cervantes' alleged anti-Church viewpoint to the idea that the text is rife with hidden allusions to historical figures. Cervantes is modern and Western; he is neither a theologian nor a socialist. As an artist, Cervantes belongs to his century; as a thinker, he belongs to posterity. Cervantes espouses the moral philosophy of his era, and in addition, in him is the germ of the philosophy of the future.

The *Quijote* is a book of inspiration, but this inspiration came from an exact knowledge of the illness which he sought to attack and the type of medicine needed. While commentaries do not furnish an answer to the meaning of Cervantes' novel, the merits of the masterpiece would not have been discovered without them. Nevertheless, a true commentary has yet to be written, for it would begin with a conscientious examination of Cervantes' era and analyze the *Quijote* as an artistic work as well as a philosophical work. In addition, to reveal the spirit of reform in Cervantes' novel, it should examine the institution of chivalry and measure its influence, its origins, and its decadence, while maintaining a philosophical perspective.

169. Apraiz y Sáenz del Burgo, Julián. "Discurso de inauguración y recepción leído en la Academia Cervántica Española el día 1 de marzo de 1873." In *Colección de discursos y artículos*, I. Vitoria: Tip. de la Ilustración de Alava, 1889, pp. 361-67.

Terence's character, the old Chremes of *The Self-Tormentor*, may have influenced the figure of Don Quijote. "I am a man," said Chremes, "I consider nothing human alien to me."

170. Asensio y Toledo, José María. *Los continuadores de El ingenioso hidalgo*. Madrid: Imp. de Noguera, 1873. 21 pages.

Spaniards were always interested in the *Quijote*; no book was more often published in the world than that one. In addition, editors have praised Cervantes' novel for many years. There is an obscure, anonymous French imitation entitled *Suite nouvelle et véritable de l'histoire et des aventures de l'incomparable Don Quichotte de la Manche* (1726), in which ninety-two chapters are devoted to the adventures of Don Quijote and ten to those of Sancho. This obscure work is tedious, the characters have no color, and the style is manneristic and lacking in truth.

171. Asensio y Toledo, José María. "¿Puede traducirse el *Quijote*?" *Revista de España* 34 (1873): 529-36.

Although translations are at times difficult, the *Quijote* has been translated successfully into many languages. The problems that can occur in the translation have to do with familiar language, ellipsis, sententiousness, and dialogues between Don Quijote and Sancho; conversations with types such as galley slaves, *dueñas*, and innkeepers also present some difficulties in an English rendition. But what makes the *Quijote* translatable is that its plot is easy to follow, its characters natural, and its language generally flexible. Certainly the crispness and fluidity of this language are hard to capture, but translation of the *Quijote* is possible and Sbarbi's standards for translating are too rigid.

172. Martínez y Saez, Jacinto María. "Oración fúnebre." *Memorias de la Real Academia Española* 4 (1873): 307-36.
    Cervantes was a moralist and a great man of wisdom and the *Quijote* is a book rich in doctrine.

173. Opiso, Antonio. "Divagaciones sobre el sentido práctico en las obras de Cervantes." In *Ateneo Tarraconense de la clase obrera al conmemorar el aniversario de la muerte de Cervantes, 1873.* [As excerpted in Rius, III, pp. 112-13.]
    Practical sense, or common sense, is Cervantes' outstanding characteristic. He knew all human weaknesses, and almost all of his characters are copied from nature. Don Quijote, though a myth, is the immortal representation of impossible feats; he is the mirror of philosophers, moralists, and artists who do not know what they are looking for, in spite of their good intentions.

174. Asensio y Toledo, José María. "Cervantes, inventor." In *Conmemoración del aniversario CCLVIII de la muerte de Miguel de Cervantes.* Seville (Academia Sevillana de Buenas Letras): Imp. de R. Baldaraque, 1874, pp. 42-46.
    One must put an end to all exaggeration and ask why Cervantes was a true genius. How could a man who never went to school or earned diplomas be considered a great inventor? One way of proving that Cervantes was a genius is to see how much he influenced later writers in Europe like Avellaneda, Pichou, Scudéry, and Goncourt, as well as many English authors.
    Cervantes was modern; he gave life to his characters that throbs within each of us; we quote them as if we knew them, and they always interest and inspire us. Moreover, Cervantes dealt a severe blow to the books of chivalry during the height of their corruption, and from the ruins of this literature he created the modern novel. By composing a perfect model of this genre and by inventing truthful characters that have found their way into modern literature, Cervantes gave this literature its primary impulse.

175. Castro y Rossi, Adolfo de. *Varias obras inéditas de Cervantes.* Madrid: A. de Carlos e Hijo, 1874, pp. 193-399.
    The name of El Toboso is not fictitious, as there is a family name of the same according to a document found in the Biblioteca Colombina with the

title "instrumentos pertenecientes a la casa del apellido Toboso en la ciudad de Córdoba." This name comes from the fifteenth century and "es de la Mancha, donde hay un lugar que lo llaman Toboso en cuyo paraje se crían muchas tobas; y las armas de los Tobosos son un escudo con un oso destroncado, atado con una cadena por medio del cuerpo, y colgando de una toba a modo del Tusson real, y orlado todo de las aspas de San Andrés, como está pintada en las casas principales de los Tobosos en esta ciudad de Córdoba."

Alarcón and Avellaneda were the same person. Evidence for this is the following: they were both American writers; ill feelings existed between Cervantes and Alarcón, much like those between Cervantes and Avellaneda; there are linguistic and technical parallels in the works of both such as the repetition of the same words; and finally, their critical thinking follows similar patterns.

176. Coll y Vehí, José. *Los refranes del Quijote ordenados por materias y glosados.* Barcelona: Imp. del Diario de Barcelona, 1874. 248 pages.

[The major portion of this book is a collection of the 263 proverbs from the *Quijote*, listed in the order in which they appear and accompanied by commentary. The remainder consists of proverbs from other works, an alphabetical listing of the proverbs of the *Quijote*, and indexes of the proverbs taken from the *Novelas ejemplares, Persiles, Viaje del Parnaso,* and Avellaneda's *Quijote*.]

While there are numerous proverbs in the *Quijote*, there are not as many as are generally supposed. Some phrases in this collection are not even true proverbs. The number 263 represents only one eighth of those listed for Cervantes' work in the dictionary of the Royal Academy. The idea of making Sancho a "padre de los refranes" must not have occurred to the author until he began Part II, for Sancho is not corrected for overusing proverbs in Part I.

177. *Conmemoración del aniversario CCLVIII de la muerte de Miguel de Cervantes.* Seville (Academia Sevillana de Buenas Letras): Imp. de R. Baldaraque, 1874. 80 pages.

[Includes J. M. Asensio's study "Cervantes, inventor" and four ballads written by admirers of Cervantes' work.]

178. J. F. F. "La novela y el *Quijote*, el *Quijote* y las conclusiones del Sr. Tubino." Artículos en los folletos de 1874 y 1875, del *Ateneo Tarraconense de la clase obrera al conmemorar el aniversario de Cervantes.* [As excerpted in Rius, III, pp. 118-19.]

Cervantes sought to organize the mind and educate the heart of the society of his times, a society that suffered from an excess of fantasy. In this sense the *Quijote* is a novel of customs. Tubino is thus incorrect in asserting that Cervantes' work is one of recreation. It would be equally mistaken to state that the *Quijote* is only a book of philosophy, for it is a mixture of the beautiful and the useful, of recreation and instruction, and neither prevails.

179. Menéndez Pelayo, Marcelino. "Cervantes considerado como poeta." In *Miscelánea científica y literaria*, 1874.[As noted by Alberto Sánchez in *Anales Cervantinos* 5 (1955-1956): 268-69.]

[Praise of Cervantes as both a lyric and dramatic poet.]

180. Opiso, Antonio. "Universalidad e inmortalidad del genio de Cervantes." In *Ateneo Tarraconense de la clase obrera, conmemoración de la muerte de Cervantes, 1874.* [As excerpted in Rius, III, pp. 113-14.]

The figure Don Quijote is comparable to Pantagruel, Faust, Hamlet, Othello, and the narrator of the Divine Comedy, characters who are transfigured by their authors. Yet the Knight is the one hero who has most penetrated the awareness of the masses. Hamlet meditates too much, which brings him to the threshold of madness; Don Quijote thinks, and the execution of his thoughts drives him mad. Like Faust, he follows an ideal, as both desire the infinite. But Faust carries within him a spark of skepticism that is unknown to the Cervantine figure. Faust appears to be more insane than Don Quijote.

Cervantes is universal. He knew action and reflexion; he joined valor to knowledge. His hero arises from a synthesis of this action and reflexion, and the *Quijote* is a great step in the grandiose history of the conscience, which began with the Bible and has not ended yet, a history written by geniuses predestined by God.

181. Pardo de Figueroa, Mariano [Dr. Thebussem]. "Las 1.633 notas de Hartzenbusch a la primera edición del *Quijote." Revista Europea* 2 (1874): 150-55.

With regard to the text of the *Quijote*, there are words in the fingida Arcadia episode that should not have been modified, because most people can understand them. Here is the proper text: "Que el gozo de Don Quijote por verse armado caballero, era tanto y tan fuerte, que saliéndose del cuerpo, atravesaba la ropa, silla y caballo, hasta salir impetuoso y reventar por las cinchas de Rocinante."

No commentator has corrected Don Quijote's response to Vivaldo: "Aunque el mío es de los Cachopines de Laredo no le osaré yo poner con el del Toboso de la Mancha . . . ." His reply should end with the words "how is it that you never heard of the name?" La Rodríguez should not carry the article "La" because it is a family name and not a first name. As it stands it has a very pejorative connotation.

The Hartzenbusch observation that foreigners can understand most everything written by Cervantes is commendable; but since even the most difficult words of the text, like *baciyelmo* or *pantalia*, have been understood by foreigners, it appears that sometimes Hartzenbusch unnecessarily annotates such locutions.

What López Fabra and Hartzenbusch have done with the text, its variants, errors, and misprints will pave the way for modern scholarship on the *Quijote*. It will reveal not only how quickly Cervantes composed his novel but also how many errors Juan de la Cuesta made in printing it.

182. Piernas y Hurtado, José Manuel. *Ideas y noticias económicas del Quijote.* Madrid: A. Aguado, 1874. 84 pages.

Sancho's character can be explained by financial interests. His family is very much concerned with money, and in the Sierra Morena and Mambrino's helmet episodes, as well as in that of the Duke and Duchess, Camacho's wedding, and the Insula Barataria, this aspect of Sancho emerges clearly. Moreover, it was Don Quijote's promise of material gain that first encouraged Sancho to travel with him. Economic interest, however, does not detract from Sancho's character. Although Don Quijote rejects wealth for himself, he condones acquiring wealth by other characters in the novel. There are not, for example, any strong attacks against owning property. The idea that Don Quijote is a socialist is wrong despite the fact that he held the idea of the golden age in high esteem when there were no Spanish equivalents of "my" and "thy"; socialism was not a school of thought in Cervantes' day. (Though it existed in the works of Plato, Cervantes seldom used Plato as a political authority.)

Cervantes obliquely criticized the *hidalguía*, and like many others of his day, he himself became a soldier out of necessity. This helps us to understand why the father of the Captive told his son that there were three true callings in this world, "iglesia, mar o casa real."

Concerning political economy, very little was permitted to be said in Cervantes' time, putting in a bolder light the scene in which Don Quijote tells Sancho (before he becomes governor of Barataria) how to curry the favor of the people by manipulating matters that concern money. The *Quijote* also touches on slavery and taxes: Sancho's suggestion of bringing slaves from Ethiopia to his isle, for instance, is a tacit way of saying such an institution existed. Also taxes are mentioned desultorily throughout the novel.

The purpose of this study has not been to look for the scientific economist in Cervantes, but to examine Cervantes' economic situation to see what social factors may have influenced his thinking. Spanish society of the time loved money and drew clear socio-economic distinctions, which emerge in the Camacho's wedding episode and in the examples of greed on Sancho's isle.

183. Díaz de Benjumea, Nicolás. *El mensage de Merlín, o tercer aviso de Cid Asam-Ousad Benengeli, sobre el desencanto del Quijote*. London: Holthusen, 1875. 110 pages.

The recondite symbolism and double meanings in the *Quijote* were recognized by Avellaneda, who censured the *Quijote* for the social ideals that the Captive represented. Also, there is evidence that the author of the apocryphal *Quijote* was the Dominican Andrés Pérez.

184. L. C. "Pensamiento filosófico-social de la obra de Cervantes." In *Aniversario de Cervantes en el Ateneo Tarraconense, 1875.* [As excerpted in Rius, III, p. 122.]

Don Quijote and Sancho were the extremes of a society that had not found the just mean. Like Rabelais, Ariosto, Pulci, and Boiardo, Cervantes is anti-feudal and anti-spiritual, and his novel has a philosophico-social goal: that of carrying out a complete revolution in the ideas and customs in the author's era.

185. Revilla, Manuel de la. "La interpretación simbólica del *Quijote*." In *Obras de Manuel de la Revilla*. Madrid: Ateneo, 1883, pp. 365-93. [Published earlier in *La Ilustración Española y Americana* 19 (1875).]

All great works are divided into two categories: the historical (or temporal) and the eternal. As a historical work the *Quijote* may be viewed as a satire against chivalry books and the Middle Ages. As the *"Quijote* eterno," however, it is about the distinction between the real and the ideal.

Cervantists of this time commit a grave error by seeing only the satirical intent of the *Quijote* and by denying the value of symbolic interpretations. If the *Quijote* were only a satire of chivalry books, its fame would not go beyond the borders of Spain. But the view that Don Quijote and Sancho are universal characters who cannot be limited to a specific time and place clearly refutes this. Thus the so-called historical opinion is faulty, not because it is wrong or untruthful, but because it is exclusivistic and incomplete. It is clear that Cervantes' stated intention was to satirize chivalry, but by doing that he unconsciously created a profound and transcendental dramatic poem beneath the surface satire. It was the *"Quijote* eterno" beneath the *"Quijote* histórico" that destroyed the chivalry book.

While some see the novel as a political satire against Charles V and others view Don Quijote as the incarnation of a revolutionary, only the idea that the *Quijote* is a dramatization of the opposition between the real and ideal is plausible, even though we must admit that this was not Cervantes' conscious intention. And it would be safe to stop there, for others who have gone beyond to create a Cervantist movement look too hard for symbolic meanings in the *Quijote* and consequently offer notions that are too vague and imprecise.

The *Quijote* is not a protest, nor is its hero a tragic figure. Nor was Cervantes an idealist when he wrote the work: he had already experienced the worst a young idealist could and was spending his life with people who were far from ideal. As we know, he came to abhor chivalry, and in a prison in Argamasilla de Alba he began to write a book against it. But was the composition of the *Quijote* motivated solely by literary preferences? As a man of the Renaissance, Cervantes did react against a literary genre that was absurd, anachronistic, and dangerous; but at the same time Cervantes was rebelling against the decadent nobility, although he did not write the *Quijote* as a specific attack on the nobility. Therefore the beauty of the *Quijote* and the truthfulness of its characters were a matter of destiny and not of purpose. Like other great men Cervantes achieved what he did not set out to do: he did not realize the ultimate value of his experiment.

The *Quijote* is not the work of an idealist, dreamer, or skeptic. It is the echo of good sense, not that of a philosophical poet who elevated his work to a transcendental level. Furthermore, realism and idealism in the *Quijote* are reconcilable; such oppositions will always exist, as will the eternal aspiration to the ideal, but these polarities do not cause comic situations, except when a person aims at false idealism. And they never lead to tragedy, which could happen only if Don Quijote were killed during one of his adventures, which, of course, does not occur in Cervantes' novel.

Thus, absurd idealism born of fantasy is what characterizes Don Quijote and is what Cervantes attacks with his humor. Don Quijote is the sort of idealist who knows no end to goodness and nothing of the real world. He is a comic figure precisely because his services are put at the disposal of the absurd. Moreover, Sancho Panza is not the figure of common sense that many think. Instead, the Priest, the Barber, and Sansón Carraso represent good sense in the novel, while Sancho, Don Quijote's opposite, is concerned totally with extravagant self-interest. Therefore, the great irony of the *Quijote* is that the antithesis does not and cannot become a synthesis: the circumstances of the lives of Don Quijote and Sancho prevent it.

186. Acosta y Lozano, Zacarías. "Demostraciones críticas contra los variantes que ha querido introducir en el texto del *Quijote* el Excmo. Don Juan Eugenio Hartzenbusch." *Crónica de los Cervantistas* 3, no. 5 (March 15, 1876): 194-96.

Hartzenbusch is wrong regarding the phrase "historia, madre de la verdad." His changing "madre" to "imagen" is objectionable because "madre" as a figurative word has been used consistently by many classical writers.

187. *Album literario dedicado a la memoria del rey de los ingenios españoles.* *(Aniversario CCLX de la muerte de Miguel de Cervantes Saavedra).* Madrid: Revista Literaria Cervantes, Tip. de Pedro Núñez, 1876. 124 pages.

[This collection contains thirty-seven short poems dedicated to Cervantes, including Juan Eugenio Hartzenbusch's "Epístola de D. Quijote" and Ventura de la Vega's "Cervantes," as well as five prose tributes to the author of the *Quijote*: José María Sbarbi's "Cervantes"; Vicente Bas y Cortés' "Noche de Concepción"; Adolfo de Castro's "Lope de Rueda y Cervantes Saavedra"; José María Casenave's "Cervantes y Cisneros"; and Manuel Tello de Amondareyn's "Ideas sueltas acerca de Cervantes y el *Quijote*."

Adolfo de Castro's article points out that Cervantes specifically acknowledged his debt to Lope de Rueda. Castro contends that Cervantes frequently borrowed Lope de Rueda's technique of mispronunciation by one character and immediate correction by another, and in addition to asserting that Avellaneda's criticism of Cervantes' "ostentación de sinónimos voluntarios" refers to Cervantes' use of this technique, he also notes various other echoes of Lope de Rueda in Cervantes' works. Also noteworthy are Manuel Tello Amondareyn's comment that each generation and each reader finds new occasion for scientific study in the *Quijote* and his subsequent summary of the many identities that the author has been given: a theologian (Sbarbi), philosopher (Federico de Castro), moralist (P. Gatell), legal expert (Antonio Martín Gamero), geographer (Fermín Caballero), navigator (Cesáreo Fernández Duro and Florencio Janer), expert in practical medicine (Hernández Morejón), politician (José de España y Lledó), and economist (J. M. Piernas y Hurtado).]

188. Alvarez Espino, Romualdo. Article written in Cádiz and found in *Cervantes* (Madrid), April 30 and May 8, 1876. [As excerpted in Rius, III, pp. 119-21.]

Descartes consolidated philosophy; Cervantes gave it a dose of common sense and beauty at a time when it seemed confused. Descartes destroys sophism and skepticism; Cervantes destroys fanaticism and pulverizes the ridiculous.

Don Quijote is the faithful representation of that nobility, mystic in soul and warlike in body, who carries scapulary and sword, who prays and strikes blows, who wears silk and steel, who makes speeches with vain emphasis and punishes with blind cruelty. Face to face with this caricature of nobility is Sancho, the symbol of the popular spirit, the sensual opposed to the mystic. There is no overall solution to the duality in the *Quijote*, for Cervantes is more artist than sociologist, and the two main characters remain independent to a certain extent—a matter which impedes harmony and produces repulsion. Don Quijote and Sancho do not die together. The Knight dies forsaking *Amadís*, and Sancho, cured of his proud ambitions, laments his disappointments among his goats.

189. Arbolí, Servando. "Oración fúnebre." In *Memorias de la Real Academia Española* 5 (1896): 283-313. [First published in Madrid: Tello, 1876.]

Cervantes and all great Spaniards are exemplary Christians, and similarly authority, faith, and patriotism are values prominent in the *Quijote*.

190. Castro y Rossi, Adolfo de. "Lope de Rueda y Cervantes Saavedra." In *Album literario dedicado al rey de los ingenios españoles*. Madrid: Tip. de Pedro Núñez, 1876, pp. 55-62.

Cervantes was a great admirer of Lope de Rueda, and we know this from the prologue to his *comedias*. He remembers having seen Lope put on productions when a young man. Cervantes' admiration for Lope is also seen in the way in which he imitated his language. The language used by Sancho in various dialogues of Parts I and II of the *Quijote* appears to parallel that of Lope's *Camila*, especially with regard to the confusion of words and Don Quijote's correcting Sancho's speech. Proverbs and everyday sayings employed in Cervantes' *entremeses* and the *Quijote* are so frequently repeated from the plays of Lope de Rueda that one could not simply consider them mere coincidences.

191. *Corona literaria dedicada al príncipe de los ingenios*. Manila: Tip. Ciudad Condal, 1876. 98 pages.

[This collection includes commentaries and poems dedicated to Cervantes on April 23, 1876, including an *oración* read by José Cueto and an essay on the *Quijote* and the Philippines.]

192. Díaz de Benjumea, Nicolás. "Cervantes y Shakespeare: analogías y diferencias." *Crónica de los Cervantistas* 3, no. 5 (March 15, 1876): 196-98.

Both Shakespeare and Cervantes lived in the same era, and interest in each was revitalized by a foreigner: Shakespeare, by Voltaire, and Cervantes, by Bowle. Furthermore, both Cervantes and Shakespeare represent the essence of their cultural backgrounds in their style, depth, and profound ideas. Spaniards are more democratic than the English, however. While the former dress their wisdom in such a way that young, old, learned, and uneducated alike may enjoy it, the English offer their treasures only to the privileged, for few have read Shakespeare, and only a limited number have seen his plays performed.

While Cervantes never knew of Shakespeare, it is possible that Shakespeare read Shelton's 1612 translation of the *Quijote*. Even the word "donkey" is perhaps derived from the name of Cervantes' hero. There are other similarities in the lives of these authors: both lived in small towns, and it is doubtful that either attended a university, though many commentators have sought to prove that each was an expert in a given field.

193. Máinez, Ramón León. "Un nuevo libro de Benjumea." *Crónica de los Cervantistas* 3, no. 5 (March 15, 1876): 169-72.

Benjumea's recently published *El despacho de Lingardeo* deserves praise for exhibiting the same adventurous spirit, critical acumen, and ingeniousness of his other books. It begins with an exhortation to readers to see the *Quijote* as more than a book about the madness of an hidalgo and the satire of a genre. The *Quijote* brings us new ideas and universal doctrines; it is a book about men who want to free themselves from slavery and a book that incarnates the principle of liberty.

Benjumea eschews the limited social approach popular in Spain at the time and favors opening up new avenues of critical awareness in Spain with his philosophical approach, because it is absolutely essential that the *Quijote* be viewed morally and socially. Furthermore, it is important to make manifest, as Benjumea does, that Cervantes fought for and died for a sublime ideal: the *Quijote*, besides being a great work of art, is a protest of an independent spirit against men's obsessions and fanaticism.

194. Máinez, Ramón León. *Vida de Miguel de Cervantes Saavedra*. Cádiz: Tip. La Mercantil, 1876. 399 pages [From vol. I of León Máinez' edition of the *Quijote*, 5 vols., 1876-1879.]

Certain legends about the composition of the *Quijote* are faulty, especially the eighteenth-century one that Cervantes wrote his novel while imprisoned in Argamasilla de Alba. There is no evidence that Cervantes was ever in that city, and it is also doubtful that Cervantes wrote his masterpiece to ridicule his wife's uncle, Alonso Quijado y Salazar, who had opposed the author's marriage to his niece, Catalina. Such frivolous motives were not what inspired the *Quijote*.

Critics of the *Quijote* are divided into three groups: (1) those who take Cervantes literally and conclude that the *Quijote* was written merely to ridicule chivalric novels; (2) those who believe that the novel was composed to mock certain individuals of the author's times; and (3) those who interpret the two protagonists from various social, religious, philosophical, and scientific points of view.

Cervantes does not attack chivalry, honor, dignity, or the Spanish character, and Lope de Vega's letter of 1604 states the erroneous view that Cervantes was an odious satirist, a view perpetuated in 1750 by Erauso y Zavaleta, who said that Cervantes was a dishonor to Spain. The *Quijote* is not a satire of chivalric novels, and it was not Cervantes but the new age of ideas and customs that put an end to that genre. Indeed, Cervantes actually praises noble chivalric ideas by contrasting them with the new and sordid ideas of his times in what is essentially a satire of all classes of Spanish society: peasants, the educated, the clergy, the nobility, merchants, and the apathetic hidalgo. The belief that Cervantes criticized individuals in his novel, like Charles V, the Duke of Lerma, the Duke of Béjar, the Duke of Osuna (Rawdon Brown), or any other person, is wrong. Furthermore, Tubino was right in challenging Rawdon Brown's opinions, which were based on certain alleged letters written by the Venetian ambassador Contareni. While Cervantes opposed the tyranny and persecution of the Inquisition, some came to wrong conclusions. Puigblanch, for example, considers the *Quijote* to be principally a censure of that institution.

The German romantic-symbolist view that the *Quijote* is only limited to poetry versus prose or idealism versus realism is too vague and fixes its attention on only two characters, Don Quijote and Sancho, assuming the other characters are mere decoration.

The style of the *Quijote* is unique and Cervantes' imagery as well as his prudence, especially his avoidance of abstruseness and affectation, are praiseworthy. In addition, Cervantes is original and V. de los Ríos and Pellicer should not have compared him with Homer or Apuleius.

Is the *Quijote* an epic? Yes, it is an extensive poem about good and evil, the high and the low. It is also more serious than comical and more profound than superficial, and the non-epic episodes in the novel do not subvert this view because the *Quijote* is original and is not bound by literary precepts.

195. Moraza, Mateo Benigno de. "Cervantes, filósofo cristiano." *Defensa de la Sociedad* (Madrid) 10 (1876): 201-17. [Discurso leído en la Academia Cervantino-Española de Vitoria en abril de 1876.]

Cervantes' genius emanated from the spark of divine philosophy. Cervantes was a philosopher without having studied philosophy, and the spirit of the *Quijote* is eminently Christian. There are philosophical maxims and ideas on every page, and at least forty can easily be cited.

196. Pascual y Cuéllar, Eduardo. "Los dos genios." *La Cuna de Cervantes*, No. 8 (April 23, 1876). [As excerpted in Rius, III, pp. 136-37.]

Shakespeare uplifted the drama while Cervantes used the novel as the most appropriate means for ridiculing the customs, correcting the abuses, and destroying the vices corrupting the social fabric of the times. Shakespeare found the terrain already prepared for his dramas, but Cervantes drew upon fantasy. Shakespeare adopted known and popular types, though he dressed them in grandeur and pathos in order to arouse emotion. Cervantes created new characters, entirely original, and full of new ideas.

Shakespeare required more than thirty works to establish his glory; Cervantes needed only one, a work in which a madman and a rustic farmer are the protagonists. With them Cervantes travels through humanity; he studies society and all its people; he analyzes the heart and penetrates the depths of the human spirit.

Shakespeare, at times, elicits tears and also laughter. But Cervantes draws forth laughter from tears, because he has the wand which makes the rainbow of laughter shine through a shower of tears.

197. Paso y Delgado, N. de. "Las mujeres del *Quijote*." *Cervantes* (Madrid), October 31, 1876. [Discurso en la Sociedad Cervantista de Granada; as excerpted in Rius, III, pp. 137-38.]

Dulcinea; Teresa Panza ("el buen sentido y la tierna solicitud de la madre de familia"); Camila ("víctima de la impertinente curiosidad de su esposo"); Clara, Luscinda, and Dorotea ("tipos magistralmente delineados del amor juvenil"); Zoraida ("acabado modelo de ternura, de fe"); Leandra ("ejemplo vivo de la mala elección"); Marcela ("cruel enemigo de los hombres"); the Duchess ("la traviesa y festiva ociosidad de su clase y tiempo"); and Doña Cristina, the wife of Don Diego de Miranda ("circunspecta")—these female characters of Cervantes will live forever.

198. Sbarbi y Osuna, José María. *Intraducibilidad del Quijote*. In *Refranero general español*, VI. Madrid: Imp. de A. Gómez Fuentenebro, 1876, pp. 198-291.

Fernández de Navarrete, Martínez de la Rosa, Mor de Fuentes, Marchena, Florian, and Capmany all found the *Quijote* to be untranslatable. It possesses words, phrases, and obscure passages impossible to translate, including "giros cervánticos, frases burlescas, equívocos, idiotismos caballerescos, sentido intencionado o picaresco, sentido histórico o meramente local, y refranes."

French and English attempts at translating parts of Cervantes' novel prove the difficulty, if not the impossibility, of translating the work. While the general plot may be adequately rendered in another language, many expressions cannot be so rendered.

199. Soravilla, Javier. "Catálogo por orden alfabético de todos los personajes que intervienen en el *Ingenioso hidalgo Don Quijote de la Mancha*." *Cervantes* (Madrid), January 8 and May 24, 1876. [As noted in Rius, II, p. 202.]

[Rius regards Soravilla's work as a curious one, and not nearly so valuable as the latter believed. Soravilla, at the end of his index, noted that the total number of characters in the *Quijote* was 669, 607 men and 62 women.]

200. Toro, Cayetano del. "Nuevo mérito del *Quijote*." [Composición leída en las Escuelas Católicas de Cádiz el 23 de Abril de 1876 para celebrar el aniversario CCLX de la muerte de Cervantes; as excerpted in Rius, III, pp. 129-30.]

Cervantes paints monomania more skillfully than famous psychiatrists, and the *Quijote* is a magnificent study of mental illness. Don Quijote is the perfect picture of chivalric madness.

201. Castro y Rossi, Adolfo de. *Juicio crítico de la velada literaria que se celebró en el gran teatro de Cádiz el 23 de Abril de 1877.* Cádiz: Alejandro Guerrero, 1877. 16 pages.

One should praise the people of the city of Cádiz for their literary celebration in honor of Cervantes and the poems they collected on the occasion. Some criticism was leveled against those involved in writing the poetry, but they should be defended for their excellent work.

202. Morés y Sanz, Julián. "Cervantes y su idioma." *La Cuna de Cervantes*, No. 49 (April 23, 1877). [As excerpted in Rius, III, pp. 141-42.]

Cervantes describes things in a simple, lively manner, presenting them as they are, revealing their essence, qualities, and circumstances. One should have pride in the richness of Cervantes' works, especially in the skill that he shows in varying the expression in a natural way, which gives greater amenity and grace to elocution and cadence. The author's discretion in the use of old and new words is in accordance with the doctrine of Quintilian. Cervantes knew well the contribution he was making to his native language, and he reveals this in the prologue to Part II, 1615.

203. Vidart, Luis. "Cervantes, poeta épico." *La Ilustración Española y Americana* 21 (1877): 226-27 and 243-46.

Cervantes is a true epic poet. The adventures of Don Quijote constitute a true poem by their breadth, grandeur, and transcendence. Cervantes is also a poet because a poet is one who makes the reader experience beauty by means of the word.

Realism is also part of poetry. Just as the French discovered realism in art by showing us how great poets allow us to see the totality of life, so does Cervantes in the *Quijote*: the novel runs the gamut from eternal love to the creation of fantasies and then to base materialism.

The *Quijote* is a Renaissance poem with a modern sensibility. That is, like the negative modern age which rejects the past and offers no substitute, the *Quijote* is a poem of this age because it is a work of negation. Those who say that Cervantes wished to make his protagonist sublime are terribly wrong. He is a ridiculous figure.

204. Araujo Sánchez, Ceferino. "¿Es posible pintar el verdadero retrato de Don Quijote?" *Revista Europea* 11 (1878): 246-49.

Unlike the painter, the poet cannot produce a complete impression of a subject for his audience; the poet often must omit details. But it is difficult to say whose aesthetic criteria are superior.

205. Coello, Carlos. *El nuevo Lázaro.* In *Cuentos inverosímiles.* Madrid: 1878. [As excerpted in Rius, III, pp. 147-49.]

The *Quijote* is a universal drama of all ages, countries, and men because in it is depicted what, on the one hand, the lofty mind conceives and the generous heart strives for, and on the other, what our wretched powers are capable of carrying out. And all this is expressed with a kind humor that does not wound and a gravity that is not disconcerting. It is told with the gentle and majestic clarity of the sun. All is noble in the *Quijote.* The two regenerating principles burn and live eternal lives in the *Quijote*: the tendency toward the ideal and the tendency toward moral and material freedom. Cervantes did not completely realize what he had done.

206. Díaz de Benjumea, Nicolás. "El progreso en la crítica del *Quijote.*" *Revista de España* 64 (1878): 474-88; 65 (1878): 42-59 and 450-66; 66 (1879): 158-72 and 329-48; 67 (1879): 519-38.

The critics of England, France, and Germany saw extraodrinary merit in Cervantes' novel when those of Spain only saw it as a work of entertainment. But it is not necessarily true that foreign criticism is superior to that of Spain in the understanding of the *Quijote.* Bowle, for example, wrongly regarded Spain as superstitious and idolatrous, and in France and Germany critics tended to seek something new to say about the *Quijote* and the lofty motives for its composition. Such studies are only of partial importance to the *Quijote* and resolve nothing.

Sismondi's melancholic view of the *Quijote* was taken from Byron when the Englishman visited Geneva. Sismondi's idea that the chivalrous Cervantes mocked himself in the *Quijote* takes all dignity away from the author and could only be true if the *Quijote* were merely an invective against chivalry, as Lord Byron avers. Cervantes, in reality, was seeking to prevent the ruin of Spain.

Clemencín accidently hit upon the truth, though he was wrong to state that Cervantes did not express himself well. Certain portions of the novel must be read in a symbolic way: for instance, when Cervantes writes that Don Quijote won Dulcinea by physical force. This is not literally correct: Dulcinea must be viewed as a symbol of truth and goodness.

Quintana was incorrect for his view that "nature" presented the figure of the Knight to Cervantes, whose imagination took over the figure, while his instinct did the rest. This statement leaves many questions unanswered, including how nature revealed the idea to Cervantes and how Cervantes' imagination took charge of the idea. The Don Quijote type always existed, but Cervantes' merit is that he saw what others did not see. Furthermore, it was not his imagination, but his intelligence, feelings, and experience that took charge; not merely luck but meditation and hard work did the rest.

Heinrich Heine did not understand the symbolism of the *Quijote* and was wrong to say that Cervantes' only *conscious* intent was to write an attack on chivalric novels while he unconsciously wrote the world's greatest satire against enthusiasm. Cervantes *consciously* sought to do much more than attack books of chivalry. Heine notwithstanding, he was not a man who thought like his contemporaries.

207. Díaz de Benjumea, Nicolás. *La verdad sobre el Quijote. Novísima historia crítica de la vida de Cervantes.* Madrid: Imp. de Gaspar, 1878. 343 pages.

Cervantes' novel is not a pure product of the imagination, but more of a "biografía de su cerebro y una fisiología de sus pasiones." The struggle of a human soul with evil and with the obstacles, passions, and the interests of the world, and failure at every step, is a noble theme, but the reality of the author's own life is transplanted into the novel. This is the mystery of the *Quijote*. It is not a question of sudden inspiration, as some contend, nor of resentment against specific individuals like Rodrigo Pacheco or groups like Manchegans. Cervantes' masterpiece is a series of contrasts between opposites: desire vs. gross reality, platonic love vs. base passions, high poetry vs. the lower prose, spiritualism vs. materialism, which lead to the comic effect in the action without diminishing the elevated state of the thought.

Cervantes is not an unconscious writer. Repeated assertions that his intention was to debunk chivalric novels were a smokescreen set up to protect his attacks first on the customs and errors that were undermining Spanish society and then on the blind faith and the Inquisition that he attacked between the lines.

Cervantes disguised the meaning of Dulcinea. The preliminary verses of "Urganda la Desconocida," where the Knight is said to have won her, cannot be taken literally, since Don Quijote does *not* actually win her. The meaning is anagogical, that is, Dulcinea is truth, light, and wisdom, which *are* achieved by the Knight.

With regard to the *Curioso impertinente* and its function in the novel, Ludwig Tieck was correct in saying that there is a thematic link between the *curioso* Anselmo and Don Quijote: both are madmen who seek an impossible ideal, absolute happiness.

If Cervantes' main object had been an end to the reading of chivalric novels, he would have continued with more mad chivalric adventures in Part II. Cervantes eventually made his hero more noble, just as he made Dulcinea the "sol y centro" in the sequel and the adventures increasingly more ideal rather than plastic. Furthermore, the hero becomes more of a critic, censor, preacher, and moralist than a battling knight-errant. Part II represents the transfiguration of both the Knight and Cervantes.

208. Milego é Inglada, S. "Cervantes." In *Estudios, disertaciones y ensayos filosófico-literarios.* Toledo: Imp. y Lib. de Fando e Hijo, 1880, pp. 123-45. [Discurso leído en la velada que la Asociación de Conferencias Científico-Literarias de Toledo celebró el día 23 de abril de 1878 en honor del príncipe de los ingenios.]

Cervantes was a man out of step with his times, a man stoically indifferent to the abuses of his epoch, its corruption, artificiality, superstition, and bad taste. Cervantes as an artist belongs to his age, but as a thinker he belongs to posterity. Like Shakespeare, Cervantes stands between two ages, contemplating the grandeur and vigor of the feudal world and looking ahead to the new century of freedom and intellectual foment. He represents the transition from the medieval to the modern, bringing to literature the change that was already taking place in the world of scientific discovery.

209. Pereira, José. "Cervantes como crítico." *Crónica de los Cervantistas* 4, no. 1 (April 23, 1878): 52. [As excerpted in Rius, III, pp. 152-53.]

Cervantes as a critic has no rival. No other works than his inform us of the habits, tastes, inclinations, and even preoccupations of his times. His short novels are accurate pictures of real characters. But we find him even more perceptive in the *Quijote*, a work in which the fatal effects of books of chivalry are revealed and where a corrective force is offered against chivalric madness in the most caustic satire that has ever been written. But above all the *Quijote* is a complete picture of Spanish customs, for in it we see all social classes. With the *Quijote* alone one may study the customs and ideas of the sixteenth century.

Cervantes as a literary critic is even more praiseworthy, comparable to Diego Hurtado y Mendoza and Diego de Saavedra Fajardo; but in none of their works does conscientious and reasoned criticism shine forth as in the chapters of the *Quijote*

210. Vidart, Luis. "Algunas ideas de Cervantes acerca de la literatura preceptiva." *La Ilustración Española y Americana* 22 (1878): 259 and 323-26.

In modern times, the idea of monarchy in the arts has become diluted, and there has been a rejection in some fashion of the so-called "appropriate" forms such as verse, reserved strictly for poetry. A prose form can encompass all literary genres and styles because it is only in the classics that form must be restricted to certain genres the way verse had been for poetry. Thus, the novel can be an epic in prose, and Cervantes could argue that the chivalry book could offer its author a chance to demonstrate his intelligence.

Cervantes was preoccupied with drama as well as prose, as evidenced by the remarks he made at the end of Part I of the *Quijote* that were highly critical of the lack of verisimilitude and the unities in Spanish drama. Here, Cervantes proposed a strictly classical approach. He was also a defender of the transcendental nature of art. He insisted on the high quality of Spanish drama and on its teaching with lofty examples of wisdom and virtue.

Another key to Cervantes' theory is his belief that the writer of imaginative literature should be as truthful as possible while being aware of the differences between poetry (fiction) and history: the poet narrates things as they should have been and the historian as they were. Thus in the *Quijote* Cervantes demonstrates artistic realism: the artist must not deny the ideal because the ideal in life is a reality, too. Although Cervantes was not primarily a theorist, he espoused significant theoretical ideas, the most important of which is "que la épica tan bien puede escribirse en prosa como en verso." Modern prose writers, that is, could reach the artistic heights of a Homer or Virgil.

211. Azaña, Esteban. *Memoria de los acuerdos del Ayuntamiento de Alcalá de Henares para la creación de un monumento a Miguel de Cervantes.* Alcalá de Henares: Imp. de F. García, 1879. 58 pages.

[The first part of this work describes all ceremonies held in honor of Cervantes between 1875 and 1879 and lists all the convocations held in Alcalá de Henares from 1833 to 1879, most of which took place on April 23. Those festivities are always described in the *Crónica de los Cervantistas* each year by its editor, Ramón León Máinez, and the Ayuntamiento of Alcalá is responsible for many of the celebrations. The journal, *La Cuna de Cervantes,* founded by F. García Carballo to honor Cervantes, describes in detail the erection of a bronze statue of Cervantes in Alcalá.

The second part of the book contains all of the speeches delivered at the festivals in Alcalá since 1875. Some express gratitude to the city of Alcalá for its library dedicated to Cervantes; others praise the publication of nineteenth-century editions of the *Quijote* and mention all of the outstanding commentators who have written on the novel. To complete the book, Azaña adds a speech of his own in praise of Cervantes and several more poems and speeches honoring the writer.]

212. Bofarull y de Brocá, Antonio de. "Observaciones sobre Cervantes y su obra maestra *Don Quijote.*" In *Don Quijote de la Mancha,* I. Barcelona: Imp. de Juan Aleu y Fugarull, 1879, pp. i-xvi.

Cervantes had profound concern for the morality of sixteenth-century Spain, especially as it is reflected in the characters of Sancho, a representative of the masses, and Don Quijote, of the *hidalguía.* Sancho is a practical man who lives simply without the habits that often mark the aristocracy, such as petulance, pride, and envy, and Cervantes is a model Spaniard who corrects with moderation the vices of his society. Cervantes revealed both the richness and the poverty of the Spanish character and showed in his ridicule of the books of chivalry how the Spaniard himself was a victim of them.

213. Hermúa, Jacinto. *Cervantes, administrador militar.* Madrid. Imp. del Cuerpo Administrativo del Ejército, 1879. 60 pages.

[Minute documentation of Cervantes' civil service career between 1587 and 1595, when he served as an administrator in the armed forces.]

214. López Fabra, Francisco. *Iconografía del Quijote.* Barcelona: Imp. de Heredero de Pablo Riera, 1879. [Vol. 4 of the facsimile of the first edition of the *Quijote.*]

[A collection of 101 drawings from the *Quijote* from editions published between 1622 and 1867. Each entry lists the year and place of the edition, its source and its title page, the title of the episode depicted, the names of the artists, and the persons who reproduced the drawings. There is both an index and a chronological list of the prints.]

215. Martínez Izquierdo, Narciso. *Oración fúnebre que, por encargo de la Academia Española, pronunció en las honras de Cervantes, el día 23 de Abril de 1879, en la iglesia de las Monjas Trinitarias.* Madrid: M. Tello, 1879. 47 pages. [As excerpted in Rius, III, pp. 155-56.]

Cervantes' great merit is that he blends the ideal with common sense. He attacks exaggerated inclinations, but without hatred. He assails the idea of a fantastic, wandering knight, but upholds, even exalts, in the same person the idea of Christian chivalry.

216. Opiso, Antonio. "Una reacción exagerada." *Parthenon* (Barcelona), April 1, 1980. [Disertación premiada en el Certamen verificado en Manila el 22 de noviembre de 1879; as excerpted in Rius, III, p. 114.]

Sismondi and Viardot said that Cervantes began with the intention of satirizing books of chivalry but later enlarged the picture and conceived the idea of presenting the struggle between the real and the ideal. Don Quijote only appears mad when he remains in the ranks of idealistic demagoguery, when he forgets that an accommodation between the ideal and the real is a fatal law of our existence, and when he ignores the historical moment in which he lives. But since the absolute ideal is so beautiful, the hero cannot help appearing to be sympathetic, even in his most violent clashes with reality. Books of chivalry were the code of absolute idealism, and for this reason Cervantes persisted in the style of satire, the most appropriate for the philosophical lesson that he had conceived. But he could never have scorned the chivalric ideal itself.

217. Revilla, Manuel de la. "De algunas opiniones nuevas sobre Cervantes y el *Quijote*." In *Obras de Manuel de la Revilla*. Madrid: Ateneo, 1883, pp. 395-430. [Published earlier in *La Ilustración Española y Americana* 23 (1879).]

Benjumea's *La verdad sobre el Quijote* is composed of hypotheses, conjectures, and unfounded, even violent, statements. It is evident that Cervantes conceived of the *Quijote* in a jail in Seville or perhaps in Argamasilla de Alba, not, as Benjumea asserts, in his anxiety to find a metaphysical-symbolic meaning to his biography in a metaphorical jail. Also faulty is Benjumea's contention that the work of Avellaneda was the result of a clerical problem; that is, that Avellaneda wrote his *Quijote* in order to make the protagonist a good Catholic, to baptize him and send him to mass, because Cervantes' *Quijote* was imbued by a spirit of paganism and liberalism. This is without basis, as Cervantes himself was a good Catholic. Furthermore, the question of the false *Quijote* has still to be resolved.

Much of the criticism that views Cervantes as a knowledgeable military administrator, navigator, theologian, doctor, etc., or some sort of Christian moralist, is fundamentally wrong. It is also incorrect to see in Cervantes' work the spirit of an idealist's protest: he was a realist and knew the real world. Apart from this, Cervantes wrote the *Quijote* in order to do away with the books of chivalry. The novel is not a protest but rather a story of an idealist's disillusionment.

That the *Quijote* was not written as a satire against chivalry and that there is an occult meaning of philosophical transcendence in the *Quijote* is absolutely false. The supposed philosophy of Cervantes is not a metaphysical conception of the opposition of the real and ideal but simply a philosophy of common sense, recognizing the absurd exercise of knight-errantry in the sixteenth century. It is chivalry itself that becomes the target of Cervantes' satire. And since Cervantes said many times that this was the sole purpose of his book, how can one see some sort of philosophical occult meaning here? If he had another motive for writing the book, then why did he not state it? The idea that the work is a recondite parody of Charles V is equally ridiculous. But such interpretation is not surprising from one who is looking for meanings that do not exist in the novel. Sancho represents the common sense of the common man and Don Quijote false idealism, the kind that accompanies a belief in the chivalry book. To try to find other meanings is an exercise in futility.

218. Alcalá Galiano, Antonio de. *Juicio crítico de Miguel de Cervantes*. Madrid: Tip. Eduardo Viuda, 1880. 16 pages. [Also Toledo: Imp. y Lib. de Fando e Hijo.]

The *Quijote* is a satire on books of chivalry as well as the people of Cervantes' time, the style and unity of Part II of the novel are suprior to

Part I, and the dynamics of Sancho's personality are especially praiseworthy. Episodes that strike the imagination are the enchantment of
Dulcinea, Camacho's wedding, the visit to the cave of Montesinos, and the
adventure in the ducal palace, where one sees considerable development in
the personalities of Don Quijote and Sancho at the same time that they
sustain their fundamental roles as knight and squire, teacher and student.

219. Ateneo Tarraconense de la Clase Obrera. *Certamen literario-artístico
en honor a Cervantes.* Tarragona: Francisco Granell y Aymat, 1880. 185
pages.

[Contains poems and plays, most of which are in Catalan, and a speech
by Agustín Musté, honoring all the young writers who contributed to a
literary contest held in tribute to Cervantes.]

220. Blanco Asenjo, R. "Cervantes y Shakespeare." *El Imparcial* (Madrid), April 26, 1880. [As excerpted in Rius, III, pp. 157-59.]

Both Cervantes and Shakespeare are men of the Renaissance who
witness the fall of the shadowy world of the Middle Ages. But Cervantes is
tranquil, while Shakespeare is somber. With Cervantes' two protagonists
the soul seems divided, but Cervantes is a synthesizer (while Shakespeare is
not), as the Knight and the Squire complement one another. Both Cervantes and Shakespeare paint humanity in its breadth and depth: Shakespeare
in the multiple variety of individual passions and Cervantes in the duality of
impulses of the soul, which at times elevates the soul toward an impossible
idealism and at other times brings the soul down to a gross materialism.
Hamlet is a sinister Don Quijote; he feels that his efforts are useless. But
Don Quijote is a man of living faith. Both, like all idealists, are conquered by
reality, but the Knight's disenchantment is placid and serene while Hamlet's
desolation is horrifying.

221. Díaz de Benjumea, Nicolás, ed. *Don Quijote de la Mancha,* I.
Barcelona: Montaner y Simón, 1880, pp. i-lxii.

The *Quijote* is more of a universal satire of human weakness and folly
than a specific satire against chivalry. One sees clearly a clash between the
real and the ideal and also influences on the *Quijote* from Cervantes' own
experiences. The evil *encantadores* were Cervantes' personal enemies, for
example.

Despite any profound ideas regarding moral conduct or political teaching, the *Quijote* is primarily a work that addresses itself to aesthetic issues.
And although critics have long said that Cervantes wrote the novel to
destroy the chivalry book, Don Quijote's conversations with the Canónigo
toward the end of Part I demonstrate that Cervantes recognized some
truth in these books. But the novel even transcends its artistic purpose: it is

is the "Biblia humana," a work that leads men along the road to eternal felicity.

222. Foronda y Aguilera, Manuel de. "Cervantes, viajero." Madrid: Imp. de Fortanet, 1880. 91 pages. [Also published in *Boletín de la Sociedad Geográfica Nacional* (Madrid), June, 1880.]

[A portrait of Cervantes' supposed travels through Spain, Portugal, Turkey, North Africa, the Azores, Italy, and France and detailed descriptions of customs of the people and places Cervantes saw. Included is a map tracing Cervantes' journeys from the Azores to Turkey, central Spain, Italy, and France.]

223. Menéndez Pelayo, Marcelino. *Historia de los heterodoxos españoles*, III: *Erasmistas y protestantes*. Madrid: Consejo Superior de Investigaciones Científicas, 1963, pp. 198-99 [First published in 1880-1882.]

Valdés' *Mercurio y Carón*, which contains a king's advice to his son, influenced Cervantes when he composed his chapters on the Knight's advice to Sancho Panza on the art of governing.

224. Pardo de Figueroa, Mariano de. [Dr. Thebussem]. "Pallida mors: Estudio sobre el *Quijote*." *Revista Contemporánea* 25 (1880): 41-50. [Also in *Averiguador Universal*, March 31, 1880.]

The *Quijote* is a "cuadro de dolores y de muerte." There are many deaths in it, but not a single birth is mentioned in the work. Do not look for recondite or symbolic meanings in the novel. Its message is found in the text itself, and those who believe that Cervantes wishes to demonstrate his expertise as an administrator, doctor, or navigator in his novel are mistaken. One often finds in the *Quijote* whatever he chooses, but one must be careful with an interpretation that is impossible to document. The *Quijote* is universal and many kinds of interpretations are acceptable. There is a limit, however, to what may be said of it.

225. Peñaranda y Escudero, Carlos. "Cervantes y sus obras." In *Artículos varios*. Madrid, 1885. [Originally "Discurso pronunciado en el Certamen literario celebrado en San Juan de Puerto Rico, el 9 de Octubre de 1880."]

The *Buscapié* is legitimate because Cervantes had to answer his critics after Part I was published. Cervantes should be placed in the line of Juvenal because the *Quijote* is fundamentally a satire against chivalry books. The novel reconciles the real and the ideal as Sancho is affected by the madness of his master, though he still possesses much wisdom when governing his isle.

226. Apraiz y Sáenz del Burgo, Julián. *Cervantes vascófilo, o sea Cervantes vindicado de su supuesto antivizcainismo.* Vitoria: Tip. de Domingo Sar, 1895. 284 pages. [First published in 1881.]

Cervantes was not anti-Basque. He had several Basque friends, including Haedo and Barrio Angulo, and merely used the Basque mode of expression for comic purposes. Cervantes actually held the Basque in high esteem, as is revealed in *La señora Cornelia.*

227. Pereda, José María de. "El cervantismo." In *Esbozos y rasguños.* Madrid: Imp. de M. Tello, 1881. 406 pages. [See final chapter.]

Cervantine criticism is a sign of the Spanish tendency to take the serious to extremes. Particularly humorous is the use of Cervantes' name for various organizations and the practice of regarding Cervantes as a theologian, lawyer, cook, sailor, geographer, doctor, military administrator, and more, which is to say, "Cervantes omniscio, y sus obras, la suma de los humanos conocimientos." *Cervantismo* has become a "fervor monomaníaco." While we owe the *Quijote* our admiration, we do not owe it with "cascabeles ni vestidos de payasos." Critics like Clemencín have sought to correct Cervantes' grammar, but it would be better that the *Quijote* be made a national monument and that no one be allowed to change the text, even if it does contain errors.

228. Asensio y Toledo, José María. "Algunas notas preparadas para un nuevo comentario al *Ingenioso hidalgo Don Quijote de la Mancha.*" *Revista de Valencia* 2 (May 1, 1882): 241; 3 (April 1, 1883): 180-84.

The attraction of Don Quijote and Sancho has to do with their innocence and naiveté because they did not see things as they were. Malice, for example, was always hidden from their eyes. They traveled the path of idealism and suffered the hard blows of reality, but goodness and innocence filled their souls as they tried to make the world a better place. As Cervantes presented the drama of their lives, he was inspired by creativity, invention, and imagination.

229. Vidart, Luis. *El Quijote y la clasificación de las obras literarias: La desdicha póstuma de Cervantes.* Madrid: Tip. de los Sucs. de Rivadeneyra, 1882. 16 pages.

The *Quijote* is an epic because of its comprehensive view of the surrounding world, its culture, customs, ideas, and aspirations. But all novels are not epics, for some do not achieve the level of grandeur of the *Quijote.*

Cervantes' novel is a negative work, that is, a work that ridicules generous intentions as well as materialism without saying where the truth lies.

230. Asensio y Toledo, José María. *Catálogo de la Biblioteca Cervantina de J. M. Asensio*. Valencia: Imp. de Domenech, 1883. 68 pages.

[Editions of the *Quijote* listed here are the seventeenth-century editions (1605-1697), with a total of twenty; eighteenth-century editions (1704-1798), with a total of twenty-six; and foreign editions, beginning 1704, in French, Dutch, Itialian, and Portuguese. The remaining sections catalogue nineteenth-century editions of Spain (1804-1883), with a total of sixty-nine entries, and contain a reprint of the front page, descriptions of printing and design, and comments about the value of each edition.

Highlighted are the following rare editions: Juan de la Cuesta, Madrid, 1605 and 1608, and Valencia, 1605; the Craesbeeck edition, Lisbon, 1605; the Rodríguez edition, Lisbon, 1605; and the *princeps* of Part II of the *Quijote*, 1615. Included as well are nineteen foreign editions of the nineteenth century, imitations and continuations of the *Quijote*, and a short essay on Avellaneda, in which Asensio states that Cervantes knew his true identity.]

231. Menéndez Pelayo, Marcelino. *Historia de las ideas estéticas en España*, II: *Siglos XVI y XVII*. Madrid: Consejo Superior de Investigaciones Científicas, 1957, pp. 264-71. [First published in Madrid: A. Pérez Dubrull, 1883 et seq.]

Laughable is the festishism that attributes scientific ideas to Cervantes and attempts to make him an expert in fields such as geography, theology, medicine, and law. A book like the *Quijote* should not be converted into an encyclopedia, since Cervantes' scientific ideas do not go beyond the limits of common sense or the sixteenth century. Cervantes is great because he is a creator of imaginative works: he needs no more than this for his glory, which only suffers when his novel is reduced to allegories, enigmas, and symbolic interpretations. It is true that geniuses have the gift of seeing with clarity and intuition what others cannot discern except through laborious intellectual effort. But this is true of all geniuses, not merely literary ones.

I mean to say that the intuition that an artist has is not the intuition of scientific truths, but only the intuition of form, which is the intellectual world in which he lives. And when he achieves the intuition of the idea, it is always found hidden and wrapped in the form. Dante and Goethe were both poets and men of science, the greatest of their respective eras. But they were not poets because of their science, nor scientists because of their poetry. Instead, they united two distinct aptitudes which aided each other marvelously. Cervantes was a poet and only a poet, an *ingenio lego*, as they said in his times. His scientific ideas could not be other than those of the society in which he lived.

It is even more specious to turn Cervantes into a teacher of literary precepts. While Cervantes did not write "unconsciously," and while his work is not irrational, his aesthetic intuition was so sharp that he, like most other artists, would not know how to tell us why he followed one road in preference to another. It is true that Cervantes had certain literary doctrines, but he did not invent these doctrines, nor did he derive them from his other works. They were exactly the same as those found in most books of literary theory, such as those of Cascales and López Pinciano. What saves these ideas from oblivion is the liveliness, the charm, and the beauty with which Cervantes used them. The aesthetic concept which is dominant in Cervantes is that poetry is a universal form, applicable to all subjects, or as he says, a *science* which includes all others.

232. Ortego Aguirrebeña, Feliciano. *La restauración del Quijote. Estudio comparativo de varias ediciones y sus respectivas notas.* Palencia: T. Martínez, 1883. 836 pages.

[Leopoldo Rius, in his *Bibliografía crítica de las obras de Miguel de Cervantes Saavedra* (Madrid, 1895-1904), concludes that Ortego's project is not the first edition of the *Quijote*, containing notes purported to be in Cervantes' own hand. He agrees with Menéndez Pelayo, who says in a letter to Rius printed in his bibliography (II, 212-15), that Ortego is profoundly mistaken: the text that Ortego used was a poorly printed copy of the second edition of Juan de la Cuesta, an edition that for a long time had been confused with the first.]

233. Pardo Bazán, Emilia. *La cuestión palpitante.* In *Obras completas*, III. Madrid: Aguilar, 1973, pp. 593-96. [First edition, Madrid: V. Saiz, 1883.]

Chivalric novels are essentially non-Spanish in origin, and the *Quijote* is a protest against this foreign literature with its false idealism and its affected language. The principal literary merit of Cervantes (leaving aside the intrinsic value of the *Quijote* as a work of art) lies in the author's having tied together again the national tradition by replacing the foreign and chimerical Amadís, Artús, and Roldán with a real hero (like the Cid), who is valorous, honorable, noble, and Christian. In addition, this hero is of flesh and blood, with emotions, passions, and even petty, human faults. However, Cervantes did not invent the Spanish realistic novel, since it already existed in the form of *La Celestina*; he created it from its predecessors. The *Quijote* and *Amadís* divide Spanish literature into two hemispheres: in *Amadís* imagination reigns; in the *Quijote* realism predominates as it did in the oldest monuments of Spanish literature.

Regarding the comparison of Cervantes and Rabelais, the latter was learned and Cervantes was not, but the Frenchman was not entirely saved from barbarity by his learning. Rabelais left France with a deformed work, while Cervantes left Spain with a finished and sublime work. Cervantes' novel is a model of style; Rabelais' is not. And Rabelais did not establish a literary school, as Cervantes did.

The *Quijote* is not only an attack on the chivalric novel but the most beautiful work in the genre of the novel.

234. Picatoste y Rodríguez, Felipe. "Cervantes." In *Estudios literarios.* Madrid: J. Gaspar, 1883, pp. 79-103.

The *Quijote* and *El rufián dichoso* are complementary works, and perhaps reflect the totality of Cervantes' thought. While the Knight and Cristóbal (the converted villain in the latter work) are very different, they do have points of contact: both realize the vanity of their prior life. Don Quijote wishes to take upon himself the realization of justice on earth and risks his life for the innocent, and Cristóbal, after he has seen the light, takes on the sins of a Doña Ana, a generous act worthy of a knight-errant within the framework of Catholicism.

235. Picatoste y Rodríguez, Felipe. "Don Juan, Don Quijote y Hamlet." In *Estudios literarios.* Madrid: J. Gaspar, 1883, pp. 49-77.

Although Don Juan is more comparable to Don Quijote than to Hamlet, Cervantes' character is most original. The Knight had no antecedents; he came from Cervantes' fantasy. Unlike the figure of Don Juan, which has been developed and modified over the centuries, no one has dared to tarnish Don Quijote's integrity.

Both Don Quijote and Don Juan are criminals in their own age. While the Knight frees galley slaves and accosts innocent people, Don Juan scales the walls of a convent and stirs up street fights: neither belongs to the quiet and orderly life. And although it is difficult to say which was more criminal, the difference in the judgment which the reader forms of the deeds of each is extreme: Don Juan's acts elicit moral indignation, Don Quijote's amazement and sad laughter, but not condemnation. The Knight is not overcome by wild passions against society or against himself. He is the man of all times—aroused by upright sentiments, attempting to right social evils, and carried away by the excitation produced by solitude. Don Quijote comes to think himself capable of reforming the world and making virtue triumph, and this madness raises the most profound, and perhaps unresolvable, questions of morality and of law. Furthermore, while Don Quijote, with his eternal aspirations, is beyond the customs of a particular society, Don Juan is a man of a particular time, who in order to exist sanely, needs a social position, an education, and certain concrete convictions.

Regarding Turgenev's essay, "Hamlet and Don Quixote," in which he asserts that we all tend to be either Quijotes or Hamlets, one should add a third type—Don Juan—since, if Don Quijote is faith, abnegation, tolerance, and courtesy, and Hamlet is cold, incredulous analysis, Don Juan is human passion, foreign to the sublimities of faith. Few follow the way of Don Quijote or Hamlet, but at a certain age all men seek pleasure and personal triumph.

Each of the three characters has a subservient figure (Sancho, Catalinón, Polonius), who represents public feeling, the judgment of the age, or the antithesis of the protagonist. The death of each protagonist offers another correspondence: Don Quijote dies quietly after recovering his reason; Hamlet dies by poison, as if the poison within him became an extension of him; and Don Juan dies by fire, which corresponds to his tumultuous life. Regarding the endings of these masterpieces, it would never occur to anyone to change the end of *Hamlet*, to have him confess and be saved; it would never occur to anyone to have the Knight die a reprobate; but various writers have changed the ending of the *Burlador de Sevilla*.

236. Gayangos, Pascual de. "Cervantes en Valladolid." *Revista de España* 97 (1884): 481-507; 98 (1884): 161-91, 321-68, and 508-43; 99 (1884): 5-33.

In this history of court festivities it is possible that one might find that the *Quijote* was known in Valladolid before it appeared in Madrid in 1605.

237. Muiños Sáenz, Conrado. "¿Cómo pronunciaba Cervantes el nombre de Don Quixote?" *Revista Agustiniana* 7 (1884): 199-204; 8 (1884): 489-97. [A continuation of an article in *El Averiguador Universal*, March 31, 1881; as excerpted in Rius, II, pp. 207, 209-10.]

With regard to the pronunciation of the *x* sound in Cervantes' era, Monlau is wrong in saying that it was similar to the soft French *ch*. The *g, j,* and *x* were generally sounded like the present guttural *j*, though uneducated people may have pronounced the sound as a dental.

238. Vidart, Luis. *El Quijote y el Telemaco: Apuntes críticos*. Madrid: Tip. de los Sucs. de Rivadeneyra, 1884. 22 pages.

In the eighteenth century *Télémaque*, by François de Salignac de Mothe Fénelon, was preferred to the *Quijote* because of the instruction and morality found in the French work. But teaching is not the primary function of literature. Fénelon's novel is worthy of praise because of the beauty of its style. *Télémaque* was born reflexively and scientifically at the hands of a learned cleric; the *Quijote* was generated artistically and intuitively by a soldier taught by adversity. Fénelon was a theoretician; Cervantes saw the dangers of excess theory. *Télémaque* is an idealistic affirmation of the perfectability of human institutions; the *Quijote* is a negation of the chivalric ideal. Eighteenth-century critics praised *Télémaque* for its optimism because they did not understand the bitterness of the *Quijote*. The neoclassical theorists of France preferred *Télémaque* because of its use of noble figures and gods and godesses, and because it was a French work.

239. Alas, Leopoldo [Clarín]. "Del *Quijote*: notas sueltas." In *Siglo pasado*. Madrid: Antonio R. López, 1910, pp. 61-72. [Listed by Luis Andrés Murillo, *Bibliografía fundamental*, no. 251, p. 57, as published in 1885; Raymond L. Grismer, *Cervantes: A Bibliography*, Vol. I, p. 20, gives 1899—*Ilustración Española y Americana*, 43, pp. 262-63.]

Signs of Spain's decadence lie in the fact that the reading of the *Quijote* is declining further when it should be reread every two or three years, and in the fact that Cervantes' novel has had little influence on recent writers. The *Quijote* is not always read by non-Spaniards either, in spite of indications to the contrary. This is a pity because now the *Quijote* could be better understood than at any other time. Shakespeare has been better studied (or *discovered*) by the critics than Cervantes, and while the *Quijote* has been translated into many languages, in translation it is not even the shadow of the original. One cannot penetrate all that is worthwhile in the *Quijote* without having Castilian in one's bones. There is no *great* non-Spaniard (*great man*, not *erudite*) who has known Spanish to such an extent.

No critic in Spain has studied the *Quijote* in depth. The *cervantófilos* and other early critics have failed. The *Quijote* enriches one's life each time it is read and it needs and deserves a truly in-depth study.

240. Asensio y Toledo, José María. *Notas de algunos libros, artículos y folletos sobre la vida y las obras de Miguel de Cervantes Saavedra*. Seville: Imp. de E. Rasco, 1885. 72 pages.

[The 260 entries (some with commentary) of this bibliography cover both works by Cervantes and critiques of those works.]

241. Ortego Aguirrebeña, Feliciano. *Desliz literario cometido por Don Marcelino Menéndez y Pelayo, cuando al examinar el ejemplar prueba del Quijote de Cervantes, no conoció tan rica joya*. Palencia: S. Peralta, 1885. 56 pages.

Menéndez Pelayo is an intolerant an careless critic. He knows little of Cervantes' poetry and has no right to conclude that the *Restauración* was done with little knowledge of the history of textual problems of the *Quijote*.

242. Campoamor, Ramón de. "Dedicatoria" to *Humoradas*. In *Obras completas*. Madrid: Aguilar, 1972, pp. 309-11. [First edition, Madrid, 1886.]

Humor is the contraposition of ideas, acts, or passions. The placing of things in an antithetical situation causes one to laugh with sadness. For example, Don Quijote's returning home, after having been drubbed for defending his ideals, while he is received by his housekeeper and his niece, representatives of common sense comfortably eating white bread and knitting, is a touch of humor which, besides making one laugh, fills one's eyes with tears.

Only Cervantes and Shakespeare offer true humor, which is serious, ingenuous, and open. If, as Cervantes states, causing laughter is a talent of geniuses, causing laughter and tears at the same time is an exceptional gift which God granted only to him and to Shakespeare, the two greatest humorous writers ever.

243. Fernández, Cayetano. "Oración fúnebre." *Memorias de la Real Academia Española* 5 (1886): 77-106.

Cervantes' harmonious language reflects his Spanish soul. There is a strong religious vein in the thinkers and heroes of Spain from the Cid to Melchor Cano, Mariana, and others in the sixteenth century.

244. Olmedilla y Puig, Joaquín. "Cervantes considerado como fisiólogo y médico." *Ilustración Ibérica* 4 (May 1, 1886): 283-86. [See also *Cervantes en ciencias médicas*, Madrid: Administración de la Revista de Medicina y Cirugía Práctica, 1905.]

Reading Cervantes involves the knowledge of many fields of scientific investigation. One of them is the causes and treatment of mental aliena-tion, or monomania, which is introduced in the *Quijote* with Don Quijote's talking to himself about chivalry. Surely, he might have been cured had he surrounded himself with friends, or so say many of the turn-of-the-century studies of the *Quijote*.

245. Pi y Molist, Emilio. *Primores del Quijote en el concepto médico-psicológico y consideraciones generales sobre la locura para un nuevo comentario de la inmortal novela.* Barcelona: Imp. Barcelonesa, 1886. 456 pages.

An insane person rarely loses all his faculties, including free will (though such faculties may be impaired), and alteration of the human organism does not completely explain the disturbance of the mind. Don Quijote did not go insane because of love but in part because he realized in his mad way that he was supposed to be in love. Another factor was excessive reading of chivalric novels and subsequent idleness and isolation.

Two fixed and related ideas, which coexist in the hero's mind, are his false belief that he is a knight-errant, with all the privileges and obligations involved, and his belief that he is in love. Other aspects of the Knight's madness arising from his *erotomanía* are an elevation of emotional and intellectual faculties, a constant feeling of moral and physical superiority, a consequent belief in the infallibility of his own judgment, and the exaggera-tion of *amour propre*, which leads to daring, arrogance, and insolence. However, madness does not change a victim completely, for religion and education remain. Thus, the Knight's sane characteristics are what make him a sympathetic figure: he is benign, courteous, compassionate, discreet, and well-read. The struggle between idealism and realism in the novel is not only between the hero and the reality of the outer world but between the hero's own inner reality and his madness.

The proper therapeutic treatment for Don Quijote is to quiet him for two years or more and to force him to act out his madness without contradicting or punishing him. The technique is very risky but can be effective.

Cervantes required Don Quijote with his madness to be a model of moral beauty (as strange and contradictory as this seems). The hero is attractive yet peculiarly mad. He is elevated in spirit, pure of emotions, and perceives ideal beauty. But psychology is the dominant feature of the *Quijote*, and hence the hero's monomania is the key to his story. Without realizing that he had penetrated a truth that was hidden from doctors, Cervantes wrote a psychiatric study even before there were psychiatrists.

246. Vidart, Luis. *Los biógrafos de Cervantes en el siglo XVIII.* Madrid: Tip. de los Sucs. de Rivadeneyra, 1886. 35 pages.

Little was known about Cervantes until a century after his death, when Luis Moreri wrote his *Gran diccionario histórico,* with an entry on the author of the *Quijote.* Lord Carteret commissioned the first biography of Cervantes, that of Gregorio Mayans in 1738, from which later biographers borrowed heavily, even though they were reluctant to give him credit.

Pellicer's biography contains erudition on every page, Vicente de los Ríos' biography is characterized by elegance and correctness of language and well thought-out literary judgment, and Quintana's work contains artistic intuition and enthusiasm for beauty. But even with these works, eighteenth-century Spaniards did not fully appreciate the *Quijote,* and neither Pellicer, Ríos, nor Quintana had revealed the full literary value of the *Quijote.*

247. Dumaine, C.-B. *Essai sur la vie et les oeuvres de Cervantès, d'après un travail inédit de D. Luis Carreras.* Paris: A. Lamerre, 1896. 332 pages. [Luis Carreras was born in 1840 in Barcelona. He lived as a political refugee in France for a number of years and died in 1888. He wrote articles on Cervantes' life and works in *El Principado* (Barcelona) in 1867 and 1868. His work on the madness of Don Quijote is listed by Grismer (I, p. 41) as appearing in *Diluvio* (Barcelona) on October 8, 15, and 20, 1887.]

[Carreras maintains that the Spanish people understand that it was because of them that the *Quijote* was written. It is, in effect, the beginning of a new literature, gay and familiar, yet positive and powerful.

Dumaine, in his introduction, states that he has revised Carreras' study with the works of certain psychiatrists, such as Pi y Molist, in view. He comments on the psychology of the Quijote figure as discussed by such alienists as Hernández Morejón and E. Esquirol. Dumaine rejects the word "monomania" used by earlier doctors. The course of the Knight's madness is traced from its basic conception of chivalric mission to the secondary "delirious" conception, the love for Dulcinea: Don Quijote's love for her is pure feeling, it is mysticism. One false idea engenders another, and Don Quijote is no more in love than he is a knight-errant. Both ideas arise from a sick mind.

Attention is devoted to the distinction between "illusion" and "hallucination." Illusion almost exclusively characterizes the Knight's illness, though some hallucinations are found in the story. Illusion is transformed sensation based on an exterior cause, whereas hallucination has no such outer impulse. Cervantes' rare use of hallucination (where Don Quijote believes he is different chivalresque figures) is not consistent with the hero's madness. Here he is recalling the *Romancero*, not writing as an alienist.

Particular note is taken of the hero's defeat, his consequent melancholy, and his desire to die. The recovery of sanity is a rare occurrence in madmen, states Dumaine, but, so long as it is possible, it is acceptable to the reader. Cervantes did not wish the reader to see Don Quijote die in madness or delirium.]

248. Martínez Duimovich, A. "La cervántico-manía." In *Literomanías*. Almería: Imp. de Comercio, 1887, pp. 143-51.

Too many critics have overstated the purpose of the *Quijote*; Cervantes was not a theologian, doctor, or navigator. This mania has gone so far as to include Cervantes' expertise in culinary arts! There has also been too much emphasis on the misery of Cervantes' life while a soldier and captive, and critics have attacked Cervantes too often for the linguistic "mistakes" in the *Quijote*, even though many of these errors were the responsibility of his editors.

249. Unamuno, Miguel de. "Espíritu de la raza vasca." In *Obras completas*, IV: *La raza y la lengua*. Madrid: Escelicer, 1966, pp. 153-74. [Lecture delivered at *El Sitio*, Bilbao, January 3, 1887.]

[Unamuno, relying on the principles of *intra-history*, or the collective unconscious, associates Don Quijote wtih Spain and also regards him as a universal type.]

250. Apraiz y Sáenz del Burgo, Julián. "Elogio fúnebre dicho en la conmemoración celebrada en el Teatro de Vitoria por el Ateneo Científico y Literario, el día 23 de Abril de 1888, aniversario CCLXXII de la muerte de Miguel de Cervantes Saavedra." In *Colección de discursos y artículos*, I: *Discursos*. Vitoria: Tip. de la Ilustración de Alava, 1889, pp. 377-404.

Juan Antonio Pellicer, Diego Clemencín, and Aureliano Fernández-Guerra are incorrect in concluding that Cervantes was anti-Basque, their opinion being partly based on an observation by Sancho at Barataria that one of his subjects, if he were also Basque, would be fit to be secretary to the emperor himself. This remark is innocent and has no hidden, anti-Basque connotation. Passages in *La señora Cornelia* and the *Viaje del Parnaso* indicate that Cervantes was pro-Basque.

251. Carreras, Luis. "Cervantes, militar, marino y diplomático." *Ilustración Artística* (Barcelona) 7 (1888): no. 325, 98-99; no. 326, 106-10; no. 327, 114-18; no. 328, 122-26.

A reading of the complete works of Cervantes will show that he had a systematically formulated idea of military strategy, even though he considered firearms diabolical inventions. Only a military engineer could write a work like *La Numancia*. Biographical studies have shown that Cervantes was a consummate soldier and that he read the works of military writers, both ancient and modern. Furthermore, Cervantes was a believer in heroism, as exemplified in *La Numancia*, and he must have had knowledge of astronomy, geography, and navigation because these sciences are required of a master of military strategy. Cervantes had a profound knowledge of diplomacy and of Spain's foreign policy through his travels in Italy, and he displays keen awareness of the question of the Turk in the *Quijote*.

252. Ortega y Rubio, Juan. *Cervantes en Valladolid*. Valladolid: Imp. Hijos de Rodríguez, 1888. 56 pages.

Cervantes was in Valladolid when he wrote the *Quijote*. Signed correspondence indicates that Cervantes was in Valladolid in 1604, requesting the rights to publish the first part of the *Quijote*. Printing was completed in the early months of 1605.

253. Rius y de Llosellas, Leopoldo. *Catálogo de la Biblioteca Cervántica*. Barcelona: López Robert, 1888. 39 pages.

[A catalogue that appears to be the genesis of Rius' masterful bibliography of 1895-1904. It lists 172 Spanish editions of the *Quijote*, from the first to that of 1887, published both in and outside Spain. This is followed by a list of translations of the *Quijote* and of Spanish editions and translations of the *Galatea*, the *Novelas ejemplares*, the *Comedias y entremeses*, and the *Persiles*. The catalogue also contains imitations of Cervantes' works and their iconography. There are 1,034 entries.]

254. Unamuno, Miguel de. "Cuestión gramatical." In *Obras completas*, IV: *La raza y la lengua*. Madrid: Escelicer, 1966, pp. 279-81. [First published in *El Diario de Bilbao*, March 27, 1888.]

Cervantes' novel is not always a model of good grammar, but one may consult it for proper usage on occasions with caution.

255. Castro y Serrano, José de. "La amenidad y salanura de los escritos como elemento de belleza y arte." Madrid: Sucs. de Rivadeneyra, 1889. 54 pages. [Discurso de recepción en la Real Academia Española; contains the reply of Duque de Rivas, entry no. 257.]

Cervantes is a universal writer and Don Quijote is a more ordinary man than the figures in the works of Calderón or Shakespeare. With the exception of his pronouncements on chivalry, we respect the knight for his sound judgments, enthusiasm, and compassion. There is no occult meaning in the *Quijote*. It is not an allegory in which Don Quijote represents a fanatic and oppressive sixteenth-century Spain, for Cervantes was too much of a Spaniard for this.

Cervantes had no one to copy, and no one could copy him, because the *Quijote* emerged from a unique set of circumstances. Rabelais, for example, could not be a precursor of Cervantes because his characters are too obscene and immoral to be compared with Don Quijote. Therefore, it is evident that Cervantes stands alone in his creation of supremely human personages.

256. Cortejón, Clemente. "Algunos secretos del lenguaje y estilo del *Don Quijote.*" *España Moderna* (Madrid) 1 (1889): 99-135.

Many criticisms of Cervantes' language are unfounded. Cervantes' style is natural, his characters speak appropriately according to their station in life, and his word choice and word placement are executed with perfection, especially in the *Quijote*. Cervantes did not write his work in a hurried fashion, as some have said. The novelist was, in fact, quite cautious in his use of language, phraseology, and expression. One will find some of the richest Spanish ever written as one peruses the *Quijote*.

257. Saavedra Remírez de Baquedano, Angel de [Duque de Rivas]. "Discurso de contestación al señor D. José de Castro y Serrano en su recepción en la Real Academia Española el día 8 de diciembre de 1889." In *Discursos, cartas y otros escritos.* Madrid: Tip. de la Viuda e Hijos de Tello, 1903, pp. 43-71. [See Castro y Serrano, entry no. 255, for an earlier version.]

Each country laughs in its own way, but there is also a universal laughter, the greatest interpreter of which is Cervantes in his *Quijote*, a marvelous book for which there have been no national barriers. It has been translated into all languages and has come to enrich all literatures. Calderón was eminently Spanish and Shakespeare essentially English: to understand them one must be a native of their countries. But to feel and understand Cervantes it is enough to be a man of any civilized nation, because even if there are in his novel the flavor of the land and telling portraits of Spaniards, the moral elements of the work are essentially human.

The character of the Knight accounts for much of this appeal. Don Quijote is made of our own substance, and apart from his lunatic streak (and perhaps because of it), he is like the mirror of our own conscience. The elevation of his character, his abnegation, and his courage conquer our spirit. Besides, who has not been a Don Quijote at one time or another?

Cervantes' story does not contain hidden meaning, although there are allusions to events and persons of the era. The *Quijote* is not a historical allegory in which the Manchegan hidalgo symbolizes the Spain of the sixteenth century, "aventurera, hazañosa, pero agresiva, fanática y opresora." Such interpretation is the extreme opinion of foreigners, seeking to make of the author a modern, liberal philosopher. Cervantes was too Spanish for such ideas to occur to him. His deep-rooted faith would not permit him to believe that the Spain of Carlos V and Felipe II was wrong in fighting Protestantism. He even loved chivalric novels, as paradoxical as this seems, and he praises the *Amadís, Palmerín,* and *Tirante.*

The heroic tone, in fusion with the picaresque (a natural consequence of the author's humble condition and his association with the lower strata of society), accounts for the originality and charm of Cervantes' immortal work. On the one side, the *Quijote* contains the elevated impulses of the author's chivalresque spirit; on the other, the festive and scornful tendency of his genius, sharpened by the vicissitudes of life and by his contact with the lower classes.

Regarding those who find Sancho to be a kind of Panurge for Don Quijote, let it be said that Panurge is obscene, clownish, vindictive, insatiable, and completely without morals, while Sancho, even though sometimes a rascal, is humble and just. Cervantes and Rabelais are not at all alike. Rabelais is a precursor of Voltaire, but he had no effect on Cervantes.

258. Unamuno, Miguel de. "En Alcalá de Henares: Castilla y Vizcaya." In *Obras completas,* I: *Paisajes y ensayos.* Madrid: Escelicer, 1966, pp. 123-33. [First published November 18, 1889 in the "Hoja literaria" of *El Noticiero Bilbaíno.*]

Alcalá recalls Cervantes, Cervantes recalls Don Quijote, and Don Quijote recalls the plains of Castile. The essence of Castile is its wide horizons, while the widespread horizons of Don Quijote are "horizontes cálidos, yermos, sin verdura." Cervantes was inspired by the landscape of Castile, and his masterpiece is a poem in which reality and life seem so small, and madness and death so great.

259. Vidart, Luis. *Los biógrafos de Cervantes en el siglo XIX.* Madrid: Tip. Sucs. de Rivadeneyra, 1889. 44 pages.

Spain did not begin to appreciate Cervantes until the English had led the way, and even at the end of the eighteenth century, Spanish critics were "semidoctos." There was a definite anti-Cervantine attitude among various Spanish critics in the first part of the nineteenth century.

While Navarrete was thorough and defended Cervantes, there is a certain lack of enthusiasm in his biography and an overemphasis on Cervantes' nobility of ancestry.

260. Vidart, Luis. "Los últimos biógrafos de Cervantes." *Ilustración Española y Americana* 33 (1889): 38-39 and 42.

León Máinez, Jerónimo Morán, M. Fernández de Navarrete, and N. Díaz de Benjumea are the leading Cervantine biographers of the nineteenth century. Navarrete stands out for the maturity of his judgments, Morán for the novelty of the data that he presents, Máinez for his generous persistence in destroying historical errors, and Benjumea for his perspicacity and liveliness of imagination.

261. López Fabra, Francisco. Review of Leopoldo Rius' *Cervantes: bibliografía e historia de la crítica*. *La Ilustración Española y Americana* 34 (1890): 390.

Rius announces his intention to publish a critical bibliography of the works of Cervantes, which was to contain some of the rarest editions of the *Quijote* ignored by critics. Rius' work became the monumental 1895 bibliography.

262. Sánchez Juárez, Francisco. *Oración fúnebre en las honras de Miguel de Cervantes Saavedra*. Madrid: Tip. de los Huérfanos, 1891. 34 pages.

The Church in which Cervantes believed knows the eternal truth, which is not the truth of science but the truth of the word of God.

263. Soravilla, Javier. "Respecto de *El Quijote*." *La Ilustración Española y Americana* 35 (1891): 11-14.

Marcela, not a kind person, but a unique one, has been drawn masterfully by Cervantes. Only Cervantes was capable of creating a character with so many contradictory aspects. She is extraordinary because she shows no hate for Grisóstomo. Don Quijote was the only member of the audience of friends who understood her. Indeed, he was the only one who had the capacity to understand her, for the world thought them both eccentric.

264. Pallol, Benigno [Polinous]. *Interpretación del Quijote: Primera Parte*. Madrid: Imp. de Dionisio de los Ríos, 1893. 527 pages.

Even though Cervantes was not an erudite thinker, he was a *sabio* in the true sense. Cervantes did not combat chivalry, for he was chivalrous and heroic himself. What he combatted was the extravagance of religion, "romanticismo de mala especie."

Cervantes wanted to present a hero who was a universal model for the enlightenment of future times, a model with the virtues of all the great historical figures. He wanted to present to us the ideal of man opposed to the obscure reality of his times and to condemn the nobility and the clergy for usurping the rights of man. Thus, he was the genius of his time because he united the two great currents of history: liberty and tyranny. But he had to disguise his ideas because of his concern for the Inquisition. While the *Quijote* is a melancholy book, there is hope to be found in it. As the author thinks of the evils of humanity, he awaits better times in resigned sadness.

Cervantes believed that the heart of evil lay in the Holy Scriptures, which, because of their absurdities (such as giants), gave rise to books of chivalry. Thus the *Quijote* is an invective against the Scriptures and their descendents.

The *Quijote* is a sublime work in spite of the fact that it is veiled and enigmatic. The hero is an example for humanity in the journey through life. His power is not in his muscles, nor in his nerves, nor in his weapons; his strength is nonmaterial like the idea.

French Criticism

265. La Harpe, J. F. de. *Cours de littérature ancienne et moderne.* 16 vols. Paris. H. Agasse, 1792-1805. [See vol. XIII.]

Both Lope de Vega and Cervantes were strangers to erudition. Although a hundred bad novels were written so that the *Quijote* could be produced, it was a work that caused the others to perish.

Cervantes' novel is too long and some people find it frivolous. Its principle disadvantage is that it treats only one (ridiculous) matter, chivalric novels. The *Curioso impertinente,* however, is one of the author's best stories.

266. Florian, Jean Pierre Claris de. "Avertissement" to *Don Quichotte de la Manche,* I. In *Oeuvres complètes.* Leipzig: Gérard Fleischer, 1826, pp. 7-9. [First published in Paris: P. Didot, 1799.]

All that Don Quijote says, when he is not speaking of chivalry, seems dictated by wisdom, and his madness is actually a misguided love of virtue. He is a fool when he acts and wise when he reasons, and since he is a good man, one never ceases to love him. One laughs at him, knows him to be mad, but listens to him. Cervantes is perhaps the only man who, by an ingenious invention, has made his readers follow at length the actions of an extravagant being who is endlessly mocked.

It is hoped that this translation will offer an idea of the book's rare union of gaiety and morality, of finesse, naturalness, imaginativeness, and purest diction. Although the 1605 *Quijote* was written in haste, as evidenced by various errors, its flaws are more than offset by the beauty of the story.

267. Feletz, Ch.-M. de. *Mélanges de philosophie, d'histoire et de littérature,* VI. Paris: Grimbert et Dorez, 1830, pp. 23-39. [Dated 1806.]

The *Quijote, Gil Blas,* and *Tom Jones* are masterpieces and the *Quijote* is the best of the three. *Gil Blas* and *Tom Jones* have the advantage of being composed during a time when civilization was more perfect, and these two novels, whose heroes are ordinary men, seem more relevant to us. But the *Quijote* surpasses the other two books in originality and brilliant imagination. *Gil Blas* and *Tom Jones* are works of two intelligent observers; the *Quijote* is the work of a genius.

Cervantes not only makes the folly of his hero interesting and probable but even makes us love and admire him: his friendly nature, openness, politeness, disinterestedness, bravery, illusions, pleasures, sorrows, and disappointments all attract us. His clear reasoning often instructs us and his good sense and eloquence charm us.

Sosie of Molière's *Amphitryon* may be compared with Sancho, who is surely one of the gaiest, most pleasant, and truest characters ever imagined. The translation of Florian is praiseworthy but the Filleau de Saint-Martin translation is poor.

268. Chateaubriand, François René de. "Voyage de Tunis et retour en France." *Itinéraire de Paris à Jérusalem*. In *Oeuvres romanesques et voyages*, II. Paris: Gallimard, 1969, pp. 1212-13. [Passage written April, 1807. First published 1811.]

[At the end of the last chapter of his *Itinéraire*, Chateaubriand states: "I left Granada for Aranjuez; I crossed the land of the illustrious cavalier of La Mancha, whom I consider the most noble, the most brave, the most lovable, and the least mad of mortals."]

269. Creuzé de Lesser, A. *La Chevalerie*. Paris: F. Ponce-Lebas, 1839, pp. 148-49. [Dated 1813.]

Cervantes destroyed many chivalric novels, but not the good ones, such as the *Amadis*. In fact, the *Amadís* acquired fame in part because of the *Quijote*, and it also clarifies a number of passages in Cervantes' work.

270. Simonde de Sismondi, J. C. L. *Historical View of the Literature of the South of Europe*, III. Translated from the original by Thomas Roscoe. London: Henry Colburn and Co., 1823, pp. 321-45. [Original version, *De la littérature du midi de l'Europe*, Paris: Treuttel et Würtz, 1813; first English version, New York: Harper, 1818.]

The *Quijote*'s most striking feature is its continual contrast between the poetic and the prosaic, between imagination and the pettiness of social life. This opposition has led some to consider the *Quijote* a melancholy book.

The book shows the vanity of noble feelings and the illusions of heroism; it also suggests that a high degree of enthusiasm is prejudicial both to the individual who sacrifices himself and to society.

Sancho is a mixture of good and bad qualities. Cervantes knew that he could not place an odious character in the foreground; at times, however, he derides both Sancho and Don Quijote. If enthusiasm suffers in the person of the Knight, egotism does not escape the Squire.

The plot of the *Quijote* is generally witty and imaginative. Cervantes, however, moves beyond wit. By creating tender and passionate romantic episodes he was able to excite interest. Indeed, the plot is infinitely varied in incident, character, and language, despite some tediousness and pedantry in the opening. The characters come alive and grow, and the language changes appropriately. The *Curioso impertinente* is faulty in the beginning but ends in a most touching manner.

The style of the *Quijote* possesses inimitable beauty, nobility, and candor. It manifests a liveliness, precision, and harmony never equaled by another Spanish writer.

271. Beyle, Marie Henri [Stendhal]. *De l'amour*. Paris: Garnier frères, 1959, p. 243. [First published, Paris: P. Mongie, 1822.]

The definition of "prosaïque" is to be found in the *Quijote* in the *perfect contrast between the Master and the Squire*: The Master, tall and pallid, and the Squire, plump and rosy; the first, all heroism and courtesy ... the second, all vanity and servility; the first, always full of romantic imaginings ... the second, a model of good behavior and wisdom; the first, always nourishing his soul with some heroic and daring contemplation ... the other, mulling over some clever plan and carefully considering all the little shameful and selfish movements of the human heart.

272. Auger, Louis Simon. "Essai sur la vie et sur les ouvrages de Cervantès." In *Histoire de l'admirable Don Quichotte de la Manche*, I. Traduction de Filleau de Saint-Martin. Paris: Delongchamps, 1825, pp. v-xi.

The vividness of the two protagonists derives from the complexity of their attitudes. Cervantes had no prior models to work with when he fashioned his two characters. Hence he is superior to such writers as Fielding (*Tom Jones*) and Lesage (*Gil Blas*).

The opposition between the hero's principles and his action, between what he seeks to do and what he believes he has done, produces comedy.

Don Quijote's madness is a form of monomania, and Cervantes' description of the condition is consistent. The frequent intervals of lucidity allow for good sense, sublime generosity, and superior intelligence. Monomania nicely suits the author's purposes of ridiculing his compatriots and charming his readers.

Sancho is no less an original figure than Don Quijote. Both are fools, though for different reasons and in different degrees. Don Quijote's folly is heroism; the Squire's folly is self-interest. The first kind of folly is rare, while the other is common.

The structure of the *Quijote* is not a chain of events tending toward a determined end. The will of the hero and chance appear to bring about events. Cervantes employs the device of the reappearing character, a technique found in romances of chivalry. Cervantes saw that the criticism of interpolated episodes in the 1615 *Quijote* was not without merit and he thus avoids them in the sequel. Also, the author reacts to the criticism of the excess drubbings of the hero.

There are two worlds in the *Quijote*, the imaginary and the real. The first world is that of the epic and the second is that of the comedy and novel of customs. Their mixture would have been bizarre and strained in any other work, but in the *Quijote* the combination arises naturally from the dual nature of the story.

Cervantes' style is simple, natural, and ingenuous as a rule. The work exhibits a sweet irony and a seriousness even in the most laughable adventures of its hero. Cervantes does not ridicule his characters; he does not give his readers the signal to laugh. He employs a "gravité plaisante," like La Fontaine and Molière.

273. Mérimée, Prosper. "Cervantès." In *Portraits historiques et littéraires.* Paris: M. Lévy frères, 1874, pp. 1-54. [Dated 1826.]

Cervantes' use of interpolated episodes is justifiable and the style of the *Quijote* is the most simple and elegant in Spanish literature. There are minor faults in Cervantes' novel, such as anachronisms and historical errors, but a more serious problem is Cervantes' tendency to seek out the comic in the suffering of the hero.

The symbolic interpretation of the *Quijote* is ingenious but not convincing. Comparing the *Quijote* with Voltaire's *Candide*, it is evident that Cervantes is content to live in society as it is, while Voltaire is not. Also, Voltaire's characters are abstract, while Cervantes' figures are real.

Cervantes indeed sought to rid the world of books of chivalry, and was successful. He disliked such books because of their affected language, not because of their incredible events.

274. Hugo, Victor. "Préface" to *Cromwell.* Paris: Garnier-Flammarion, 1968, p. 75. [Dated October, 1827.]

The development of the grotesque in the Middle Ages reaches its peak in the sixteenth century. Its verve, vigor, and creative force produce three contemporary, comic Homers: Ariosto, in Italy, Cervantes, in Spain, and Rabelais, in France.

275. Denis, Ferdinand. "Essai sur la philosophie de Sancho." In *Le Livre des proverbes français.* Paris: Paulin, 1842, pp. vii-xxvii. [First published in Paris: Abel Ledoux, 1834. Spanish version of essay on Sancho by J. M. Sbarbi, *Refranero general español*, V, Madrid, 1876.]

Proverbs arose as a form of consolation especially from poverty. Proverbs incorporate both a sublime and a grotesque element. They are primitive poetry, containing the psychology and thinking of the earliest ages. That Spain is particularly rich in proverbs is attributable to Moorish and Jewish influences. Cervantes undoubtedly was familiar with Juan de Mal Lara's collection of proverbs, *La filosofía vulgar*, 1568.

276. Janin, Jules. "Don Quichotte." *L'Artiste* 9 (1835): 50-51.

Don Quijote is the bravest, worthiest, most disinterested, and wisest of men, possessed of the sweetest, most honorable, and most saintly form of madness. Don Quijote and Sancho are as inseparable as body and soul. Sancho is common sense, Don Quijote is poetry; Sancho is fact, Don Quijote is dream; Sancho is the earthly, Don Quijote is the ideal. Without Don Quijote, Sancho is a caricature. The two are held together in an indissoluble artistic and philosophical unity.

277. Viardot, Louis. "Notice sur la vie et les ouvrages de Cervantès." In *L'Ingénieux Hidalgo Don Quichotte de la Manche*, I. Paris: J.-J. Dubochet et Cie, 1836, pp. 1-48.

Cervantes began the *Quijote* with the sole intention of ridiculing chivalric novels, and at first Don Quijote was a complete fool and Sancho a self-seeking, simple-minded peasant. Yet the author grew fond of his two characters and bestowed understanding on the Knight and common sense and natural integrity on the Squire. Don Quijote's monomania became that of an honorable man, revolted by injustice. Outside of chivalry he was an able reasoner and an eloquent speaker. Sancho, like his master, had only a grain of folly. At first, the two protagonists invited mockery; then they aroused pity and sympathy. They revealed the vices and the foolishness of those who derided them. In the 1615 sequel, written after Cervantes had matured and experienced the world, the *Quijote* became a book of practical philosophy.

The *Quijote*'s various virtues are its perfect unity of plan, its diversity of details, its fertility of imagination, its intimate and natural combination of the ridiculous and the sublime, and its magnificent and harmonious language.

278. Littré, E. "*Don Quichotte de la Manche* par Miguel de Cervantès, traduit et annoté par Louis Viardot." In *Littérature et histoire*. Paris: Didier, 1877, pp. 176-92. [First published December 30, 1837 in *Le National*.]

Problems in translating the Spanish of Cervantes' times into nineteenth-century French include the difficulty of finding equivalents for puns. The Viardot translation is excellent and the sketches of Johannot effectively transpose the author's ideal into pictorial form.

Cervantes' original purpose was merely to banish romances of chivalry. As the plot advances, however, the hero changes: he becomes less mad and more intelligent, elevated, and noble.

Cervantes' great contribution came from his understanding of the important connection between hallucination and reason. Hallucination has played a greater role in human affairs than is generally supposed. Certain men like Christ and Saint Paul, for example, have felt themselves in communication with supernatural powers and have achieved results on behalf of morality and justice. On the other hand, belief in the supernatural realm has produced evil as well. Cervantes was a consummate psychologist who understood the human mind and mysteriously put into play the hidden powers which the human spirit conceals. He created a hero in whom hallucination and reason coexist without harm.

279. Esquirol, Etienne. *Des maladies mentales.* New York: Arno Press, 1976, p. 47. [Reprint of first edition, Paris: J.-B. Ballière, 1838.]

In the *Quijote*, the author gave a perfect description of erotomania, which was almost an epidemic in Cervantes' era and which was modified by the chivalresque customs of the fifteenth century.

280. Nisard, August. "Cervantès: *Don Quichotte—Les Nouvelles.*" *Revue Française* 7 (1838): 299-327.

Through all his hardships Cervantes never lost his sense of justice. The *Quijote* is the truest and sincerest book ever to come from the mind of man, and its power derives from the author's difficult life.

The book goes beyond pure satire. While Cervantes seeks to ridicule the chivalric genre he also exalts *quijotismo*. He elevates both the Knight and the Squire. The friendship between Don Quijote and Sancho is one of the most touching features in the novel. In fact, Sancho is Cervantes' favorite character.

281. Rosseeuw Saint-Hilaire, E. F. A. *Etudes sur l'origine de la langue et des romances espagnoles.* Paris: Guiraudet et Ch. Jouaust, 1838. 33 pages.

The man who gave chivalry its most deadly blow was Miguel de Cervantes, an ungrateful son of the land in which poetry and religion had given birth to so many miracles. Cervantes ridicules all generous instincts in a sublime fool. Byron's condemnation of Cervantes will live as long as Cervantes' immortal parody.

282. Vigny, Alfred de. *Le Journal d'un poète,* I. In *Oeuvres complètes.* Paris: Louis Conard, 1935, pp. 547-58. [February or March, 1840.]

When Cervantes lay dying, he was asked whom he intended to depict in the person of Don Quijote. "Myself," he replied; "I wanted to express the misfortune of imagination and enthusiasm misplaced in a vulgar and materialistic world."

283. Gautier, Théophile. *Voyage en Espagne.* Geneva: Slatkine Reprints, 1978, p. 193. [Reprint of the 1883 Charpentier edition; first published in Paris: Charpentier, 1843.]

One cannot take a step in Spain without finding the trace of Don

Quijote, for so deeply national is the work of Cervantes. The Spanish character is marked by chivalresque exaltation, the adventurous spirit joined to common sense in a sort of jovial fellowship full of delicacy.

284. Puibusque, Adolphe de. *Histoire comparée des littératures espagnole et française*, I. Paris: G. A. Dentu, 1843, chapts. 6 and 7.

Don Quijote is a fool who has common sense, and Sancho a sensible man who falls prey to folly. One is poetic and questing for glory; the other is prosaic and looking for a fortune. Sancho is just as credulous in his materialistic dreams as his master in his illusions of heroism.

Cervantes remains a poet without going beyond reason: he brings back chivalry and makes it more interesting than ever before. At one stroke he creates the comic and the ethical novel. No successor equals him, though Sir Walter Scott, a man of reason and good spirits, is his best heir. Other writers, such as Quevedo, Vélez de Guevara, Lesage, and Espinel, cannot match the scope of his originality.

Cervantes knows how to be true without ceasing to be comic; he excels at talking about everything. Cervantes knows the human spirit intimately, and his rendering of the Knight's monomania is superb.

285. Mennechet, Edouard. *Matinées littéraires*. In *Cours complet de littérature moderne*, II. Paris: Garnier frères, 1868, pp. 31-44. [First published in Paris: Langlois, 1846-48.]

The *Quijote* was begun while its author was imprisoned by the mayor of a town in La Mancha because of some unknown dispute. The *Quijote* is to an extent a satire of chivalry; however, by placing noble virtues in his hero, Cervantes paid tribute to true chivalry and only mocked knight-errantry, which had become useless after the imposition of laws.

The most brilliant aspect of the novel is not the comedy but the dialogue. Never have the human heart, mind, and spirit been studied so well. Never has the good sense of the people, in their appetites and vulgar instincts, rung so true.

As for the characters, Don Quijote displays the noblest qualities of our nature, and yet he does a thousand foolish things because his passion interferes with these high qualities and renders them useless. This is too often the history of the human soul. Sancho exhibits sensuality, gluttony, cowardliness, laziness, and vanity, but is tempered by a sort of goodness and sensitivity. Above all, he shows the instinct of self-preservation.

Don Quijote and Sancho imitate the relationship of soul and body. The former seeks to lead the latter toward goodness but almost always travels toward evil; the latter struggles against the will that controls him and yet obeys because he cannot do otherwise. Don Quijote aims at spiritual heights but is held back by Sancho, who clings to earth.

Cervantes' philosophical suggestions may have been formed unconsciously. As Diderot noted, a man of genius may produce a masterpiece
without being completely aware of its value.

286. Noriega, François de Paul. *Critique et défense de Don Quichotte, suivies de
chapitres choisis de L'Ingénieux Hidalgo de la Manche.* Paris: Maquet, 1846. 286
pages.

Concerning the relative merits of a free as opposed to a literal
translation of the *Quijote*, a free translation involves attempting to think the
way Cervantes may have thought while composing the original. A literal
translation may result in the loss of color but permits the correcting of
mistakes in the original. Many French translators improved Cervantes'
language so that the text now reads the way it should have read had
Cervantes not been so careless. In effect, Cervantes' reputation remained
intact because of his translators.

287. Magnin, Charles. "De la chevalerie en Espagne et le *Romancero.*"
Revue des Deux Mondes, August 17, 1847: 494-519.

The purpose of the *Quijote* was not to contrast heroic and ideal
generosity with prosaic and vulgar reality. It was to contrast false and
chimerical enthusiasm with the true and practical heroism of historical
figures and to contrast ethereal love with true, natural love. Cervantes also
sought to censure foreign literature, full of folly and license, which had
caught the public imagination and was altering national customs.

288. Mazade, Charles de. "La Comédie moderne en Espagne." *Revue des Deux
Mondes*, August 1, 1847: 432-61.

The *Quijote* is a true human comedy, a sincere and vigorous raillery by a
man who looked on human nature without astonishment and who could
reproduce the totality of human qualities, including good sense, triviality,
vanity, chivalresque exaltation, folly, and abnegation.

289. Chasles, Philarète. *Etudes sur le seizième siècle en France.* Paris: Aymot,
1848, pp. 83-85.

Chivalric novels are the common property of the European feudal
heritage, and Ariosto's *Orlando furioso* and Cervantes' *Quijote* are works that
are characteristic of their national literature. Cervantes' work is also an
amusing epitaph to chivalric literature. He makes us admire chivalry while
destroying it with ridicule. Perhaps the *Quijote* is the only example of irony
that is both sweet and forceful.

290. Chateaubriand, François René de. *Mémoires d'outre-tombe*, I. Paris:
Pléiade, 1962, p. 165. [Dated October, 1821; first published in 1848.]

I cannot understand Cervantes' novel and its cruel gaiety except upon sad reflection: Considering the human being as a whole, weighing the good and the bad, one would be tempted to desire anything which would lead to oblivion as a means of escaping oneself; a joyous drunk is a happy creature. Religion aside, happiness is being unaware of oneself and arriving at death without having experienced life.

291. Sandeau, Jules. A comment on Saint-Evremond's passage dealing with the *Quijote*, as reprinted by Wolfgang Wurzbach in *Zeitschrift für Romanische Philologie* 47 (1927): 603-04. [From the years 1850-1852 (?).]

The bourgeoisie look favorably on the *Quijote* because they consider it an ingenious satire on poetic and chivalresque sentiments. However, they are mistaken, for Cervantes' novel is the most cutting satire possible of the dastardly society of the times.

292. Flaubert, Gustave. *Correspondance*. In *Oeuvres complètes*. Paris: Louis Conard, 1927. [A letter dated November 22, 1852.]

[In the *Troisième série* (1852-1854) of the Conard edition is found the oft-quoted passage of Flaubert in regard to the *Quijote*: "Ce qu'il y a de prodigieux dans *Don Quichotte*, c'est l'absence d'art et cette perpétuelle fusion de l'illusion et de la réalité qui en fait un livre si comique et si poétique. Quels nains que tous les autres à côté! Comme on se sent petit, mon Dieu! Comme on se sent petit!"]

293. Baret, Eugène. *De l'Amadis de Gaule et de son influence sur les moeurs et la littérature au XVIe et au XVIIe siècle avec une notice bibliographique*. Paris: Firmin-Didot frères, fils et Cie, 1873. 234 pages. [First published in 1853.]

J. Chapelain's admiration for the heroism of the books of chivalry and his condemnation of Cervantes for mocking such stories without considering the times and customs of the era in which the deeds took place are worth pointing out. And at the time of the *précieuses* (mid-seventeenth century), military chivalry had grown anachronistic, perhaps as a result of the satire of Ariosto and Cervantes.

294. Latour, Antoine de. "Cervantès à Séville." In *Etudes sur Espagne: Séville et Andalousie*, I. Paris: Michel Lévy frères, 1855, pp. 253-91.

For Morejón, Cervantes is not only an admirable novelist, a great moralist, and an eloquent portrayer of the human heart, he is also an able doctor. But this is somewhat dubious and Morejón should be criticized for treating the novel as a case study in the cure of a mental disorder.

295. Jullien, August. *Le Véritable Sancho Panza, ou choix de proverbes, dictons, adages, colligés pour l'agrément de son neveu E. L.* Paris: Hachette, 1856. 240 pages.

[A collection of 2,700 proverbs in French. Despite the title, there appears to be no relationship between the proverbs presented and Sancho Panza (or the *Quijote*).]

296. Vacquerie, Auguste. "Don Quichotte." In *Profils et grimaces*. Paris: Pagnerre, 1864, pp. 394-404. [Dated February, 1856.]

The relationship of Don Quijote and Sancho demonstrates profound truths. Too much practicality, for example, is just as foolish as excessive idealism. Truth is neither material nor spiritual; it is both. Spiritual errors, however, are less dangerous than venial mistakes. As the novel progresses, Cervantes moves his characters toward a middle ground. In Part II he makes his hero less of a fool and the Squire less of a glutton. Don Quijote gains more victories, his credulity is less dense, and Cervantes insists on the good side of his hero, making his madness a halo.

297. Anonymous. "Nouvelles." *Bulletin du Bibliophile* (Paris), 13th Series (June, 1857): 331-32.

[An attempt to prove that Cervantes was unoriginal in his conception of the *Quijote* by pointing out variations in the *privilegio* of the 1605 edition and the appearance of the Don Quijote figure in three works previous to Cervantes' novel.]

298. Baret, Eugène. "Cervantès." In *Espagne et Provence*. Paris: A. Durand, 1857, pp. 323-48.

The *Quijote* lacks unity and its author's purpose is not clear, even though Cervantes himself and many critics assert that his only aim was to attack chivalric novels. The book contains a multitude of reflections, observations, and judgments on matters much more important than the question of romances of chivalry. Indeed, *Don Quijote* ranks high in world literature because of its seriousness. Furthermore, various symbolic elements in the novel do not primarily relate to chivalry. The metaphorical suggestion of imagination and common sense in the protagonists is an example. Cervantes attacks only certain unrealistic elements of the medieval epic and does not attack chivalry itself, as some have wrongly concluded.

The novel's interpolated elements are somewhat disparate. Fragments of diverse genres were placed in the novel for no other reason than to please and attract the reader.

299. Anonymous. *Don Quichotte expliqué par Goetz de Berlichingen*. Oporto: 1858. [As excerpted in Rius, III, pp. 294-95, and by C. A. Sainte-Beuve, *Nouveaux Lundis*, VIII, p. 32.]

Goethe's Goetz von Berlichingen was obviously inspired by the figure Don Quijote, and the German author followed Cervantes from beginning to end without knowing it.

The *Quijote* is not merely an attack on chivalry, for Don Quijote represents more than one epoch. He is the idealistic type of all ages who comically clashes with reality. A great deal of Cervantes' life is reflected in his novel. He was a man who took refuge in fantasies and launched a satire of his own age, a satire understood only by posterity.

300. Asselineau, Charles. "Mon cousin Don Quixote: physionomie d'un Philhellène." In *La Double Vie*. Paris: Poulet-Malassis et de Broise, 1858, pp. 69-91.

[A philosophical short story about a quixotic cousin, Captain Francheville. The author regards Don Quijote as the personification of courage and regrets that anyone who should seek to redress wrongs or protect the weak would be treated with derision.]

301. Furne, Charles. "Prologue" to *L'Ingénieux Chevalier Don Quichotte de la Manche*. Paris: Furne, 1858, pp. v-xxviii.

The principal aim of the *Quijote* was not to destroy books of chivalry. Rather, Cervantes wanted to express his deep resentment of the people and the institutions of his day. Despite his achievements as a soldier and writer, he received little money, gratitude, or recognition. In illustrating injustices, Don Quijote is Cervantes himself. Cervantes' true aim in the *Quijote* was to exonerate himself and to rebuke his critics. Because emotions had festered a long time in him, Cervantes was driven to write a novel full of irony and satire.

302. Gautier, Théophile. *Histoire de l'art dramatique en France depuis vingt-cinq ans*. 6 vols. Paris: Edition Hetzel, 1858-1859. [See first three vols.]

The *Quijote* is one of the funniest and merriest of books, but it leaves an impression of profound melancholy. While the original intention of its author was merely to satirize books of chivalry, his purpose expanded. Don Quijote became the symbol of spirit, poetry, and enthusiasm, a man who ignored material things. Sancho represents practical reason and responds to his master's lyrical enthusiasm with common sense. A writer of genius usually produces only one great character in his lifetime, yet Cervantes produced two.

303. Barthélemy, Charles. "Cervantès, libre penseur." In *Erreurs et Mensonges*, IX. Paris: Blériot frères, 1880, pp. 218-41. [First published in 1863-1864.]

Certain commentators (such as Geoffroy, 1783) convert skeptical writers into freethinkers. Cervantes, however, exhibits deep faith, in contrast to Voltaire's premeditated sacrilege. Cervantes revealed serenity of soul up to the last moments of his life.

304. Hugo, Victor. "Les génies." *William Shakespeare*. In *Oeuvres complètes* XL. Paris: Albin-Michel, 1937, pp. 41-44. [Translated into English by Melville B. Anderson, Chicago: A. C. McClurg and Company, 1911, pp. 76-80. Dated 1864.]

There are between the Middle Ages and modern times two comic Homers—Rabelais and Cervantes. Both epitomize horror in jest, but the raillery of Cervantes has nothing to do with the broad grin of Rabelais.

Cervantes' jesting is neither coarse nor cynical. His satire is fine, polished, delicate, almost gallant, and his poetic Renaissance spirit saves his work from becoming petty.

Cervantes' intuition, complex thinking, and creative energy produce unexpected marvels of imagination. He seems to possess a new and complete chart of the human heart, and he creates characters simultaneously universal and unique. He functions as more than an imaginative writer, however.

The advent of common sense is the great fact in Cervantes. Common sense is not a virtue; it is self-interest. But in the face of selfish and ferocious monarchies, dragging their unhappy peoples into their own private wars, decimating families and driving men to kill each other with all those fine words—"military honor," "glory," "obedience to orders," etc.— this Common-Sense is an admirable personage, arising suddenly, and crying out to the human race, "Take care of your skin."

The ideal is in Cervantes as in Dante; but it is called impossible, and is scoffed at. Beatrice has become Dulcinea. Cervantes, however, only seems to rail at the ideal; in reality, he sides with Don Quijote, as Molière sides with Alceste. One must learn how to read between the lines, especially in the books of the sixteenth century. There is in almost all, on account of the threats hanging over freedom of thought, a secret that must be unlocked but whose key is often lost.

305. About, Edmond. "*Don Quichotte* illustré par G. Doré." *Nouvelle Revue de Paris*, February 15, 1864: 63-82.

Cervantes is not audacious (like Rabelais) nor revolutionary. He is tolerant toward hypocrisy; and while he praises liberty, he would restrain its excesses. Cervantes is not a liberator of the spirit (like Voltaire), nor painter of customs (like Lesage), nor a standard-bearer of progress (like Beaumarchais), nor an olympian skeptic and passionate searcher after truth (like Goethe). Cervantes has an honest soul; he is essentially bourgeois. His merit lies in his ability to create graphic literary types. Four new and distinctive figures appear in the novel: Don Quijote, Sancho Panza, Rocinante, and Dapple, and they exist in artistic harmony despite their differences.

306. Latour, Antoine de. "Cervantes." In *Etudes littéraires sur l'Espagne contemporaine*. Paris: M. Lévy frères, 1864, pp. 293-314.

For Benjumea, the *Quijote* represents an apology of chivalric novels, not an attack on them. It also forms a vast allegorical system. Dulcinea, for example, represents science, wisdom, civilization, *l'ame objective du héro*. In addition, Benjumea believes the novel is autobiographical; particularly, he suggests that Cervantes used his work to attack Juan Blanco de Paz, who had persecuted him both in Algiers and in Spain.

Benjumea's ideas are highly imaginative but false. Cervantes' greatness stems from his generous human instincts and his ability to speak strongly and in a manner understandable to all intellects. As an allegory filled with hidden doctrine the *Quijote* would have no charm. As for autobiography, Blanco de Paz may be personified in the novel, but the *Quijote* is too varied and grand a book to represent a diatribe against one person.

307. Sainte-Beuve, Charles Auguste. "Don Quichotte." *Nouveaux Lundis*, VIII. Paris: C. Lévy, 1879, pp. 1-68. [Articles dated May 9, 16, and 23, 1864.]

The *Quijote* is a most enjoyable book. While it was begun almost at random and had as its goal only the satire of books of chivalry, it quickly became a complete mirror of the world in which its author chastises humanity without ever being offensive.

There is little hidden meaning in the novel, and Cervantes should be praised for the vivacity of his characters. Regarding the readers, those with cold judgment prefer the 1615 *Quijote*, while those who are more poetic, who enjoy fantasy, prefer the earlier part.

Certain critics, such as Germond de Lavigne, were wrong to prefer the spurious *Quijote* of Avellaneda and to find Cervantes to be "un esprit léger, frivole et vagabond." Also to be condemned are those who assert that the *Quijote* contains political or historical satire. Sismondi, with his philosophical and aesthetic interpretation of the novel, is mistaken to view the *Quijote* as a sad and serious work about a noble figure. This approach does not grasp its light and satirical style.

Cervantes was a man of genius who retained his humor, compassion, and imagination through a life of extreme misfortunes. It is impossible to find either the bitterness of Alceste or the fine satire of Lesage in the *Quijote*.

308. Chasles, Emile. "Cervantès." *Revue des Cours Littéraires de la France et de l'Etranger*, April 15, 1865: 326-29. [Soirées littéraires de la Sorbonne. Conference de M. Emile Chasles.]

Cervantes drew freely on his life in composing the *Quijote*. He amused himself by painting his self-portrait in the adventures of the sublime, incorrigible, ragged hidalgo. Before beginning the book when he was sixty, the author had lived as an enthusiast and as a knight. The *Quijote* was an act of courage as well as genius.

Cervantes was trying to tell Spain about its problems. The author broke with the intellectual regime of his times; he studied Spain and pronounced judgment on it. Thus Cervantes served his homeland with enthusiasm as a young man and with joyous and healthy irony when he grew old. Cervantes was wise but not prophetic. In his writings Cervantes sought to avoid pedantry, falsehood, and cruelty. He believed in good humor; his break with his own contemporaries did not have to be either an insult or an apostasy. His love for Spain, his enthusiasm for the arts, his noble taste for speaking and doing good all burst forth in a marvelous work.

309. Gautier, Léon. *Etudes littéraires pour la défense de l'église*. Paris: Poussiel-gue et fils, 1865, pp. 80-81.

Hugo's inclusion of Lucretius, Rabelais, and Cervantes in his list of fourteen great writers is objectionable. Including Cervantes among those who have guided humanity is scandalous. Genius is joyous, not derisive, and since Cervantes ridiculed chivalry (and would have gladly crushed it under his heel), he cannot be termed a genius.

310. Reynald, M. H. "Don Quichotte." *Revue des Cours Littéraires de la France et de l'Etranger*, July 22, 1865: 559-65.

Books of chivalry are flawed by their extravagant and absurd deeds, impossible style, and advocacy of rashness and idolatry. In contrast, Cervantes' style brings characters to life and represents a middle ground between the idealistic (heroic) and the realistic (picaresque). Cervantes' gaiety should be contrasted to the bitter irony of Swift, the cruelty of Voltaire, and the despair of Byron.

Don Quijote is a monomaniac who is insane on the subject of chivalry, but otherwise sensible, and whose good traits include courtesy, bravery, delicacy, and generosity. Cervantes comes to love his hero and the other characters and communicates this feeling to the reader. In Part II, trans-formation toward goodness occurs without loss of unity of the characters. Just enough of chivalric madness in the Knight and of drollness in the Squire carry over, but Sancho is less gluttonous and more wise, while Don Quijote becomes somewhat saner.

The two protagonists personify the Spain of the author's era: Sancho is the old Christian and Don Quijote is the defender of Church and Crown, a man whose brave but foolish acts typify those of his people.

Cervantes' novel is comparable to the works of Rabelais and Ariosto: all three writers attack the Middle Ages, its ideas, and institutions. However, Rabelais represents an uproarious return to Nature and Ariosto lightly attacks the chivalric deeds of true heroes. Cervantes goes not as far as Rabelais but farther than Ariosto.

311. Chasles, Emile. *Michel de Cervantès: sa vie, son temps, son oeuvre politique et littéraire.* Second edition. Paris: Didier et Cie, 1866, pp. 287-345 and 444-51. [First edition also 1866.]

Cervantes' novel is a mixture of diverse elements: it is a personal creation by an independent-minded author and a universal judgment on all of Spain. Cervantes wants Spain to recognize itself in the image that he presents. However, Cervantes was not a malcontent, as Lord Byron suggests; his only goal was to criticize false ideas and sentiments such as platonic love, feudal pride, and chivalresque madness. He fought for truth, which he believed to be more beautiful than beauty itself.

Numerous previous interpretations of the *Quijote,* including Ticknor's view that the popularity of the chivalric novel was due to Catholic credulity, are mistaken. Cervantes' contemporaries did not understand his novel; the true interpretation is to be found in the author himself. Cervantes joined art to the observation of man: he saw what was mysterious in the human soul. At the bottom of the novel is a monologue as in the works of Saint Augustine and Rousseau.

As for the Knight and the Squire, Cervantes does not favor one or the other. At first, Sancho seems to represent common sense, and Don Quijote foolishness, but if one meditates over the book, the suggested meanings are more complex. To understand the *Quijote,* one must follow Cervantes' thought between 1598 and 1616 and listen to what he says when he speaks directly of poetry, literature, and Spanish society.

312. Saint-Victor, Paul de. "Don Quichotte." *Hommes et dieux.* In *Etudes d'histoire et de littérature.* Paris: M. Lévy frères, 1867, pp. 441-56.

While the *Quijote* was first considered a masterpiece of pure buffoonery, it later came to be seen as a heroic-tragic drama. Don Quijote is the last representative of chivalry. He, unlike such figures as Panurge, Falstaff, and Scapin (Molière), engenders respect while he makes us laugh. He conceals the soul of a hero beneath the disguise of a fool, and his most absurd acts are the deviations of a sublime idea. Don Quijote's only crime is having been born three centuries too late. He is the living anachronism of the Cid and of Bernardo del Carpio. His folly is only a monomania: outside his *idée fixe,* Don Quijote is the wisest and the most eloquent of men.

Cervantes conceived his hero in a burst of laughter and finished him with a tender smile. In Part I of the work Cervantes treats his hero cruelly, but his lucid intervals increase as the novel moves along. Sancho is influenced by the Knight's ideals and becomes less vulgar and less gluttonous. In his devotion to his master he is purified.

313. Chasles, Philarète. "Cervantès et ses contemporains." In *Voyages d'un critique à travers la vie et les livres: Italie et Espagne.* Paris: Didier, 1868, pp. 219-66.

Cervantes was a heroic individual who, in all his hardships, never grew cynical, servile, or misanthropic. He always managed to maintain a good smile. His heroism was of the past, but his spirit, of the future. Cervantes was an abolitionist, a writer devoted to human rights and opposed to the low moral standards of his time.

The *Quijote* is a model of philosophical satire, replete with contradictions and incongruities. Cervantes could not satisfy fantasy, good sense, and the reader all at the same time.

314. Poitou, Eugène. *Voyage en Espagne*. Tours: Alfred Mame et fils, 1869, pp. 47-54.

Cervantes is charming, profound, original, truthful, and eternally admirable. The *Quijote* outgrew its initial satirical purpose and became most instructive and kindly. It belongs to all times and to all human life; it is a living image of humanity in its myriad aspects.

The Spanish character is bloodthirsty and enamored of the gruesome, but Cervantes, while in most regards Spanish, is full of human feelings; human miseries sadden him. Sometimes he laughs at sorrows, but he does so without bitterness; and if he exaggerates noble sentiments, he does not ridicule them. The golden mean lies between the chimerical enthusiasm of the Knight and the commonplace world of the Squire. Here true courage and true wisdom lie.

315. Lacroix, Octave. "Michel de Cervantès." *Journal Officiel de l'Empire de France*, January 18, 1870: 116-18. [A review of Emile Chasles' *Michel de Cervantès: sa vie, son temps, son oeuvre politique et littéraire*.]

Spaniards of Cervantes' times only saw the gaiety and irony of the *Quijote*, and most regarded the novel as merely a satire directed at books of chivalry. Cervantes deserves from Spaniards the kind of patient study given to Dante by the Italians.

316. Puymaigre, Comte de. "La Bibliothèque de Don Quichotte." *Correspondant* (Paris) 93 (November 10, 1873): 548-62.

Censured books in Don Quijote's library shed light on the novel. Among them is *Amadís de Gaula*, an influential and stylistically admirable chivalric novel published in twenty-two editions between 1510 and 1587. *Amadís de Gaula* can be read without the difficulty presented by many books of the chivalric genre, such as the *Sergas de Esplandián* and the *Amadís de Grecia*.

Olivarte de Laura and *Felixmarte de Hircania* are rare volumes included in Don Quijote's library. The latter was supposedly translated from the Italian. Racine describes both the *Felixmarte* and its translation this way: "Point n'ont voulu l'avoir fait l'un ni l'autre?" Another volume, *El Caballero de la Cruz*, was supposedly written first by an Arabic chronicler, and this may have given

Cervantes the idea for his fictitious historian, Cide Hamete Benengeli. *Palmerín de Inglaterra* is similar to *Amadís de Gaula* in characters and style.

Tirante el Blanco, supposedly translated from the English, has been viewed as a precursor of the *Quijote* because of its ironic attitude toward the chivalric ideal. Many of the editions of this work, such as the 1511 Spanish translation of Valladolid, are extremely rare.

The pastoral novels in the collection were influenced by the *Arcadia* of Sannazaro. They are a strange mixture of paganism, magic, nymphs, muses, chivalry, Christians, and Moors. Although their verse is pleasant at times (Montemayor's *Diana*), they are often tiresome reading. Alonso Pérez' sequel to the *Diana* is not as successful as Gil Polo's. Antonio Lofrasso's *Diez libros de fortuna d'amor* was mocked in the *Quijote* and in the *Viaje del Parnaso*. Montalvo's *Pastor de Fílida* is an unusual work in that all the characters are courtiers instead of shepherds. In the *Galatea* many characters are real people: Cervantes is Elicio, and Galatea is either a mistress or the wife of Cervantes. This book gives clues to Cervantes' mature works.

To understand the *Quijote* better, one should be familiar with the works in Don Quijote's library, despite difficulty in locating them.

317. Gebhart, Emile. "La Bibliothèque de don Quichotte." *Revue Bleue, Politique et Littéraire* 17 (1876): 567-70.

The *Quijote* is a book that marks the moment when Spain, influenced by the intellectual life of Europe, joins in the critical spirit of the Renaissance. Chivalric tales had grown popular in Spain as they were being killed by the analytical spirit in the rest of Europe, but the senseless readers of books of chivalry were the true wise men: at least they were happy. The day Don Quijote came to understand the vanity of his idle fancies, he died of a broken heart.

318. Louveau, E. *De la manie dans Cervantès*. Montpellier: Imprimerie Centrale du Midi, 1876. 54 pages.

Cervantes was a born psychiatrist who sought to reveal in one being all the manifestations of madness that he had observed in a number of cases. There are causes, physical symptoms, and hallucinations evident as Don Quijote's madness progresses from an ill-defined state to a definitive fixation. There exists a contrast between the Knight's indifference to his stallion and Sancho's healthy feelings for Dapple. Generally, Cervantes contrasts Don Quijote's unusual intelligence and perverse emotions with Sancho's healthy state.

319. Mérimée, Prosper. "Dialogue: La Comtesse—Le Chevalier." *La Gazette Anecdotique, Littéraire, Artistique et Bibliographique* (Paris) 1 (November 30, 1876): 294-97.

[In reply to the Comtesse's assertion that the *Quijote* is a book for children, the Chevalier (Don Quijote) states that the pleasantries of the story are unique. He declares that the book is not only amusing but also a fine painting of Spanish customs: Its style mixes the light with the serious and the characters are original.]

320. T. B. "Ecrits sur Cervantès." *L'Intermédiaire des Chercheurs et des Curieux* 10 (1877): 251.

[T. B. briefly notes various works by nineteenth-century critics of the *Quijote*, including Morejón, Sainte-Beuve, Inglis, Roscoe, and Biedermann.]

321. Starn, René de. "Voltaire et Cervantès." *L'Intermédiaire des Chercheurs et des Curieux* 12 (1879): 91-92.

On two occasions Voltaire referred to Cervantes: (1) Letter V to the Prince of Brunswick; (2) a letter to the King of Prussia, November 11, 1740.

322. Demogeot, J. "Italie-Espagne." In *Histoire des littératures étrangères.* Third edition. Paris: Hachette et Cie, 1892, pp. 254-65. [First published in 1880.]

Cervantes had no clear purpose when he began his work. His thought developed as the writing progressed. At first the *Quijote* is a parody of a gentleman who reads so many books of chivalry that he takes them to be true history and goes out ill-prepared to save the world. However, the novel develops into a tableau of true and living characters. Don Quijote becomes a real individual and the author comes to know and love him. He gives him a generous spirit, a sense of honor, and such nobility and love that the reader shares the author's affection and even admiration for him.

Sancho's development is even more noticeable. He begins as merely a foil to his master. Yet the Squire, with the Barataria episode, becomes a subtle mixture of credulity and astuteness.

Critics such as Bouterwek, Simonde de Sismondi, and Baret have turned the two protagonists into symbols of poetry and prose, while others see them representing imagination and common sense. But this was not Cervantes' intention. Such a lengthy symbolic novel was not characteristic of the era. Cervantes was not a systematic thinker, and his main characters are too complex to be mere symbols in the Benjumean sense.

323. Montégut, Emile. "Don Quichotte." In *Types littéraires et fantaisies esthétiques.* Paris: Hachette, 1882, pp. 43-92.

Don Quijote symbolizes the painful contrast between the aspirations of noble souls and commonplace reality. He also represents his author through his adventures and his spirit. However, it is doubtful that the adventures of the Knight and the Squire stand for the struggle of mind and body.

To consider Don Quijote a personification of sixteenth-century Spain does not strain the text. The tragic story of the Spanish soul is told with a silent rage by a witness to the pointlessness of its grandeur and the folly of its heroism. The *Quijote* is the work of a saddened patriot whose reason conflicts with his heart and who cannot help loving what he curses. Despite this mixture of feelings, the story remains harmonious.

Don Quijote is more than a symbol of Spain. He was and is a largely historical figure. He is also a fool, but for only the first three chapters of Part I. Later, the folly of heroism becomes the folly of love. Don Quijote is not really mad; his illness is only a hallucination. He lacks the necessary vanity for madness, vanity being the basis of all insanity.

324. Larroumet, Gustave. *Marivaux: sa vie et ses ouevres d' après de nouveaux documents*, III: *Le Romancier*. Geneva: Slatkine Reprints, 1970, pp. 328-32. [Reprint of Paris edition of 1882.]

Pharsamon ou les folies romanesques, Marivaux's parody of chivalric love, is the story of a Don Quijote of a more common sort. Recovered from his fantasies, Cervantes' hero does not care to go on living; Pharsamon, having recovered from love, quickly consoles himself in a rather ignoble state of comfort. While the good Knight of La Mancha is generous and concerned with justice and honor, the village gentleman of Marivaux is petty, flighty, and full of hollow phrases. The squire Cliton would like to resemble Sancho, but does not succeed. In vain he responds to the platonic effusions of his master with tirades that are trivial. He lacks everything needed to equal his model: basic goodness, humor, and enthusiasm.

The battle of Pharsamon with the apprentice cooks is somewhat witty but still imitative of Don Quijote's more energetic combat with the muleteers; the country wedding of Pharsamon is but a faint echo of the wedding of Camacho. Also, in Marivaux's work the plot is loose, characters are barely described, episodes are too long, and action is too deliberate. Worst of all, Marivaux completely misunderstood what attracts interest in Cervantes' novel. The *Quijote* is amusing because it contrasts the ideas and behavior of a former age, adopted by the hero to the best of his ability, to the completely different ideas of a society which no longer understands anything about chivalry. This contrast does not exist in Marivaux's novel. Pharasmon lives among people as foolish as he, and his misadventures never result from an opposition between the chimera of the past and the reality of the present. Thus Marivaux's hero lacks interest and his work fails.

325. Scherer, Edmond. *Etudes sur la littérature contemporaine*, VII. Paris: C. Lévy, 1882, pp. 84-97.

In Part II of the *Quijote* adventures tend to become mystifications and

Sancho is the real hero. The 1605 *Quijote* is better because the continuation has a burdensome burlesque tone. Also, the episodes in Part II are too short, too dull, and too vague to achieve verisimilitude, and the protagonists often step out of character. Much would be lacking if Cervantes had not completed his novel, but the second part itself would not have been a masterpiece.

Cervantes wrote the *Quijote* partly to earn money and partly to satirize books of chivalry. The true artist does not proceed in order to prove a thesis; the reader must search for Cervantes' hidden purpose. A writer's work is more revealing than his announced intentions.

Cervantes is more than a comic writer; he is a humorist, that is, he satirizes not with self-assured detachment, but with compassion, regarding folly as the common lot of man. Cervantes' humor consists more of things and deeds than of words. The amusing effects arise more from the hero's character and adventures than from Cervantes' own intrusions.

The novel's originality lies especially in its presentation of characters. Paradoxically, the hero is foolish and mad, but he makes us admire him because of the loftiness of his sentiments. Don Quijote is the visionary hero grappling with the vulgarities of real life. Sancho, on the other hand, is vulgarity struggling with heroism. His simplicity is redeemed by his good sense.

326. Gautier, Léon. "Dédicace" to *La Chevalerie*. Paris: La Palmé, 1883, pp. ix-xi.

The author of the *Quijote* unwittingly dealt chivalry a fatal blow. Cervantes did in Spain what Rabelais had done in France: he destroyed love of the ideal and replaced it with love of the real. Cervantes' great fault was in not foreseeing the consequences of his work.

327. Laffitte, Paul. "Cervantès et son *Don Quichotte*." *Magasin Pittoresque*, Série II, vol. 1 (September, 1883): 297-306.

Cervantes' life has influence on his work. For example, in the 1605 *Quijote*, written when Cervantes was living an itinerant life, the order of the adventures is not important. Episodes in the 1615 sequel, however, written when the author was leading a sedentary life in Madrid, are well tied together. The hero seems to grow old with Cervantes himself, and at the end they become almost inseparable. Cervantes deliberately put a part of himself in his spiritual son, Don Quijote. The comic element is dominant in Part I of the novel, while Part II fully illuminates the noble and elevated elements in the hero's character.

Adolfo de Castro was right in saying that Cervantes wrote the *Entremés de los romances*, but he developed the earlier figure Bartolo, adding many sympathetic traits, as he created Don Quijote.

328. Gebhart, Emile. "Préface" to *Le Roman de Don Quichotte*. Paris: Imp. Jouaust et Sigaux, 1884, pp. 1-11.

The *Quijote* is among the most popular foreign books in France. It is the patrimony of all civilized peoples.

Spain was the most naturally chivalric country of Christendom during the Middle Ages. At that time the Spaniards fought the Reconquest and then remembered it in their literature. In the fifteenth and sixteenth centuries chivalric literature was revived, but the Spanish did not treat it with the irony seen in other European literature. An ironic view of chivalry did not appear in Spain until the literary manifesto of Part I of the *Quijote*, and even there the irony was tempered. Don Quijote was a man whom chivalry made demure, loyal, and even heroic. He lived, however, in an unsuitable age.

There is an autobiographical element in the novel as hardships and misfortunes of heroes were part of Cervantes' own experience. He had fought in Italy and Africa and taken part in the supreme victory over the Turks at Lepanto. As his own hero travels through Spain, he too suffers much travail.

As for the characters, Don Quijote has been seen as poetic and Sancho as prosaic. The latter is gluttonous and lazy, yet sensible. He also is faithful to a master affected with madness.

Sancho surely deserves to be the protagonist temporarily. As it turns out, he becomes the leading character in the novel when he acts as governor of the promised island. The two characters illuminate each other, while conflict and human contradictions abound.

Despite its Spanish origins, the *Quijote* is the most European of all novels.

329. Daudet, Alphonse. *Tartarin de Tarascon*. Paris: E. Flammarion, 1887, pp. 34-36.

Our protagonist combines elements of the Knight and the Squire: The soul of Don Quijote, full of chivalresque impulses, heroic ideals, and grandiose madness, was contained in a fat, clumsy, and soft body of bourgeois appetites. Don Quijote and Sancho Panza in the same man! You understand what a bad combination this must make; what struggles, what contradictions!

330. Hignard, H. "Etude de littérature comparée: *Don Quichotte et Pickwick-Club.*" *Revue du Lyonnais* 5 (1889): 180-92.

Dickens' Pickwick was evidently influenced by Don Quijote. The two works have similar frameworks and heroes. Both men seek to aid humanity and both are a bit foolish (though Pickwick is certainly less foolish than the Knight). Yet neither is a purely comic figure, for each provokes thought.

Both heroes have companions who tell droll stories, use earthy expressions, and represent common sense.

331. Monge, Léon de. "Don Quichotte." In *Etudes morales et littéraires*, II. Louvain: Ch. Peeters, 1889, pp. 276-313.

[In a fictitious conversation about the *Quijote*, Le Président, L'Abée, and L'Archiviste participate, and their principal subject is the anti-heroic interpretation of Léon Gautier, who admired Cervantes the man but was repelled by the anti-chivalric tone of his novel. Le Président vehemently disagrees with Gautier's view. Instead, he regards the *Quijote* as the revenge of common sense and Christianity against the contagious folly of books of knight-errantry. It is not a pessimistic work, in his view.

The trio also discuss the life of Cervantes, the meaning of the title *caballero* in the author's time, Don Quijote's literary love for Dulcinea, and the interpolated tales. While conceding that Don Quijote has a generous side, Le Président refuses to accept the belief that Cervantes attacked that aspect of his hero's character. For Le Président, the Knight is a man who will not examine himself in good faith and only begins to doubt during the cave of Montesinos episode.]

332. Barbey d'Aurévilly, Jules. "Avellaneda." In *Les Oeuvres et les hommes*. Paris: Alphonse Lemerre, 1890, pp. 95-106.

Cervantes' novel mocks the past, insults tradition, and attacks the most beautiful customs that have ever existed. It is a work of old age that derides the youthful preoccupations of the author. If the novel is funny, its melancholy is more powerful.

Don Quijote is comparable to Job because both retain something of the ideal. Sancho is comparable to Panurge, Falstaff, and Figaro in his worldly wisdom. In the Avellaneda continuation, the Squire has grown dense and coarse, and Don Quijote has become a complete fool.

333. Morel-Fatio, Alfred. "Comment la France a connu et compris l'Espagne depuis le moyen âge jusqu'à nos jours." In *Etudes sur l'Espagne*, I. Paris: E. Bouillon, 1890, pp. 1-114.

The *Quijote* is a novel in which the philosophical import equals, if not excels, the charm of its invention and style.

334. Morel-Fatio, Alfred. "Duelos y quebrantos." In *Etudes romanes dédiées a Gaston Paris le 29 decembre, 1890*. Paris: E. Bouillon, 1891, pp. 407-18.

Regarding attempts to explain the expression "duelos y quebrantos," which is used in the first chapter of the 1605 *Quijote* to describe Don Quijote's Saturday diet, the views of Oudin, L. Franciosini, Pellicer, Puigblanch, Quevedo, and the Royal Academy should be noted. The expression refers to the custom of semiabstinence, the eating of only entrails (*grosura*) on Saturdays.

335. Wyzewa, T. de. "Les Allusions contemporaines dans le *Don Quichotte.*" *Revue des Deux Mondes,* November 15, 1894: 452-56.

The *Quijote* has a continuing popularity in Spain, and there is a constant flow of books about Cervantes' novel. For Benigno Pallol, who seeks to determine the hidden meaning in the novel, Don Quijote was born in La Mancha to signify that we are all born with the stain (*mancha*) of ignorance, etc. J. M. Asensio's notes on the *Quijote,* published in *España Moderna,* deal in detail with such matters as the early editions of the novel and the corrections and suppressions. Asensio also discusses efforts by the Royal Academy to recover two supposedly lost chapters of the *Quijote;* he also mentions an Italian edition of the *Quijote* in which the dedication to the Duke of Béjar is replaced by a dedication to Count Vitaliano Visconti. Asensio does not regard the novel as a caricature of Charles V, as certain of Cervantes' contemporaries may have done. Asensio does concede that there are personal allusions in the story, but he believes they will never be unraveled.

336. Cabanès, Dr. "Cervantès médecin." *Chronique Médicale,* March 15, 1895: 173-79.

Both Louveau and Morejón regarded Cervantes as a gifted psychiatrist. Morejón dealt at length with the various causes of Don Quijote's madness, including poor diet, lack of sleep, transition from activity to inactivity, and excessive reading. For Louveau, Cervantes sought to sum up in one person the physical and moral manifestations of madness that he had observed in a large number of individuals. Louveau's ideas are superior to those of Morejón in view of the progress of psychiatry in the late nineteenth century.

Don Quijote did not die sane; he was born mad, lived mad, and died of melancholy.

German Criticism

337. Schiller, Johann Christoph Friedrich. "Vorrede zur ersten Auflage." *Die Räuber.* In *Sämtliche Werke*, I. Munich: Carl Hanser Verlag, 1965, p. 486. [Dated 1781.]

A protagonist's false concept of his power and influence, when it supersedes all laws, must naturally collide with established society. If we add to these enthusiastic dreams of greatness and unbounded activity a feeling of bitterness against an imperfect world, then we have in full form the strange figure of Don Quijote, whom we abhor and love, admire and pity, in the thief Karl Moor.

338. Heinse, Johann Jakob Wilhelm. *Sämtliche Werke*, VIII. Edited by Albert Leitzmann. Leipzig: 1925, pp. 253-54. [Dated 1790. Heinse's views on the *Quijote* are discussed by Werner Vordtriede in "Wilhelm Heinse's Share in the German Interest in Spanish Literature," *Journal of English and Germanic Philology* 48 (1949): 88-96.]

[Heinse's first interpretation of the *Quijote* was rationalistic—an attack on excessive enthusiasm (Don Quijote) and an affirmation of reason (Sancho Panza). However, after a trip to Italy, between 1780 and 1783, where he became aware of the *Quijote* in the original, Heinse moved away from the orthodox Enlightenment view of that novel. Even before such writers as Herder and the romantics, Heinse came to recognize the national character of the *Quijote* as well as the necessity of the interpolated episodes, the novel's realism, and the naïve directness of the artistic experience, which is in direct opposition to the moralizing tone of rationalistic writing.

Although Heinse realized that Don Quijote was ridiculed by Cervantes, he came to regard the Knight, rather than Sancho, as the true hero of the work. Nevertheless, Heinse does complain of the excessive drubbings Don Quijote receives and believes that Cervantes should have heightened the romantic aspect of Spain.]

339. Herder, Johann Gottfried. "Rittergeist in Europa." *Ideen zur Philosophie der Geschichte der Menschheit*, IV, Buch 20. In *Sämtliche Werke*, XIV. Hildesheim: Georg Olms, 1967, p. 460. [Dated 1791.]

[Herder notes how deep-seated chivalric roots were in Spain and briefly considers Cervantes' use of such sources in the *Quijote*.]

340. Herder, Johann Gottfried. "Blumen aus morgenländischen Dichtern gesammelt." In *Sämtliche Werke*, XVI. Hildesheim: Georg Olms 1967, p. 23. [Dated 1792.]

Proverbs are a reflection of a people's way of living and thinking. Sancho Panza, whose only wisdom is a treasure of proverbs, has since been treated widely in literature. Proverbs are short, powerful, and often ingenious sayings that serve as axioms of moral thought.

341. Tieck, Johann Ludwig. *Shakespeares Behandlung des Wunderbaren*. In *Kritische Schriften*, I. Leipzig: Brockhaus, 1848, pp. 49-50. [Dated 1793.]

Cervantes could have ended his novel more satisfactorily if he had put merely one adventure in his hero's way that his fantasy could not distort. This would have enabled Cervantes to rid his hero little by little of his delusions and he would have gained the means of separating error from truth.

342. Schiller, Johann Cristoph Friedrich. *Über naive und sentimentalische Dichtung*. In *Gesammelte Werke*, V. Berlin: S. Mohn, 1961, pp. 517-23. [First published 1795-1796 in *Die Horen*.]

A satirical writer is one who contrasts reality with the ideal, and Cervantes is a satirist striving for an ideal.

343. Herder, Johann Gottfried. "Brief 88." *Briefe zu Beförderung der Humanität*. In *Sämtliche Werke*, XVIII. Hildesheim: Georg Olms, 1967, p. 57. [Dated 1796.]

When I read the works of Dante, Petrarch, Ariosto, and Cervantes I seek to understand only the author and his circumstances. Cervantes belongs to that group of writers who tend to participate in their own works.

344. Tieck, Johann Ludwig. Letter to A. W. von Schlegel, December 23, 1797. In *Ludwig Tieck und die Brüder Schlegel: Briefe*. Munich: Winkler Verlag, 1972, pp. 24-27.

Bertuch, in his translation of Cervantes' novel, is wrong to omit certain portions of the novel, such as poems and love episodes. The translator has no feeling for the romantic tone of the story, its wonderful verses, and its tender descriptions of love. In addition, the true glory of the *Quijote* is largely unrecognized and it is still generally considered to be merely a book of drolleries.

345. Schlegel, August Wilhelm von. "*Leben und Thaten des scharfsinnigen Edlen Don Quixote von La Mancha*, von Miguel de Cervantes Saavedra. Übersetzt von Ludwig Tieck. Erster Band. Berlin, 1799." In *Sämtliche*

Werke, XI. Leipzig: Weidmann'sche Buchhandlung, 1847, pp. 408-26. [First published in *Allgemeine Literaturzeitung*, Nos. 230-31 (1799).]

When Cervantes destroyed the absurd and colossal novelistic world of chivalric romances, he created a new romantic realm based on native customs of his times. Some readers complain of the endless beatings which Cervantes gives to his hero, and the dosage is strong, but Cervantes' imitative powers must be praised, especially his depiction of the lower classes.

Considering the relevance of the *Curioso impertinente* to the overall plot, the *Quijote* would be defective *if* cause and effect of the episodes were the criterion. However, the novel as a genre is episodic; interpolated episodes can be found even in Homer's *Odyssey*. Those who find the 1615 *Quijote* to be inferior to Part I are mistaken; it is only natural that Don Quijote should not clash as violently with society in the continuation.

346. Schlegel, Friedrich von. "Tiecks Ubersetzung des *Don Quixote* von Cervantes." In *Kritische Schriften*. Munich: Carl Hanser Verlag, 1971, pp. 256-58. [From *Athenäum* 2 (1799).]

Tieck's manner of capturing the tone and color of Cervantes' novel is praiseworthy. Readers should no longer consider Cervantes a purely comic writer, but see his subtle skills. Cervantes wrote unique prose; Lope de Vega's was raw and common, and Quevedo's bitter and harsh.

347. Tieck, Johann Ludwig. *Prinz Zerbino oder Die Reise nach dem guten Geschmack*. In *Schriften*, X. Berlin: G. Reimer, 1828, pp. 278-80. [Dated 1799.]

The character Nestor says that he considers the *Quijote* a funny book, but wonders what the interpolated tales are doing in it. In his reply to Nestor, Cervantes observes that Don Quijote raised the same question.

348. Humboldt, Wilhelm von. "Der Montserrat bei Barcelona." In *Werke*, III: 1799-1818. Berlin: B. Behr, 1904, pp. 30-31. [As reprinted in Berlin by W. de Gruyter, 1968. Dated 1800.]

In order to understand a people's character and literature thoroughly, one must visit their country. This is especially true in the case of Cervantes, for his Knight and Squire are taken from Spanish life itself. Those who have not visited Spain and met the types that Cervantes describes would falsely conclude that his two protagonists are mere caricatures.

349. Schlegel, August Wilhelm von. "Cervantes." In *Sämtliche Werke*, I. Leipzig: Weidmann'sche Buchhandlung, 1846, pp. 338-43. [Dated 1800.]

[Schlegel presents six sonnets on Cervantes' life and works: "Sein

Leben," "Galatea," "Das Trauerspiel Numancia," "Die Leiden des Persiles und der Sigismunda," "Don Quixote de la Mancha," and "Die Reise auf den Parnass." The sonnet to Don Quijote contains the oft-quoted contrast of Don Quijote and Sancho as that of "Ritterpoesie" and "Prosa," in continuous dialogue.]

350. Schlegel, August Wilhelm von. "Soltau, Uebersetzung des *Don Quixote*, 1800." In *Sämtliche Werke*, XII. Leipzig: Weidmann'sche Buchhandlung, 1847, pp. 106-33. [From *Athenäum* 3 (1800).]

The Soltau translation of the *Quijote* contains significant errors, and Soltau fails to distinguish the spontaneous speech of Cervantes' era from the antiquated style used at times by Don Quijote. He also mishandles both the wordplay and the comic portions of the novel, often overdoing them. The beauty, artistic structure, symmetry, and the tender, spiritual charm of Cervantes' work, all of which are lacking in Soltau's translation, are present in Tieck's translation.

351. Schlegel, Friedrich von. "Gespräch über die Poesie." In *Kritische Schriften*. Munich: Carl Hanser Verlag, 1971, pp. 473-529. [From *Athenäum* 3 (1800).]

The 1605 *Quijote* is the principal work of the second phase of Cervantes' career in which extravagance of audacious inventiveness prevails. Some of the humorous *novelas* were also written during this period. In the 1615 *Quijote* Cervantes did take note of the criticism of Part I, but nevertheless remained able to satisfy himself by turning this criticism back on itself as he used it.

352. Herder, Johann Gottfried. "Von romantischen Charakteren." In *Sämtliche Werke*, XXIII. Hildesheim: Georg Olms, 1967, pp. 175-80. [From *Adrastea* 1 (1801).]

Romantic characters appear to be from and belong to another world; they love the unusual rather than everyday goals. Sometimes a romantic character will burst forth in his later years, like Don Quijote, who read books of chivalry night and day until he lost his senses. The proselytizing leaders of this day should also be considered romantic figures, comparable to Don Quijote, who endeavors to convert Sancho Panza. The more out of touch with reality a given sect is, the more zealous it is.

353. Schelling, Friedrich W. J. von. *Philosophie der Kunst*. Darmstadt: Wissenschaftliche Buchgesellschaft, 1960, pp. 311, 318-19, and 320-24. [Lectures delivered at Jena and later at Würzburg, 1802-1805.]

The *Quijote* is not a satire but an example of mythology created by an individual genius, because Don Quijote and Sancho are mythological figures and their adventures are mythological sagas. What might have seemed to be a satire of a madman Cervantes turns into a universal portrait of life. Its two parts might be considered the *Iliad* and the *Odyssey* of the novel.

The overall theme of the work is the conflict between the real and the ideal. In Part I, 1605, the ideal is treated naturalistically and realistically (i.e. the ideal of the hero clashes with the everyday world); in Part II, 1615, the ideal becomes *"mystificirt"* (i.e. the world with which the ideal comes in conflict is itself an ideal, not the usual world). The mystification, to be sure, becomes ridiculous so that the idealism of Don Quijote is weakened underneath. Yet, it appears to be triumphant in contrast to the extraordinary commonness of the antagonists (such as the Duke and Duchess). Thus, Cervantes' novel depends on an imperfect, even mad, hero, who is nonetheless noble and understanding. Cervantes predominantly draws on everyday events and people such as galley slaves, a puppet show, and a lion in a cage; love, on the other hand, always takes place in romantic surroundings, so that the whole novel is set under open skies in warm air and heightened by southern color.

354. Tieck, Johann Ludwig. *Die altdeutschen Minnelieder*. In *Kritische Schriften*, I. Leipzig: Brockhaus, 1848, pp. 207-08. [Originally published in 1803.]

Cervantes, seeing how far poetry had become separated from life in the *Amadís* and its successors, invented out of love of poetry and the marvelous a most daring joke in order to join poetry and life together again despite their disharmony. His *Don Quijote*, which consciously and unconsciously influenced the entire age, reflects an unfathomable spirit in which parody is constanty genuine poetry in such a way that one cannot determine if the poetry is not to be entirely construed as parody. Such a bright humor flashes through the entire work, and one is never certain whether he is seeing clearly or is merely being deceived.

355. Bouterwek, Friedrich. *History of Spanish Literature*. Translated from the German by Thomasina Ross. London: David Bogue, 1847, pp. 230-53. [From vol. 3 of *Geschichte der Poesie und Beredsamkeit seit dem Ende des dreizehnten Jahrhunderts*, Göttingen: Röwer, 1804.]

The *Quijote* is much more than an attack on chivalric romances. It is an original conception concerning the restoration of the past by a man of elevated character, heightened by Cervantes' poetic inspiration along with his classical perfection of expression. Cervantes combines his knowledge of mankind, gained through experience, with the most delicate satire, and as a result renders his comic romance a book of moral inspiration. Particularly praiseworthy are the vivid characters portrayed in the novel, as well as the use of solemn language to give relief to the comic scenes.

Episodes are varied, and the romantic portions prove that Cervantes was not merely interested in inciting laughter. With regard to style, the author used an indeterminate tone, between pure poetry and mere prose, without which the *Quijote* would not be considered the first modern novel, because the modern reader desires a certain union between poetry and prose. At the same time, Cervantes restored to poetic art its place in the composition of romance.

356. Herder, Johann Gottfried. "Von der komischen Epopee als einem Correctif des falschen Epos." In *Sämtliche Werke*, XXIV. Hildesheim: Georg Olms, 1967, pp. 362-68. [From *Adrastea* 6 (1804).]

The *Quijote* eradicated the Spanish taste for books of chivalry. What lecturing could not accomplish, the first of all European comic epics was able to achieve.

357. Eberhard, Johann August. "Zweyhundert und erste Brief." In *Handbuch der Aesthetik für gebildete Leser aus allen Ständen*, IV. Halle: Hemmerde und Schwetschke, 1805, pp. 286-87.

The *Quijote* is an attack on the ignorance of the masses and the Catholic Church.

358. Richter, Jean Paul. *Vorschule der Aesthetik*. In *Sämtliche Werke*, XI. Weimar: Hermann Böhlaus Nachfolger, 1935. [First published in 1805.]

Cervantes' genius was too great for a long, drawn-out joke about an accidental case of madness and common simplicity. The novelist carried out, less consciously perhaps than Shakespeare, the humorous parallel between realism and idealism and body and soul in an unending comparison.

359. Bouterwek, Friedrich. "Vorwort" to *Aesthetik*, I. Vienna-Prague, 1807, p. 385. [As quoted by Werner Brüggemann in *Cervantes und die Figur des Don Quijote*, p. 93, fn. 104.]

The idea of the true novel was developed with the *Quijote*, in which poetry and prose meet. The novel then became narrative character portrayal which shifts, in spirit and style, in many diverse ways: one moment toward poetry, another moment toward prose. Then it quickly becomes lost in poetry.

360. Beneke, J. B. W. *Spanisch-deutsches Wörterbuch zum Don Quixote*. Neue wohlfeile Ausgabe. Berlin: Carl J. Klemann, 1841. [First and second editions are in 1808 and 1821 under different titles.]

[The first edition of this dictionary appears to have been published in connection with the publication of a Royal Academy edition of the *Quijote* in

Germany. This is a dictionary designed for German readers who want to read Cervantes' masterpiece in the original.]

361. Schlegel, Friedrich von. "Goethes Werke nach der Cottaschen Ausgabe von 1806." In *Kritische Schriften*. Munich: Carl Hanser Verlag, 1971, pp. 288-322. [Dated 1808.]

In the *Quijote* and Goethe's *Wilhelm Meister* there is a conflict between the heroes' idealism and reality and a certain disillusion in both works. But this similarity is only superficial, for these two works are significantly different. The *Quijote* is romantic throughout, in spite of its irony; *Wilhelm Meister* is not, because in Goethe's work it is not the inner conflict of the hero and his clash with reality that are poetized, but the whole modern world with all its petty details.

362. Schlegel, Friedrich von. "Elfte Vorlesung." *Geschichte der alten und neuen Literatur*. In *Kritische Friedrich-Schlegel Ausgabe*, VI. Munich: Ferdinand Schöningh, 1961, pp. 251-73. [Vienna, 1812.]

Cervantes' novel deserves the fame and admiration throughout Europe which it has had for two centuries. It is noteworthy for its perfection of presentation, its rich invention and genius, its epic picture of Spanish life and character, and the youthful charm it manages to retain, while its many imitators in Spain, France, and England have grown old and been forgotten.

Cervantes, with his rich supply of poetry and interpolated tales, has a right to all liberties which he takes. Those who seek out only the pure satire from Cervantes' novel and ignore the poetry are unquestionably very wrong. In the *Quijote* joking and seriousness, wit and poetry are joined together most fortunately in a rich picture of life, and therefore the *Quijote* is a unique jewel in Spanish literature. Spaniards can justifiably be proud of a novel that is so completely representative of its national character. It is a richly profound view of the life, customs, and spirit of Spain, comparable to an epic poem, but also forging a new and original genre of its own.

363. Schlegel, Friedrich von. "Zwölfte Vorlesung." *Geschichte der alten und neuen Literatur*. In *Kritische Schriften*. Munich: Carl Hanser Verlag, 1971, pp. 601-32. [Vienna, 1812.]

The *Quijote*, a work that is unique in its form, has affected the whole genre of the novel and has inspired a number of unsuccessful imitations among Frenchmen, Englishmen, and Germans. Setting aside Cervantes' genius, the conditions under which the novelist wrote were more favorable than those of his successors, for real life in Spain was at that time more knightly and romantic than in any other land in Europe.

Despite the subsequent efforts to elevate prosaic reality (whether it is through wit and adventure or through genius and the arousing of emotions), novelists are now looking for its poetic future: an artist's life in Italy or life in the American West.

364. Hegel, Georg Wilhelm Friedrich. *Aesthetics: Lectures on the Fine Arts.* 2 vols. Translated by T. M. Knox. Oxford: The Clarendon Press, 1975. [First published in 1835; original title is *Vorlesungen über die Aesthetik*, 1818.]

Adventurousness becomes ridiculous when Cervantes insists that his hero is the sole, legitimate righter of wrongs and helper of the oppressed. In other words, adventurous independence of knights-errant is out of tune with the modern world.

While Ariosto developed the fairy-tale aspect of adventure, Cervantes developed its romantic dimension. Don Quijote is a noble man in whom chivalry becomes lunacy because we find that his adventure-seeking disturbs the stability of the real world. This provides a comic contradiction between the intelligible self-ordered world and an isolated mind that proposes to create order and stability by itself and by chivalry. Despite this comic aberration, however, there is in Don Quijote what we previously eulogized in Shakespeare. Cervantes, too, has given his hero a noble nature, equipped with many spiritual gifts, which truly interest the reader. In his lunacy, Don Quijote is a heart completely sure of itself; in fact, his only madness is that he remains so sure of himself and his business. Without this lack of reflection with regard to the object and outcome of his actions, he would not be genuinely romantic, and this self-assurance is adorned with the finest traits of character. Even so, the whole work is on the one hand a mockery of romantic chivalry, genuinely ironical from beginning to end, while in the case of Ariosto adventure remains, as it were, only a frivolous joke. On the other hand, adventure in the *Quijote* is only the thread on which a chain of genuinely romantic tales is strung in the most charming way.

Cervantes' work is deeper than that of the Italian poet. Cervantes had chivalry behind him, which could enter present-day life only as an isolated illusion and a fantastic madness, and yet, in its noble aspects, it overpowers what is clumsy, senseless, and trivial in commonplace reality, bringing the world's deficiencies vividly before our eyes.

365. Goethe, Johann Wolfgang von. "A Conversation reported by Chancellor von Müller on February 1, 1819." In *Gespräche*, III. Zurich and Stuttgart: Artemis, 1965-1972, pp. 98 et seq. [Spanish version in Rius, III, p. 213.]

Cervantes had the good sense to want to end with the second part because the real motifs had been exhausted by then. As long as the hero has illusions, he is romantic; when he is merely fooled and mystified, all true interest ceases.

366. La Motte-Fouqué, Friedrich Baron de. "Etwas über den *Don Quixote* des Cervantes, nebst einer Nutzanwendung." In *Gefühle, Bilder und Ansichten*, II. Leipzig: Gerhard Fleischer, 1819, pp. 180-94. [Spanish excerpts in Rius, III, pp. 237-39.]

Don Quijote's windmills and fantasies would not be enough to carry the reader over the long run, unless a special principle enlivened or even transformed it into something important. The spirit with which the unfortunate hero is possessed is a certain obsession with identity, but who among us has not at sometime in his life played a particular person that he was not? While this is characteristic of youth, with Don Quijote it takes hold in his mature years, and moreover, he even swaps one foolish scheme (chivalry) for another (pastoral). This leads us to ask if one can ever be sure if his mind is twisted, a dilemma for which Cervantes offers two answers: First, only at the joking Duke's palace does Don Quijote feel that he is a true knight. We all know what monstrous things he had suffered previously because of his conviction, yet he only half believes in the truth of his scheme until tempted. The second which Cervantes offers, and which brings his hero to reflection, is serious and sad. It is the aspect which the world and our aspirations take on at the hour of death, when all that is a lie in us falls away. But this could be a painful and perhaps terrible experience if we did not rid ourselves not only of sin but also of madness, which makes us pass for something other than what we are. Thus, in the last moments, one must realize Don Quijote was never in life either a true knight-errant or a true Arcadian shepherd—a frighteningly painful thought!

367. Schopenhauer, Arthur. *Die Welt als Wille und Vorstellung, Drittes Buch*. In *Sämtliche Werke*, I. Stuttgart: Cotta-Verlag, 1916, p. 338. [First edition is 1819. Translated into English by E. F. J. Payne as *The World as Will and Representation*, I, New York: Dover Publications, 1966, p. 241.]

The *Quijote* and *Gulliver's Travels* are cryptic allegories. The *Quijote* in particular is an allegory of the life of any person who does not look after his own welfare, but pursues an ideal goal that has taken possession of his thought and will.

368. Goethe, Johann Wolfgang von. An 1823 review of a collection of Spanish romances, noted by Eric A. Blackall in *Goethe and the Novel*. Ithaca and London: Cornell University Press, 1976, p. 142. [Blackall cites the 1948-1960 Artemis edition of Goethe's works, *Gedenkausgabe der Werke, Briefe und Gespräche*, edited by Ernst Beutler, Zurich and Stuttgart, XIV, p. 508.]

Cervantes should be praised for maintaining the relationship between the lofty and the ordinary.

369. Bouterwek, Friedrich. *Aesthetik*, II. Dritte, von neuem verbesserte Auflage. Göttingen: Vandenhoeck und Ruprecht, 1825, pp. 268-69.

Satirical novels will remain popular when they achieve a tone that later generations will be willing to listen to. This the remarkable *Don Quijote* has already been able to do as one of the ever-popular novels and an unequaled model of a satire on the unbridled enthusiasm (*Schwärmerei*) which can derange the mind of a great and noble-minded person.

370. Tieck, Johann Ludwig. *Der spanische Dichter Vicente Espinel*. In *Kritische Schriften*, II. Leipzig: Brockhaus, 1848, pp. 68-69 and 74. [Dated 1827.]

Those who call the arrangement of the episodes in the *Quijote* capricious and fortuitous have not understood the novel and are incapable of perceiving the profound plan of a work of art. It is true that the episodes of *Lazarillo de Tormes* and *Guzmán de Alfarache* are not closely tied together and the presentation of scenes in *Gil Blas* is neither original nor exemplary, but the technique of using such tales in the *Quijote* is masterful. The only isolated and therefore often criticized story is the *Curioso impertinente*, but this makes the way in which Cervantes wove this story into his book of chivalry all the more skillful.

371. Heine, Heinrich. *Die Reisebilder* (Italien: Die Stadt Lucca). In *Werke*, VIII. Berlin: Bong & Co., 1908, pp. 193-95. [First published in Hamburg: Hoffman und Campe, 1828.]

Don Quijote's deeds are more praiseworthy in view of the meagerness of his frame, the brittleness of his armor, and the worthlessness of his palfrey. As I was reading I grew to despise the base mob who treated Don Quijote with rudeness, and even more the mob of higher rank, who scorned a man who was in strength of soul so immeasurably their superior.

372. Tieck, Johann Ludwig. *Goethe und seine Zeit*. In *Kritische Schriften*, II. Leipzig: Brockhaus, 1848, p. 184. [Dated 1828.]

Cervantes' *Quijote* is probably the only book in which humor, mirth, jest, parody, poetry, and wit, along with the most daring elements of fantasy and the most bitter elements in real life, have been elevated to a truly artistic level. The poem not only reaches the highest spheres of reason, but is poetic necessity, which governs all from a central place and illuminates everything. What is more, at no single moment does one become disturbingly aware of the necessary limitation of poetic reason because here everything seems to be cheerful caprice and jest.

373. Tieck, Johann Ludwig. *Kritik und deutsches Bücherwesen*. In *Kritische Schriften*, II. Leipzig: Brockhaus, 1848, pp. 147-51. [Dated 1828.]

[In an imaginary conversation with a fictitious friend, Tieck examines whether Cervantes indeed sought to rid the world of the false novels of chivalry. His friend takes the position that the extraordinary effect of the *Quijote* is that even years later it presents reality without false decoration, and that it represents both the marvelous and the poetic. Tieck muses that it is even more striking that the Spanish people continue to love this false and unrealistic literature, which Cervantes was unable to drive away. In reality, Tieck believes that Cervantes himself was a lover of chivalric novels and even in his old age was not able to abandon this proclivity altogether.

With the friend's statement that Cervantes mocked enthusiasm and an earlier more beautiful age Tieck takes issue, stating that those who believe this misunderstand the *Quijote*, for true chivalry had long been dead when Cervantes wrote his novel. The wonderful thing about the *Quijote*, argues Tieck, is that the reader can both admire and laugh at the hero. Moreover, Cervantes' novel is a work filled with genuine enthusiasm for the fatherland, heroism, the life of the soldier, the chivalric way of life, and the king.]

374. Solger, K. W. F. *Vorlesungen über Aesthetik.* Leipzig: Brockhaus, 1829, pp. 296-97.

Nowhere are the episodes more beautiful than in Cervantes' *Don Quijote*, where the interpolated short stories are essential and always have an allegorical relationship to the whole. They also reveal the work's relationship to the epic.

375. Wolf, Ferdinand Joseph. *Historia de la literatura española, escrita en alemán por Bouterwek . . . Studien zur Geschichte der spanischen und portugiesischen Nationalliteratur.* Berlin: A. Asher, 1859, p. 19. [First appeared in *Jahrbücher der Literatur* (Vienna) 55, 56, 57, 58, and 59 (1831-1832).]

Cervantes, like other geniuses, almost unconsciously includes the universal in the particular, so that at the same time he depicts, with tragic irony, in this amusing contrast between the ideal and real that which is eternally human. And all this in a work that serves as the unrivaled model of Spanish prose.

376. Heine, Heinrich. *Die romantische Schule.* In *Sämtliche Werke*, III: *Schriften zu Literatur und Politik*, I. Munich: Winkler-Verlag, 1972, pp. 325-27. [English translation by Charles Godrey Leland (Hans Brietmann) in *The Works of Heinrich Heine*, V, London: William Heinemann, 1892, pp. 353-58. Heine's preface is dated June 30, 1833.]

Both *Hamlet* and the *Quijote* open up the tragedy of our solitude. While some prefer *Hamlet*, those who have come to see that all human effort is useless prefer the romance of Cervantes, for they see inspiration satirized in it and regard all knights who fight and suffer for ideas as so many Quijotes.

Did Cervantes mock mankind, depicting the soul in the form of Don Quijote and the body in the form of Sancho? Is the *Quijote* a mystery in which the spiritual and the material conflict? This much I see: The material Sancho must suffer for the spiritual Don Quijote, and the body seems to have more insight than the soul. The author of the *Quijote* may merely have meant to see in Don Quijote those who wanted to restore medieval chivalry and call again to life a perished past. Yet if this is so, it is then ironic that it was the Romantic School itself which gave us the best translation of a book in which its own folly is most delightfully satirized.

377. Tieck, Johann Ludwig. *Zur Geschichte der Novelle*. In *Kritische Schriften*, II. Leipzig: Brockhaus, 1848, p. 381. [Dated 1834.]

It is a popular but erroneous belief that Cervantes wrote the *Quijote* to ridicule books of chivalry. If the origin of his book had been no deeper, his work would have been forgotten long ago. But Cervantes' great genius went beyond that to reveal how the everyday and trivial can take on the glow and color of the marvelous. Since Cervantes, we possess tales and presentations from the real world, those incidents and weaknesses of life which have not rejected even the lowest wretchedness. Since Cervantes, no distinguished narrator has been heard from in Spain.

378. Schleiermacher, Friedrich. *Vorlesungen über die Aesthetik*. Berlin: C. Lommatzch, 1842, pp. 647-702. [Photocopy by Walter de Gruyter, Berlin-New York, 1974 from *Sämtliche Werke*, Berlin: G. Reimer, 1835-1864.]

Exaggerated language had long been used in the writing of short stories (*Novellen*) in order to build up what was essentially trivial, and character description was generally subordinated to plot, whereas in the novel (*Roman*) the essential thing is the description of characters. Thus even though Don Quijote and Sancho stand out in Cervantes' novel, in the aggregate the composition is a series of *Novellen* in which these stories become more valuable as they represent various classes of society. The overall plot would acquire a quite different character if the *Novellen* were removed.

379. Tieck, Johann Ludwig. *Eine Sommerreise*. In *Gesammelte Werke*, VII. Berlin: Georg Reimer, 1853, pp. 46-48. [First edition of *Novellen*, Breslau: J. Max, 1835-42.]

[In the course of this short story, the characters Walther and Ferdinand discuss the relevance of the *Curioso impertinente* to the main plot of the *Quijote*. Walther asks whether most critics rightly regard the tale as superfluous. Ferdinand replies that the interpolated tale illuminates Don Quijote's madness from another angle: Anselmo seeks to possess the invisible, which can only be possessed through faith, just as Don Quijote seeks to possess the ideal Dulcinea.]

380. Biedermann, F. B. Franz. *Don Quichotte et la tache de ses traducteurs: Eclaircissements nouveaux sur le style et l'esprit de l'original*. Paris: Delaunay, 1837. 79 pages.

Cervantes' Spanish and Viardot's French are somewhat imperfect. Studying classical Spanish in the present time is like studying Classical Latin, in that it is very difficult to know the language Cervantes wrote more than 200 years before. Translations that have appeared make this clear, for many of them indicate that what Cervantes was praised for is simply not praiseworthy after all. Translations do not recognize the faults of Cervantes' language, for he mixes the good and the bad, the high and the low.

Criticism of Viardot's translation of the *Quijote*'s prologue is necessary to arrive at a more accurate rendition of the Spanish original. A list of all the mistaken words and expressions in the text appears at the end of this study. It is hoped that some day there will be an excellent French translation, and that these corrections will serve this end.

381. Heine, Heinrich. "Einleitung zum *Don Quixote*." Stuttgart: Verlag der Classiker, 1837-1838. [As reprinted in Heine's *Sämtliche Werke*, IV: *Schriften zu Literatur und Politik*, II: *Vermischtes*, Munich: Winkler-Verlag, 1972, pp. 554-71.]

What was Cervantes' basic motive in writing the *Quijote*—was it merely to destroy the popularity of books of chivalry, or did he seek to satirize the institution of chivalry itself? On the surface, it is the former, for he accomplished that in Spain. But the pen of the genius is always greater than the writer himself; the pen reaches far beyond contemporary interpretations. Cervantes wrote the greatest satire against enthusiasm without being aware of it.

As for the supposed originality of both Cervantes and Shakespeare, neither was original in the modern sense of the word. Yet Cervantes was not a mere product of his times, for he was the germ of the future and the founder of the modern novel: he featured the life of the common people. In other words, as Cervantes satirized the chivalric novel, he created the prototype of what we call the modern novel. Cervantes was not one-sided in his presentation of life; he mixed the lowly with the noble and showed not only that one serves the other, but also that one is as powerful as the other. In the eighteenth century the noble element was lost to the novel, although Sir Walter Scott brought this element back to it. But Scott cannot be compared to Cervantes, nor are Scott's works truly novels. Cervantes,

Shakespeare, and Goethe are the true literary triumvirate: Cervantes the epic, Shakespeare the dramatic, and Goethe the lyric. Cervantes' great contribution lies in the natural dialogue of his two lasting figures.

382. Schopenhauer, Arthur. "Zur Metaphysik des Schönen und Aesthetik." In *Sämtliche Werke*, VI. Wiesbaden: Eberhard Brockhaus Verlag, 1947, p. 469. [First edition, Frankfurt, 1837.]

The more a novel represents inner life and the less it represents outer life the greater its value will be. The ratio between the two will supply a means of judging any novel. *Don Quijote* has relatively little action, and what there is of it is unimportant in itself because it is introduced merely for the sake of fun. The business of a novelist is not to relate great events but to make small ones interesting.

383. Tieck, Johann Ludwig. "Einleitung" to *Die Leiden des Persiles und der Sigismunda*, I. Leipzig: F. A. Brockhaus, 1837, p. x. [As briefly discussed by Werner Brüggemann in *Cervantes und die Figur des Don Quijote*, p. 67.]

Cervantes was aroused by the bad literary tastes of his times, but in addition to the satire of such tastes there is in the *Quijote* the noblest poetry, wisdom, and knowledge of human nature, bound together on every side with joy and pleasure.

384. Grillparzer, Franz. "Cervantes." In *Sämtliche Werke*, XIII: *Studien zum spanischen Theater*. Leipzig: Max Hesses Verlag, 1903, pp. 192-94. [Also in *Sämtliche Werke*, II: *Ausgewählte Briefe, Gespräche, Berichte*, Munich: Carl Hanser, 1964, pp. 407-11. Dated 1839-1842.]

In the interpolated stories, like Dorotea's tale, Cervantes' style is affected. Also, the *Curioso impertinente* is rather weak, and if its purpose (as Tieck alleges) is to raise prosaic reality to the level of the poetic, its inclusion was an artless effort.

Mistaken is Tieck's view that the interpolations are an advantage. Cervantes avoids them in Part II, since he realizes that the variety and the poetic element should be woven into the main plot. Tieck sees the *Quijote* in a false light, as he sees everything else, for what Cervantes only allowed to shine forth out of the background (the hero's essentially noble character and his lucid intervals) Tieck would like to bring into the foreground and make the hero a martyr of chivalry instead of the fool that he is. The hero's lucid intervals would probably have been fewer if Cervantes had not decided to bring in his own views on many matters. Lord Byron's idea that Cervantes laughed Spain's chivalry away makes much more sense, for Cervantes continually uses his talent to make his hero ridiculous to amuse the reader.

385. Notter, Friedrich. "Anmerkungen" to *Die Pruefungen des Persiles und*

der Sigismunda: Eine nordische Geschichte von Miguel de Cervantes Saavedra. 2 vols. Stuttgart: Verlag der J. B. Metzler' schen Buchhandlung, 1839. [As noted by Harry Meier, "Zur Entwicklung...," p. 244.]

Cervantes is a friend of the socially oppressed *moriscos* and an opponent of the reactionary Philip III.

386. Deutinger, Martin. "170. Die Nachklänge der romanisch-epischen Dichtkunst in Ercilla, Camoens und Cervantes." In *Grundlinien einer positiven Philosphie als vorläufiger Versuch einer Zurückführung aller Theile der Philosophie auf christliche Principien,* V: *Das Gebiet der dichtenden Kunst.* Regensburg: 1846, pp. 498-502. [As reprinted in 1967, Frankfurt.]

Aristophanes, the Greek playwright, relates his comedies to tragedy as Cervantes relates the *Quijote* to the romantic epic, and the general scenario of *The Birds* is comparable to the nonsense in Cervantes' work.

The *Quijote* reveals the complete dissolution of the historical foundations of the Middle Ages, and consequently life, as far as it could be presented poetically, had to take on a new form. Higher forms of perception could come no longer from natural powers, but from the power of the free will, which joins objective belief with subjective insight. Epic life turns into an irony of itself in which there comes forth the profundity of subjective life, of feeling, and of will. No matter how laughable Don Quijote seems in his contradiction with the outer world, his heart and will are honorable, and Sancho, in his devotion (as little as this that can be free from self-interest), is a person full of inner truthfulness, who seems laughable only because of his lack of imagination. Sancho represents the people, who are always pragmatic, but who nevertheless let themselves be dragged into untenable speculations when they find a fool who believes in his own dreams.

387. Eichendorff, Joseph von. *Der deutsche Roman des achtzehnten Jahrhunderts in seinem Verhältnis zum Christentum.* In *Sämtliche Werke,* VIII. Regensburg: Josef Habbel, 1965, pp. 58 and 132. [First published in 1851.]

Humor is the natural reaction of healthy forces against the general sickness of the times, and the greatest humorist in this sense is without doubt Cervantes. His famous novel is, in spite of its absurdity, about the tragic defeat of knighthood. Thus, it often occurs to us that it is not Don Quijote who has gone mad, but only the world around him.

Cervantes wrote during a period when chivalry was popular in a romantic sense and when there was an almost completely developed national poetry. For that reason, the *Quijote* is the prototype of all modern novels. Considering the general meaning of the *Quijote,* it is an antidote for certain forms of mental feverishness, rather than a call to madness.

388. Lemcke, Ludwig. "Cervantes." In *Handbuch der spanischen Litteratur*, I: *Die Prosa*. Leipzig: Friedrich Fleischer, 1855, pp. 371-470.

While at the core of the *Quijote* is the idea of reviving chivalric institutions, the work goes far beyond this original idea. Yet the American critic Ticknor, who found Bouterwek wrong in believing the *Quijote* was philosophical satire, was himself mistaken in thinking that this form of satire did not coincide with Cervantes' times or personality. Cervantes' novel is an attack on aggressive Spanish attitudes brought on by reading chivalric romances, not merely an attack on the romances' literary flaws.

389. Rosenkrantz, Karl. "Cervantes." *Poesie und ihre Geschichte*. In *Eine Entwicklung der poetischen Ideale der Völker*. Königsberg: Gebrüder Bornträger, 1855, pp. 588-94.

Cervantes should be praised for sweeping above the spirit of his age and being a genuine Spaniard. Only the critical spirit that lived in him and the urge to reform that controlled him were strange to his culture. Herein lies the universality of his world view, the rational freedom of his judgment, and the humanity of his poetry.

Cervantes did not only contrast the real and ideal, but he also revealed the irreconcilability of these extremes, even though both are needed for freedom. Don Quijote can talk reasonably, and Sancho can dream; and hence arises the subtle irony of the *Quijote*, which is equaled by only that of Shakespeare. Cervantes goes beyond the romantic ideals of his day, but does not partake of Quevedo's bitterness. And yet, Cervantes did not stop at irony; he went beyond to create a modern, romantic novel by lifting the pastoral and the picaresque through tragicomedy.

390. Ebert, A. "Literarische Wechselwirkungen Spaniens und Deutschlands." *Deutsche Vierteljahrsschrift*, No. 2 (1857): 86-121.

[In this study only casual allusions are made to the *Quijote*. Ebert refers to early German translations, musical adaptations, Wieland's imitation, *Don Sylvio von Rosalva*, Tieck's translation of 1799, and the general interest of the German romantics in Cervantes' works.]

391. Frenzel, Karl. *Dichter und Frauen*, II. Hannover: Carl Rümpler, 1860, pp. 139-203.

Shakespeare is tragic in his emphasis on guilt and in his tendency to oppose man's freedom and nobility with feebleness: man in Shakespeare's work shakes the world and returns to dust. Cervantes, on the other hand, denies human significance as well as guilt: he sees the error of hopes, the denigration of virtue, and the victory of cowardice.

Regarding Boccaccio and Cervantes, the latter emphasizes the ideal in his *Novelas ejemplares*, while there is an utter lack thereof in the *Decameron*.

And yet, Cervantes is at his best only when he portrays the life of the people.

The *Quijote* is a sad book, yet a work full of the liveliest Homeric humor; sad because chivalry is trod upon by galley slaves, muleteers, and filthy animals. We do not laugh at Don Quijote, but at ourselves, for we all have lofty yearnings. The same sadness exists in Part II; the novel becomes tragic when others seek to intervene in the hero's mad world. Yet, after his defeat, we see that despite his folly and sorrows, beauty and worthiness are after all imperishable. There is a note of apology in the final pages of the work, as the author gathers strength and seems to be asking the reader's forgiveness for having treated his hero so ignominiously.

392. Carus, Carl Gustav. [Comment in Rius, III, p. 299 and based on Edmund Dorer's *Cervantes und seine Werke nach deutschen Urtheilen*, pp. 35-36. From 1861?]

Cervantes' profound knowledge of human extravagance, his happy genius, and his serene mind are commendable. The *Quijote* reflects all the madness of humanity. Who has not felt only partially sane at times and who has not armed himself with Mambrino's helmet?

393. Baumstark, Reinhold. "Das Cervantesdenkmal und sein Gegenstand." In *Mein Ausflung nach Spanien im Frühling 1867*. Regensburg: Georg Joseph Manz, 1868, pp. 451-72.

There are superb, simple sentences in Cervantes' prose comparable to those of Julius Caesar, and the character descriptions are peerless. Yet, does the original aim of the book, to destroy the popularity of novels of chivalry, continue to account for the greatness of the *Quijote*? This greatness lies in two things: First, for Spaniards, Don Quijote and Sancho are the picture of the Spanish people; the Knight's *idée fixe* is in large part identical to the false way that Spain has developed, while Sancho represents the realistic aspect of the Spanish people and their richness of spirit. Secondly, for non-Spaniards, the *Quijote* reveals that Cervantes was a first-rate authority on humanity; he observes and understands the human heart.

Cervantes did not intend to embody theoretical concepts in his protagonists, but sought to describe people and their spirit. Cervantes, a creative genius, could have hit upon the idea of revealing the sum of his practical wisdom by showing the contrast of the two complementary human figures. In addition, one can find consolation and wise counsel in the *Quijote* for any situation. Particularly praiseworthy is the hero's death, for while he dies as a result of madness, he does not die insane.

394. Dohm, Hedwig. "Cervantes." In *Die spanische National-Literatur in ihrer geschichtlichen Entwickelung*. Berlin: Gustav Hempel, 1867, pp. 242-301.

The style of the *Quijote* is almost unimportant compared to the content, which is so rich in inventiveness and spirit. The *Quijote* is a wonderful combination of serious ideas, high-spirited humor, biting scorn, and beautiful poetry. It is also a colorful picture of Spanish life and a book so full of truth and power, which make it a national epic.

With the appearance of Sancho, the story changes: here Don Quijote ceases to be a mere fool, and the struggle between the ideal and the real begins. As the novel moves along, Cervantes takes the side of his hero, who is enthusiastic for all that is good, beautiful, and magnanimous. His foolishness seems to us eventually a touchingly sublime misfortune, and he is gradually glorified until he dies almost a saint.

Cervantes' original aim was probably to write only a satire of chivalric novels. The work itself lifted him above and beyond his particular time and drove him to present something for all times. Thus, this simple satire, planned as only a parody, achieved significance for everyone. While Don Quijote may have yearned for the ideal of the past, Cervantes longed for the ideal of the future. The *Quijote* is not merely the satire of chivalric literature but of romanticism, for it depicts the idealism of the past becoming the foolishness of the present.

In Part II of the novel the satire dissolves into parody, especially when the real Don Quijote criticizes the false knight of Avellaneda. But no matter how great the faults of the *Quijote* may be, it is and remains the first classical novel of the modern world. Never was a book loved by so many people.

395. Fastenrath, Johann. "Die Bedeutung des *Don Quijote.*" In *Das Buch meiner spanischen Freunde*. Leipzig: Eduard Heinrich Mayer, 1870, pp. 8-10.

[A free German verse translation of the closing lines of Juan Eugenio Hartzenbusch's play, *La hija de Cervantes*, in which Don Quijote and Sancho are said to represent all mankind with their mixture of lofty aspiration and lowly self-interest. The *Quijote*, the poem states, was begun by the author when he suffered in Algiers; the author put part of himself in his hero and gave us a mixture of serene poetry and bitter truth.]

396. Ludwig, Otto. *Epische Studien*. In *Werke*, VI: *Ausgewählte Studien und kritische Schriften*. Neue vermehrte Ausgabe. Leipzig: Adolf Bartels (Hesse & Becker Verlag), n.d., pp. 411, 424, 432, and 434-35. [Ludwig's critical works appear to have been first published in 1871-1873 by Moritz Heydrich and later expanded and arranged by Eric Schmidt and Adolf Stern in 1891-1892.]

In drama it is the hero who is imposing, while in the epic and the novel it is the world that is imposing. While drama is based on ethics and the novel on positive law or custom, the epic is based on natural law. Yet the *Quijote* seems to play on all three. The hero takes the initiative, and this work would be dramatic if the world condition which the hero is attacking were not so overwhelming. Indeed, if this attack were in truth an attack, and the entire struggle were not just a fantastic fiction of Don Quijote's, but a real struggle, the novel would be dramatic. But it is the unsuitability of the hero that negates the dramatic and makes this a novel. What might be genuinely serious is turned into the ridiculous.

Tragedy, defined as the high feeling of freedom and of self-determination on the part of the hero, can be found in the *Quijote*, just as strongly as in Shakespeare. In fact, the charm of the *Quijote* lies in the contrast between the ironic freedom of the author and the reader and the naïveté and repressed state of the protagonists. Because the other characters are aligned with the author and the reader in their relationship with the heroes, we are especially affected when one of them falls into the restrained state of the protagonist, as when the *dueña* Rodríguez in all seriousness calls on Don Quijote's chivalry to her own service.

Considering an author's attitude toward his hero, Cervantes clearly states that Don Quijote is a fool, so the reader cannot avoid thinking the same. Dickens, for example, softens the blunt Cervantine narrator and transforms the interest from the general to the specific, and thus Pickwick seems to have neither the foolishness nor the romantic spirit of the Knight. The difference is that we love Pickwick for himself, but we love the humanity in Don Quijote and Sancho Panza (glorious and inane human nature, not merely a simple charming example of it!).

In the *Quijote* lies the tragic and the comic, the great and the small, that which we admire in human nature, and that which we must laugh at. Further, the conflict between idealism and realism remains unresolved. At the end they oppose one another just as at the beginning, even when seen from the ideal standpoint. *Pickwick* is merely the incidental story of a charming and original individual. The *Quijote* is a work of objective humor. But we must remember that both writers shared the same intention, namely, to influence humanity and to show that human folly is another side of that which is noble in people.

397. Klein, J. L. "Miguel de Cervantes Saavedra." In *Geschichte des spanischen Dramas*, II. Leipzig: T. O. Weigel, 1872, pp. 258-410.

Cervantes was a man who sought to free Spain from self-deceit. Thus, the cause of Don Quijote's madness was the fanatical religion of the times. Yet critics forget that a poetic spirit like Cervantes was not depicting the society of his times like a portrait painter, nor was he writing for the mere fun and amusement of his contemporaries. Instead, Cervantes took two character types of the day and transformed them into archetypes, without allowing them to lose their individuality. That is not to say that Bouterwek and Sismondi, who believed that Cervantes was consciously symbolic, were correct. The true author pictures idea and image in one movement; he does not picture the idea first and then give it a human form.

It is wrong to put Cervantes' novel on the stage, where it loses its impact, its thoughtful observations about man, and its warning against foolish undertakings.

398. Nietzsche, Friedrich. *Briefwechsel mit Erwin Rhode*. Leipzig: Insel, 1923, pp. 370-71. [Letter dated December 8, 1875.]

Read the *Quijote*, not because it is cheerful reading, but because it is most bitter (*herbste*). I once took the *Quijote* on a summer vacation and after reading it felt that all my sorrows seemed small.

399. Baumstark, Reinhold. *Cervantes. Ein spanisches Lebensbild.* Freiburg im Breisgau: Herder'sche Verlagsbuchhandlung, 1875. 185 pages.

[Baumstark here devotes nine chapters to Cervantes' life and works, but his remarks on the *Quijote* are virtually a verbatim repetition of his early observations in *Mein Ausflug nach Spanien*, 1868.]

400. Dorer, Edmund. *Die Cervantes-Literatur in Deutschland: Bibliographische Übersicht.* Zurich: Fusseli & Co., 1877. 29 pages.

[This a list of German literary histories that have commentary on Cervantes, all German translations of Cervantes' works, imitations and dramatic adaptations of the *Quijote* and other works, and all Spanish editions of Cervantes' works published in Germany.]

401. Dorer, Edmund, ed. *Cervantes und seine Werke nach deutschen Urtheilen.* Leipzig: W. Friedrich, 1881. 177 pages.

[Dorer presents lengthy excerpts by Germans on the subject of Cervantes and his works. Among them are passages from Bodmer, Herder, Goethe, Schelling, Hegel, Schopenhauer, Carl Gustav Carus, Tieck, A. W. Schlegel, F. Schlegel, Eichendorff, Richter, and Heine. The appendixes deal with such matters as translations, imitations, and adaptations of Cervantes' works. A general bibliography is included.]

402. Braunfels, Ludwig. "Einleitung" to *Der sinnreicher Junker Don Quijote von der Mancha.* 2 vols. Stuttgart: Deutsche Hand-und-Haus Bibliothek, 1883. [As discussed by Werner Brüggemann in *Cervantes und die Figur des Don Quijote*, pp. 313-14, and as excerpted by Rius, III, pp. 371-77.]

Cervantes does not merely copy chivalric material but transports it into modern times. Finding in the material a moral and poetic problem of a totally different class, Cervantes placed his hero in continual conflict with real life and brought him into situations and relationships which do not permit any solution. And yet, Don Quijote must realize the falseness and madness of his chivalry—if only in his death. Cervantes destroyed the ideal of three centuries when his laughter killed off inverisimilitude.

Yet the *Quijote* goes beyond the author's original intention of attacking books of chivalry. The characters grow both inwardly and outwardly, revealing the noble side of chivalry, until the notions of the hero become ideals. The hero is an idealist who seeks only goodness and beauty, and as he becomes the image of true wisdom, we follow his path from simple alienation toward the idealization of his acts and efforts.

Subsequently, Cervantes became fond of his hidalgo and made him likeable. In the *Quijote*, for the first time in literature, idealism appears in open combat with realism. But Cervantes did not merely place idealism face to face with realism. He also placed idealism at the side of realism in the form of the faithful squire Sancho Panza, a contrast and a complement to Don Quijote. Sancho too wins the heart of the author and reader, as he becomes increasingly astute and eventually even the voice of the people.

The *Quijote* is not a success, then, because the reader believes it is an attack on chivalric novels, but because the reader sees in the work the marvelous and true picture of the eternal struggle between desire and ability, between the elevated and the lowly, between the ordinary humor of daily life and the tragic nature of existence.

403. Haller, Joseph. *Altspanische Sprichwörter und sprichwörtliche Redensarten aus den Zeiten vor Cervantes.* 2 vols. Regensburg: Published by the author and in Commission G. J. Manzschen Buchhandlung, 1883.

Cervantes could be called a collector of proverbs. Many sayings in the *Quijote* are not found in collections available during his time, although they were in circulation among the people of his age. Among other things, his ingenious and witty work will always remain a rich source of Spanish proverbs.

404. Michaëlis, C. T. *Lessings Minna von Barnhelm und Cervantes' Don Quijote.* Berlin: R. Gaertners Verlagsbuchhandlung, Hermann Heyfelder, 1883. 44 pages.

There are various similarities between Lessing's play *Minna von Barnhelm* and Cervantes' novel, among them a parallel in the choice of the time of year and the use of an inn. There are also similarities in the relationship between master and servant in both works, even a likeness in the choice of words employed. Finally, there is repeated use of pairs of lovers with resemblances between Dorotea and Minna, Don Quijote and Tellheim, Sancho and Just.

405. Brandes, Wilhelm *"Minna von Barnhelm und Don Quijote?"* *Akademische Blätter* (1884): 51-54.

Michaëlis' earlier work on the influence of the *Quijote* on Lessing's play *Minna von Barnhelm* is contrived. Lessing drew upon his own living environment and not upon previous literary models in writing this drama.

406. Dorer, Edmund. "Deutsche Uebersetzer des *Don Quijote.*" *Das Magazin für die Litteratur des In- und Auslandes*, Jahrgang 54, no. 46 (November 14, 1885): 726-27.

By 1700 there were as many editions of the *Quijote* published outside Spain as there were within that country, and in the fifty years prior to the date of this article, there were more editions printed in Germany than in any other country. Especially praiseworthy is the Ludwig Braunfels edition and the abridged edition by Ernst von Wolzogen, accompanied by Doré's illustrations. Other German editions worthy of note are the anonymous translation of 1682 (Frankfurt and Basel) and the editions of Bertuch, Tieck, Soltau, Keller, and Zoller.

407. Vollmöller, Karl. "*Der sinnreiche Junker Don Quijote von der Mancha* von Miguel de Cervantes Saavedra. Uebersetzt, eingeleitet und mit Erläuterungen versehen von Ludwig Braunfels. 4 Bände ... Stuttgart: W. Spemann, 1883." *Göttingische gelehrte Anzeigen* 7 (April 1, 1885): 281-91.

The Braunfels translation of the *Quijote* is the best German version ever published. Detailed attention to errors made in earlier translations, such as those of Oudin-Rosset, Duffield, Bertuch, Soltau, and Tieck, should be recorded and noted.

408. Nietzsche, Friedrich. *Zur Geneologie der Moral.* In *Werke in Drei Bänden*, II. Munich: Carl Hanser Verlag, 1977, pp. 807-08. [First edition in Leipzig: C. G. Naumann, 1887.]

We read the *Quijote* with a bitter taste on our tongue, with almost a feeling of torture, but our interpretations would seem strange to Cervantes and his contemporaries, who read the story with a clear conscience as the most cheerful of books.

409. Amyntor, Gerhard von. "Eine Urteilsrevision in Sachen Don Quichotes." *Das Magazin für die Litteratur des In- und Auslandes*, Jahrgang 57, no. 39 (September 22, 1888): 611-14.

Is the *Quijote* a truly humorous work? The novel would be much more humorous if the beatings were sharply reduced.

410. Gessner, Emil. *Das Vorbild des Don Quijote.* [Berlin: 1891.] 47 pages. [Title page missing.]

The intense popularity of chivalric customs in Spain long after the decline of chivalry in the rest of Europe might be explained by the long struggle between Christians and Moors on the Iberian Peninsula. Yet the Spaniards did not seek their poetic ideal in their own *romances* but in a fantastic, utterly nonhistorical literature—the novel of chivalry—, whose only function was to present a perfect hero.

Various attempts to drive this genre out of existence failed, however, until Cervantes used the device of parody. Cervantes did not exaggerate when he depicted the second innkeeper's obstinate insistence on the veracity of such absurd stories.

The knighting ceremony in the *Quijote* is consistent with chivalric literature, though exaggerated for parodic effect. Among the other elements in the *Quijote* which seem capricious or overly imaginative, but which are actually taken from chivalric novels, are unprovoked battles with animals and the custom of placing the lady-love before God, which Cervantes satirizes in the conversation between Don Quijote and Vivaldo.

411. Fischer, Hermann. "Don Quijote in Deutschland." *Vierteljahrsschrift für Litteraturgeschichte* 5 (1892): 331-32.

[Describes a celebration on June 13, 1613, honoring the marriage of Friedrich V of the Palatinate to Elizabeth, daughter of James I of England, at which the figure Don Quijote appeared carrying a sign describing his exploits.]

412. Bahlsen, Leopold. "Spanische Quellen der dramatischen Litteratur, besonders Englands zu Shakespeares Zeit." *Zeitschrift für vergleichende Litteraturgeschichte* 6 (1893): 151-59.

Beaumont-Fletcher's *Knight of the Burning Pestle* was undoubtedly influenced by the *Quijote*.

413. Dühring, Eugen Karl. "Drittes Capitel. Vorerscheinungen und Ankündigungen des neuern Völkercharakters. Cervantes und Shakespeare." In *Die Grössen der modernen Literatur populär und kritisch nach neuen Gesichtspunkten dargestellt*. Zweite verbesserte Auflage. Leipzig: C. G. Naumann, 1904, pp. 47-100. [First published in 1893.]

Cervantes and Shakespeare can be viewed as a literary introduction to a new era: Both writers are relatively free of classical influence and both look upon the Middle Ages, if not negatively, and even though not actually in a modern way, at least with an awareness that the new era has come.

Part I of the *Quijote* would have been more unified if the reader had actually known of the protagonist's death, the natural conclusion of the novel, rather than merely hearing it mentioned. Nevertheless, Part I is superior to Part II in originality and consistency of style. The interpolated stories of the 1605 *Quijote* furnish a serious contrast to the humor of the main plot. Because no work of art can rest entirely on humor, the error of inserting serious interpolated stories actually mitigates the problem of letting humor stand alone.

414. Epstein, S. Sigismund. "Don Quixote in entwicklungsge schicht-licher Beleuchtung. Eine litterarisch-psychologische Studie." *Die Gesell-schaft* 10 (1894): 1482-90.

Neither Bodmer nor Saint-Evremond looked for any profound meaning in Don Quijote. We owe to Kant the search for a guiding idea and also a certain tendenciousness in literature and criticism at the beginning of the nineteenth century. Don Quijote and Sancho became symbols, with Bou-terwek being the first to find Don Quijote a *weltschmerzlerische* figure, the representative of enthusiasm for an ideal, and Sancho a symbol of everyday life.

British Criticism

415. Anderson, James. Essay No. CLXX. In *The Gleaner*, IV. London: Printed for Suttaby, Evance, and Co., 1811, pp. 273-84. [From *The Bee* 15 (June 26, 1793): 265 et seq.]

The *Quijote*, more than any other work, has suffered at the hands of translators, who have made both Don Quijote and Sancho Panza absurd. Sancho is converted into an impossible combination of pertness and ignorance, and the Knight, a mixture of meanness and stateliness, whereas in the original the latter is kind, humane, and honorable, and the former is extraordinarily simple and good-hearted. In English it is difficult to avoid a tone of bold familiarity in Don Quijote's attitude toward Sancho and a tone of impertinence in the Squire's attitude toward his master.

416. Wordsworth, William. *The Prelude*: Book V. London: Oxford University Press, 1966, lines 28-139. [1805 text.]

[Describing a friend who falls asleep while reading the *Quijote* near the sea, Wordsworth creates a dream or vision of a part-Arab, part-Quijote figure, "craz'd by love and feeling and internal thought." The poet expresses a feeling of reverence, rather than pity, for this strange figure. For Wordsworth, reason lies couched in the madness of the Arab Don Quijote.]

417. Lamb, Charles. "The Second Part of the Honest Whore." In *Specimens of English Dramatic Poets, Who Lived About the Time of Shakespeare.* London: Longman, Hurst, Rees, and Orme, 1808. [From *Lamb as Critic*, Lincoln and London: University of Nebraska Press, 1980, p. 118.]

The fondness with which Cervantes dwells upon Don Quijote's library suggests that he had been a great reader of books of knight-errantry and perhaps at some point in his life had even been in danger of falling into those very extravagances which he ridicules in his hero.

418. Dunlop, John Colin. "Don Quixote." In *History of Prose Fiction*, II. New York: AMS Press, 1969, pp. 313-23. [A reproduction of the 1906 London edition. First published as *The History of Fiction*, London: Longman, 1814.]

Cervantes did not attack the spirit of adventure, but parodied those who spent their time reading and writing romantic compositions. Also, the excellence of the *Quijote* lies in the readiness with which the hero conceives and the gravity with which he maintains the most absurd and fantastic ideas that always bear some analogy to the adventures in romances of chivalry.

The *Quijote* is occasionally hampered by the number of characters, though worthy of note is the novelty of the work's design and the pleasure it affords, since readers first behold objects as they are in reality and then see them metamorphosed by the imagination of the hero. Don Quijote is a double character, a man of good sense, who is irrational on the subject of chivalry. Sancho, too, has a different disposition when under the influence of his master's frenzy. Other characters who intervene in the action have two appearances—that which they possess in reality and that which they assume in Don Quijote's imagination.

Part II is inferior to Part I because we feel hurt and angry at the cruelty of the deceptions practiced by the Duke and Duchess. Images which spontaneously arise from natural objects are more entertaining than those which are forced by artificial combination and the machinations of others.

419. Godwin, William. *Lives of Edward and John Philips, Nephews and Pupils of Milton.* London: Longman, Hurst, Rees, Orme, and Brown, 1815, pp. 240-60.

> An examination of John Philips' translation of the *Quijote* (1687), the first English translation since that of Shelton (1612 and 1620), shows that it is certainly a work of great power and spirit, but it is the spirit of Philips, not of Cervantes. Especially unfortunate is the translator's love of beastly allusions and his tendency to revel in slang. Philips takes more liberties than any other translator, though his English versions of Cervantes' poetry are good. Subsequent English translations include those of Motteux (1700), Stevens (1706), Ozell (1719), Jarvis (1742), Smollett (1755), and Wilmot (1774).

420. Cunningham, John William. *Sancho, or the Proverbialist.* Third edition. Printed by Ellerton and Henderson For T. Caldwell and W. Davies, 1817. 178 pages. [Preface dated November 7, 1816.]

> [This fictive, fifteen-chapter autobiography of Sancho is accompanied by his Aunt Winifred's running list of proverbs, and, at times, her explanations of them. The author wryly observes that all of her maxims may be found in the works of Cervantes, Poor Richard, or any other collection of sayings of which no one knows the author.]

421. Coleridge, Samuel Taylor. "Lecture VIII: Don Quixote. Cervantes." In *The Literary Remains of Samuel Taylor Coleridge.* New York: AMS

Press, Inc., 1967, pp. 113-31. [A reprint of the 1836 edition, London: William Pickering. Dated 1818.]

Shakespeare and Cervantes personify astuteness and reflection, respectively. Cervantes' style is more spirited than Addison's and similar in tenseness to Swift's, although this tenseness is blended with an exquisite flow. Underlying every passage is the idea, "Brethren! with all your faults I love you still!"

Don Quijote is a man no longer tempted by base passions or even interested in science or art, but who is also a man estranged from observation by self-interest and a person whose judgment has lain fallow. And yet the dependency of our nature demands some confirmation from without, though it be only from the shadows of other men's fictions.

The world was a drama to Cervantes. His own thoughts, in spite of poverty and sickness, perpetuated for him the feelings of youth. He painted only what he knew and observed, but he knew and had looked into much indeed; and his imagination was ever at hand to adapt and modify the world of his experience.

422. Scott, Sir Walter. *An Essay on Chivalry, Romance, and the Drama.* In *Complete Works*, I. New York: Conner & Cooke, 1833, pp. 29-43. [From the year 1818.]

It was against the extravagances of chivalric romances, their character and style, that the satire of the *Quijote* was chiefly directed. Almost the whole library of Don Quijote belongs to this genre, a fact, no doubt, that contributed much to ending the vogue.

423. Hazlitt, William. "Lecture VI: On the English Novelists." *Lectures on the Comic Writers, etc. of Great Britain.* In *The Complete Works of William Hazlitt*, VI. New York: AMS Press, Inc., 1967, pp. 108-12. [First edition of *Lectures . . .* is 1819.]

Don Quijote presents something more stately, more romantic, and at the same time more real to the imagination than any other hero on record. We not only feel the greatest veneration and love for the Knight himself, but a certain respect for all those connected with him. Perhaps no other work combines so much whimsical invention with so much truth.

To consider the *Quijote* merely a satirical work or a vulgar attempt to explode the long-forgotten order of chivalry is a great mistake because Cervantes had no need to destroy what no longer existed. Besides, Cervantes was a man of the most sanguine temperament, and even through the crazed and battered figure of Don Quijote, the spirit of chivalry shines undiminished. Cervantes saved the flame of Spanish liberty, which might consume tyranny, and kept alive the spark of generous sentiment and romantic enterprise from which that flame must be kindled.

Cervantes' intuitive perception of the hidden analogies of things is called the instinct of *imagination,* and it works unconsciously. What seems to be involuntary unity in the novel, particularly in the unsettled, rambling humor that extends itself to all the subordinate parts and characters of the work, that aspiration toward imaginary good and indescribable longing after something more than we possess, flows through all of the *Quijote.*

As for the leading characters in the *Quijote,* they are strictly individuals; that is, they do not so much belong to as form a class by themselves. Their actions and manners do not arise out of the actions and manners of those around them or the situation of life in which they are placed, but out of the peculiar dispositions of their own persons, operated upon by certain impulses of caprice and accident. Yet these impulses are so true to nature, and their operation so exactly described that we recognize both the fidelity of the representation and its originality at the same time. They are, therefore, originals in the best sense of the word.

One test of the truth of Cervantes' characterizations is the number of allusions which the *Quijote* has furnished to the whole of civilized Europe; that is, Cervantes gives us nearly the same insight here into the characters of innkeepers, barmaids, hostlers, and puppeteers that we have in Fielding, for instance, although there is a much greater mixture of the pathetic and sentimental with the quaint and humorous in Cervantes' work than in Fielding's.

There is little to warrant the idea that Fielding was an imitator of Cervantes, except his own declaration in *Joseph Andrews,* the romantic turn of the character of Parson Adams, and the proverbial humor of Partridge. Fielding's novels are, in general, thoroughly his own and thoroughly English.

424. Frere, John Hookham. Review of *The Comedies of Aristophanes,* translated by T. Michell. *Quarterly Review* 23 (May-June, 1820): 474-505. [Reprinted in *Works of John Hookham Frere,* I, London: Basil Montague Pickering, 1872, pp. 167-200.]

There are two eternal character types in Aristophanes: on the one hand, Lamachus of the Acharnians—proud, haughty, courteous, romantic, adventurous, and imaginative; on the other, Dicaeopolis—shrewd, calculating, peaceful and sensual, humble or saucy, as circumstances may require or permit. Not individuals but pure abstractions, they are the permanent contrasts of human nature, who, like Don Quijote and Sancho Panza, belong to all times.

Aristophanes' technique of "marking a person" (as a drunk, for example), then modifying him (causing him to be sober, even eloquent) is like Cervantes' development of Don Quijote, describing him in the first chapters as a mere madman, yet towards the conclusion modifying him so that he becomes a vehicle for communicating many of the author's own sentiments and opinions.

425. Scott, Sir Walter. "Prefatory Memoir" in *The Novels of Henry Fielding, Esq.* London: Hurst, Robinson, and Co., 1821, pp. xi and xvii-xviii. [*Ballantyne's Novelist's Library.*]

The heroic style both in *Joseph Andrews* and *Tom Jones* is closer to the *roman comique* of Scarron than it is to the *Quijote*. However, the inclusion of such interpolated tales as "The Old Man of the Hill" in *Tom Jones* and "The History of Leonora" in *Joseph Andrews* is attributable to the influence of Cervantes, and they are equally artificial. There is also a parallel between the excessive beatings received by Parson Adams in *Joseph Andrews* and those received by Don Quijote, especially as both are bastinadoed without being degraded.

426. Scott, Sir Walter. *Biographical Memoirs of Eminent Novelists and Other Distinguished Persons*, I. In *Miscellaneous Prose Works*, III. Edinburgh: Robert Cadell; London: Hurst, Robinson and Co., 1834. 464 pages. [From 1820 to 1824, in *Ballantyne's Novelist's Library.*]

Smollett uses an interpolated tale in *Peregrine Pickle* ("Memoirs of a Lady of Quality") "in the manner introduced by Cervantes," and there are certain quixotic traits in the character Mr. Mackercher. Lesage uses such interpolated stories as the "History of the Count of Belflor" and the "Force of Friendship," though Lesage's style is completely different from that of Cervantes.

427. Digby, Kenelm Henry. *The Broad Stone of Honour, or Rules for the Gentlemen of England*. London: C. & J. Rivington, 1823, pp. 173-79. [First edition is 1822.]

While no man can deny the genius and inimitable humor of the *Quijote*, the moral tendency of the work and its effect on the ordinary class of mankind is a legitimate subject for debate. Many are the men of reflection who think with me that it is a book never to be read without receiving melancholy impressions, without feelings of deep commiseration for the weakness and for the lot of human nature.

Don Quijote is a man possessing genius, virtue, imagination, and sensibility, all the generous qualities which distinguish an elevated soul, with all the amiable features of a disinterested and affectionate heart. This is the man whom Cervantes has represented as the subject of constant ridicule and of occasional reproach. There is an important lesson to be derived from the whole: the necessity of prudence and good sense, of moderation and respect for the institutions of society, of guarding the imagination from over-excitement. However, this is a lesson to be gently hinted to men of virtue, not to be proclaimed to the profane amidst the mockery of the world. This is not the lesson that the ordinary class of mankind will derive from it, any more than it is the one they need. Like Sismondi, we can pronounce in favor of the moral tendency of the whole, but we can never agree to the justice of his conclusion. In other words, there is much to be apprehended from the ridicule which is cast upon sentiment. What Cervantes can never be forgiven for is that in exposing the danger and absurdity of chivalrous sentiment, he held up to mockery not alone the excess and the abuse, but the very reality of virtue.

The institution of chivalry lost its empire; and, at length, the romance of Don Quijote, by its success, concealed under an attractive fiction, completed the ruin by fixing ridicule even upon its own memory.

428. Lockhart, John Gibson. "Introduction" to *Don Quijote*, translated by P. Motteux. London: J. M. Dent & Sons Ltd.; New York: E. P. Dutton & Co., Inc., 1943, pp. vii–xxx. [Originally published in Edinburgh: A. Constable and Co.; London: Hurst, Robinson & Co., 1822.]

That Cervantes attacked the sacred spirit of chivalry is an exaggerated and out-of-date attitude. Cervantes does not confuse the absurdities of knight-errantry with the generous aspirations of the cavalier. One respects Don Quijote despite his madness, and while one pities his delusion and laughs at the situation, he always reveres the noble spirit of the Castilian gentleman. One feels, on every page, that he is reading the work of an enlightened mind in which true wisdom had grown up beside true experience, of a man who knew human nature too well not to respect it, and of a writer who beneath a mask of apparent levity, aspired to commune with the noblest principles of humanity to give form to the noblest feelings of the national character of Spain. Wit, satire, and eloquence are only the lesser ornaments of national life and manners, yet they are by far the most glowing that were ever embodied in one composition. But while *Don Quijote* is the property of Spain, it is also the property and pride of the whole cultivated world. Don Quijote is not only a Spanish cavalier filled with a Spanish madness, his is a more universal madness. He is the symbol of imagination continually struggling with reality; he represents the eternal warfare between enthusiasm and necessity—the eternal discrepancy between the aspirations and the occupations of man and the omnipotence and vanity of human dreams.

429. Byron, George Gordon, Lord. *Don Juan*: Canto XIII, stanzas viii–xi. In *The Works of Lord Byron*, VI. London: John Murray; New York:

Scribner's Sons, 1903, pp. 458-86. [1823 text.]

I should be very willing to redress
Men's wrongs, and rather check than punish crimes,
Had not Cervantes, in that too true tale
of Quixote, shown how all such efforts fail.

Of all such tales 'tis the saddest, and the more sad,
Because it makes us smile; his hero's right,
And still pursues the right,—to curb the bad
His only object, and 'gainst odds to fight
His guerdon: 'tis his virtue makes him mad!
But his adventures form a sorry sight;—
A sorrier still is the great moral taught
By that real Epic unto all who have thought.

Redressing injury, revenging wrong,
To aid the damsel and destroy the caitiff;
Opposing singly the united strong,
From foreign yoke to free the helpless native:—
Alas! most noblest views, like an old song,
Be for mere fancy's sport a theme creative,
A jest, a riddle, Fame through thin and thick sought!
And Scorates himself but Wisdom's Quixote?

Cervantes smiled Spain's chivalry away;
A single laugh demolished the right arm
Of his own country; seldom since that day
Has Spain had heroes. While Romance could charm,
The world gave ground before her bright array;
And therefore have his volumes done such harm,
That all their glory, as a composition,
Was dearly purchased by his land's perdition.

430. Landor, Walter Savage. "XVIII. Peter Leopold and President Du Paty." *Imaginary Conversations: Italian.* In *Complete Works*, III. New York: Barnes & Noble, Inc.; London: Methuen & Co., Ltd., 1969, pp. 112-70. [First published, 1824-1829, in London, in five volumes, by various publishers; additional material was published in 1826 and 1846.]

[This imaginary conversation is a debate over the religious implications of the *Quijote*, with President Du Paty claiming that the "most dexterous attack ever made against the worship of the Virgin" is that of Cervantes. When Peter Leopold replies that Cervantes also wrote some sacred poetry, Du Paty retorts that this was perhaps "a cover to his other book"; he insists that irreverent allusions abound, and indeed, that "throughout *Don Quijote*, Dulcinea was the peerless, the immaculate, and death was denounced against all who hesitated to admit the assertion of her perfections." Later, Du Paty (probably speaking for Landor) claims that Cervantes was not really ridiculing either knight-errantry or chivalric literature: "He delighted the idlers of romance by the jokes he scattered among them on the false taste of his predecessors and of his rivals; and he delighted his own heart by his solitary archery, well knowing what amusement those who came another day would find in picking up his arrows and discovering the bull's-eye hits."

Du Paty is also sure that Don Quijote was Charles V, "devoting his labours and vigils, his wars and treaties, to the chimerical idea of making minds, like watches, turn their indexes, by a simultaneous movement, to one point." Sancho, he sees as a symbol of the people, "possessing sound sense in other matters, but ready to follow the most extraordinary visionary, and combining implicit belief in him with the grossest sensuality."

The passage also hints that Cervantes may have been attacking the Trinity when he wrote "Triante el Blanco" instead of "Tirante el Blanco." But while he contends that allusions are made to the Catholic Church by more than one character, he ends with the observation that Cervantes had the good sense, not to mention the prudence, to avoid continuing the allegory in so long a work, and to make it yield to character.]

431. Carlyle, Thomas. "Jean Paul Friedrich Richter." In *Works*, XXVII: *Critical and Miscellaneous Essays*, I. New York: AMS Press, 1974, pp. 1-25. [Essay dated 1827.]

Compared to Swift, Shakespeare, Ben Jonson, Sterne, Lessing, and Wieland, Cervantes is the purest of all humorists. So gentle and genial, yet so ethereal is his humor, and in such accordance with itself and his whole noble nature.

432. Coleridge, Samuel Taylor. "Table Talk." In *Coleridge: Select Poetry and Prose*. London: The Nonesuch Press, 1962, p. 502. [First published in 1835, as recorded by H. N. Coleridge in *Specimens of the Table Talk of the Late Samuel Taylor Coleridge*, 1832.]

Don Quijote is not a man out of his senses, but a man in whom imagination and pure reason are so powerful as to make him disregard the evidence of sense when it opposes those impulses. Sancho, on the other hand, is the common sense of the social man-animal, unenlightened and unsanctified by reason, and capable of revering his master at the very moment he is cheating him.

433. Anonymous. "Don Quixote's Library." *Fraser's Magazine* 7 (May, 1833): 324-31 and 565-77.

[After listing the thirty-two literary works mentioned in chapters six and seven of the 1605 *Quijote*, the writer points out that fourteen of them are chivalric romances, while the remainder are either pastoral romances, in prose or verse, or poems which claim epic status. The rest of the article is devoted to the *Dianas* of Montemayor and Gil Polo and to Cervantes' *Galatea*. Plot summaries are furnished, and a few words are dedicated to the general merits of each work.]

434. Lamb, Charles. "John Martin." In *Last Essays of Elia*. London: Moxon, 1833. [From *Athaneum*, January 12, 19, 26, and February 2, 1833. As found in *Lamb as Critic*, Lincoln and London: University of Nebraska Press, 1980, pp. 346-47.]

Cervantes sought to bring forth tears, not laughter, and he who laughs while reading the *Quijote* misinterprets the author's purpose. It is regrettable that in illustrations the Knight is always accompanied by his Squire, because in the first adventures Cervantes wanted to keep the heroic attributes of Don Quijote in the mind of the reader and shield him from the debasing fellowship of the Squire.

Cervantes must have been stung by the public's love of Sancho's foolishness and its disfavor toward Don Quijote's generosities, and that is why, in the 1615 sequel, he let his pen run riot, lost harmony and balance, and yielded to the taste of his contemporaries. In effect, Cervantes abandoned Don Quijote and set up the Squire as his hero. In Part I Sancho respects his master, while in the continuation he becomes a downright knave, only following the mad Knight for his own ends and threatening to harm his former master. From the moment that Sancho loses his respect for Don Quijote, he becomes a treatable lunatic.

435. Cruikshank, George. *Illustrations of Popular Novels and Romances*. London: Charles Tilt, 1834.

[Each of the three paperbound volumes in this set contains five sketches, all by Cruikshank, of episodes in the *Quijote*. Each illustration is accompanied by a brief description of the passage it pertains to.]

436. Coleridge, Samuel Taylor. "Cervantes [Don Quixote]." *Miscellaneous Criticism*. In *Coleridge: Select Poetry and Prose*. London: The Nonesuch Press, 1962, pp. 331-32. [From the Eighth Lecture, 1818. First published in *Literary Remains*, 1836; see entry no. 421.]

Don Quijote resorts to novels of chivalry because he does not like a narrow sphere of power, and the character's genius is of the limited sort which must restlessly seek a vivid representation of its own wishes. The more improbable these romances are, the more they are akin to Don Quijote's will, and, as the novel proceeds, the hero begins to dismiss what

vestiges of common sense he has. The fervor of critical controversy with
the Priest and Barber, for instance, feeds his passion which gives its own
reality to objects; thus his mental striving becomes a madness, a circling in
a stream instead of linear and adaptive thought. Therefore, Don Quijote
grows at length to be a man out of his wits; and as he does so, he becomes
a living allegory, the personification of reason and moral sense divested of
judgment, while Sancho is the converse. He is common sense without
reason or imagination. In other words, Cervantes shows the power of
reason in Don Quijote and the power of common sense in Sancho.
Together the characters form a perfect intellect, but separated, one will
gain mastery over the other, for common sense, although it may see the
practical inapplicability of the dictates of the imagination or abstract
reason, cannot help submitting to them. They are alternately and inter-
changeably the cheater and the cheated, the impersonation of which is one
of the highest creations of genius, achieved by Cervantes and Shakespeare
almost alone.

437. Hallam, Henry. *Introduction to the Literature of Europe*, III. London:
John Murray, 1864, pp. 379-85. [First published in 1837.]

   The *Quijote* is to Europe what Ariosto is to Italy and Shakespare to
England: It is a book rich in allusions and multiple meanings. Readers did
not find any deeper meaning than that which the author announced, nor
did they delay their enjoyment for any metaphysical investigation of
Cervantes' plan until the nineteenth century. The change came with the
new criticism of the German school, namely that of Bouterwek and
Simonde de Sismondi, who regarded the *Quijote* not merely as a satire but
as a book about the eternal contrast between the spirit of poetry and that
of prose. The German school is acute, ingenious, and eminently successful
in philosophical (or, as they denominate it, aesthetic) analyses of works of
taste, but they glide too much into conjectural hypothesis and have a
tendency to mislead men of inferior capacities into mere paradox and
absurdity. For instance, since the group tends to see Don Quijote as a
noble and elevated character, it is no wonder that many have been led to
think of the *Quijote* as a melancholy and even immoral work.

   Cervantes' main intention was not to ridicule the enthusiastic do-
gooder. Don Quijote (especially in the 1605 *Quijote*) is mad and vainly
regards himself as inconquerable. In short, he is a punctilious imitator of
the romances that drove him mad, but has no character when it comes to
ideals; he is the echo of romance.

   However, in the 1615 *Quijote* the case is altered; the hero becomes
more rational, acute, profound, sarcastic, and cool-headed. Thus there are
two Don Quijotes: the first, who is foolish and frantic, and the second,
who is highly gifted, a model of perfect chivalry, but scathed in one part of
his mind by an inexplicable visitation of monomania.

Few books of moral philosophy display as deep an insight into the mechanism of the human mind as *Don Quijote*. And when we look into the fertility of its invention, the probability of its events, and the general simplicity of its story, Cervantes fully deserves the glory of his genius.

While there is improvement in Don Quijote's mind in the 1615 *Quijote*, the sequel is inferior to the 1605 *Quijote*, especially in the realm of verisimilitude.

438. Inglis, H. D. *Rambles in the Footsteps of Don Quixote*. With Illustrations by George Cruikshank. London: Whittaker and Co., 1837. 203 pages.

[Inglis' work consists of twenty-eight chapters in the form of a loose itinerary of Don Quijote's sallies. Having wanted to follow the Knight's footsteps since his boyhood, Inglis first traveled to the village of Miguel Esteban, where he happily met a barber who claimed that the village was indeed the true home of Don Quijote. This same barber later became not only Inglis' guide but literary companion. Thus, in addition to landmarks, this journal also records their debates about the novel's chief merits (Inglis states that it is its humor; the barber insists that the humor is only incidental) and the interpolated tales (Inglis concludes that it is folly to try to separate Don Quijote's adventures from the stories, which are essential to the continuation of the main narrative.) From time to time Inglis himself inserts interpolated stories as told by characters whom he meets.]

439. Anonymous. "Dickens' Tales." *Edinburgh Review* 66, no. 137 (October, 1838): 41-53.

[The critic refers to Pickwick and his man Weller as "the modern Quixote and Sancho of Cockaigne." Since this 1838 article, most scholars of *Pickwick Papers* have assumed the affinity between Cervantes and Dickens without bothering to examine the validity of the claim.]

440. Roscoe, Thomas. *The Life and Writings of Miguel de Cervantes Saavedra*. London: T. Tegg, 1839. 412 pages.

The *Quijote* is not only the liveliest and most delicate satire, but also the most original and effective. Although Simonde de Sismondi states that the *Quijote* is one of the most melancholy books ever written, the novel demonstrates how prejudiced a high degree of enthusiasm can be both to the individual and to society. But the contrast between the heroic world and the vulgar world and the raillery of enthusiasm were not the only objects Cervantes had in view. The *Quijote* was, in addition, an attack on the literature of the time, the wretched compositions on chivalry, which perverted national tastes and had no basis in reality.

441. Ruskin, John. *The Diaries of John Ruskin*, I: 1835-1847. Selected and edited by Joan Evans and John Howard Whitehouse. Oxford: Clarendon Press, 1936, p. 625. [Dated December 15, 1840.]

    Don Quijote is so intensely amusing that the want of plan is easily forgiven.

442. Dickens, Charles. Seventeen brief allusions to the *Quijote* over a period of 28 years, beginning with the preface to the third edition of *Oliver Twist*, 1841. [For a discussion, see Steven H. Gale's "Cervantes' Influence on Dickens, with Comparative Emphasis on *Don Quijote* and *Pickwick Papers*," *Anales Cervantinos* 12 (1973): 135-56.]

    [Found in six novels, three collections, and in various letters, Dickens' allusions are very brief, but he generally praises Don Quijote's idealism and wishes to show some fascination with his library.]

443. Ruskin, John. "Introductory" to *Modern Painters*, Part I. In *The Works of John Ruskin, M. A.*, VI. New York: Thomas Y. Crowell & Company, 1901, p. 73. [First edition is London: Smith, Elder & Co., 1843.]

    There is a hierarchy of interpretations among readers of the *Quijote*: The lowliest mind would find perpetual and brutal amusement in the misfortunes of Don Quijote and perpetual pleasure in sympathy with his Squire, while a mind of average feeling would perceive the satirical meaning of the book and appreciate its wit, elegance, and truth. However, only elevated and peculiar minds would discover the moral beauty of truth in the character of the hero and understand its manifestation and expression of fortitude, self-devotion, and universal love.

444. Ford, Richard. *A Hand-book for Travelers in Spain and Readers at Home*, I: *Preliminary Remarks, and Andalusia*. Carbondale, Illinois: Southern Illinois University Press, 1966, pp. 471-77. [First published in London: J. Murray, 1845.]

    Don Quijote was not written to criticize knight-errantry, because that had passed with its age and with it the love for reading the ponderous folios of romance. Had *Don Quijote* been a mere parody or satire on them, both the conqueror and the conquered would long ago have been buried in the same grave and forgotten. Instead, it is "Cervantes loquitur" all through the story. The novel is made the vehicle for Cervantes' own chivalric temperament, for his philosophical comment on human life, and for his criticism of manners, institutions, and literature. Don Quijote is a delineation of the former highbred Spaniard, a hater of injustice and lover of virtue; he is a monomaniac. But the last is not a quality unbecoming to a Castilian hidalgo, for although the sweet bells of his intellect are jangled and out of tune, he is always the gentleman, always generous, elevated, and beneficent. Moreover, our feelings of pity and sympathy, always strong in his favor, increase when he recovers his senses in the second part. This may be because Cervantes did not anticipate the spirit of ridicule which he excited against the chivalric. Thus the tone and character of his hero rise in Part II.

It is also a mistake to consider Sancho Panza (Paunch) a vulgar clown. A homely, shrewd, natural, sanguine, and self-deluding native of La Mancha, he may be compared with the gravediggers in *Hamlet* or the *Demos* in Aristophanes. In spite of his preferring his belly to honor, and his *bota* to truth, not to mention his ambition and his truly Spanish reference to self and his own interest, one loves him for the affection which he bears to his master, for his Boswell-like admiration; that is, he believes everything in spite of his master's eccentricities, even though he notices and condemns them.

As for the wit that pervades the *Quijote*, it is enhanced by Cervantes' ability to bring the sublime into constant contact with the ridiculous. The never-failing charm of the conversation of master and man is only one example for such contrasts throughout the novel. Moreover, if real wit consists in bringing together things which have no apparent connection, then all books must yield to the *Quijote*.

Cervantes, like Shakespeare, is distinguished from his contemporaries by an avoidance of those coarse and indecent allusions so prevalent in picaresque literature of the time. Instead he prefers light burlesque and irony. Want of decency was a want of sense for Cervantes. He also eschewed the affected euphemisms of the day. While Cervantes' tact and judgment always kept his wit and ridicule in its proper place, the rich air of poetry and his dramatic delineation of character show that he was not merely a writer of novels but of tragedy that reached almost epic proportions.

445. Ross, Thomasina. *El Buscapié, by Miguel de Cervantes, with the Illustrative Notes of Don Adolfo de Castro. Translated from the Spanish, with a Life of the Author, and Some Account of his Works*. London: Richard Bentley, 1849. 235 pages.

Adolfo de Castro's *Buscapié* is authentic. Other critics only conjecture as to the contents of the legendary *Buscapié*—a sort of key to the *Quijote* in which the persons alluded to were named. In Adolfo de Castro's version this is not true, and those who consider the *Quijote* a satire on Charles V or the Duke of Lerma are without justification in doing so.

446. Anonymous. Review of *El Buscapié, by Miguel de Cervantes, with Illustrative Notes of Don Adolfo de Castro. Translated from the Spanish, with a Life*

of the Author, and Some Account of his Works, by Thomasina Ross, London, 1849. *Dublin Review* 26 (March, 1849): 137-52.

The *Buscapié* was supposedly written in defense of the *Quijote* to vindicate it from the unjust criticisms, by which it had been assailed, and to show that it was worthy of being read by the wise and the learned. Cervantes' masterpiece is still not understood by the multitude, who do not see the noble sentiments, the lofty aspirations, and the loving genuine chivalry of the hero.

447. Anonymous. Review of *History of Spanish Literature,* by George Ticknor. *The Quarterly Review* 87, no. 174 (September, 1850): 289-330.

The tiresome, interminable romances of chivalry, whether lay or clerical, have had their day. Peace to their ashes, and forgiveness, for to them we owe *Don Quijote.* While gunpowder practically reduced knighthood to the ranks, Cervantes, in his immortal work, laughed Spain's chivalry away and dissipated the glorious dream. The very masterpiece that sent them to the collector's shelf testified to the extent of their previous vitality. Cervantes' acquaintance with them was intimate, and the fact that they had engaged the essentially chivalrous nature of his genius is evident in every chapter of *Don Quijote.*

448. Ruskin, John. *Ruskin's Letters from Venice, 1851-1852.* Edited by John Lewis Bradley. Westport, Connecticut: Greenwood Press, 1978, pp. 78-79. [Letter dated December 3, 1851.]

[In this letter to his father, Ruskin asks why Henry Hallam's comments on the *Quijote* annoyed him, and reflects: "I think when I read it next—for it is long now since I looked at it—I may perhaps be a little doubtful about the main scope of the book and purpose of it, things which in old times I troubled myself little about." As it is, though, Ruskin is beginning to wonder about the moral value of the novel because, as he puts it: "I believe there is by no means enough Knight-Errantry in the world—a good deal of Errantry without the Knighthood—but little of that Spirit which Cervantes has at once raised and ridiculed in this marvellous portraiture; and, in nine minds out of ten, the *Quijote* is merely ridiculous, so that I imagine the book, in the long run, to have done great harm."]

449. Clarke, Mary Cowden. "The Women of the Writers." *The Ladies' Companion* (London), 2nd Series, 2 (1852): 16. [As summarized by Richard D. Altick in *The Cowden Clarkes,* London: Oxford University Press, 1948, and by Arthur Efron, "Satire Denied..." pp. 133-34.]

Marcela, Luscinda, Dorotea, and Zoraida are sweet-natured, active, prompt, energetic beings full of generous emotions. Their actions are all in consonance with their sentiments. They are beautiful in person, graceful in demeanor, and capable of the utmost warmth and tenderness of devotion. They are also gentle, yet not feeble, soft and kindly of manner, yet spirited in conduct.

450. Chambers, William and Robert Chambers. "Miguel de Cervantes." In *Chambers' Repository of Instructive and Amusing Tracts*, VIII, no. 55. London and Edinburgh: W. and B. Chambers, 1853. 32 pages.

The *Quijote* is not an attempt to discredit books of chivalry, but an excuse for Cervantes to talk at length about his favorite form of literature. His satire is much too good-natured to have proceeded from a hostile pen.

Don Quijote is an original and innately excellent figure, though at times tedious, while the interpolated tales are uninteresting or absurd. The *Curioso impertinente*, for instance, is a horrid tragedy, inconsistent in many of its incidents with nature, and Italianate in content. Similarly, the African adventures are dull, although the Dorotea episode is one of the most beautiful parts of the novel.

There is even less imagination, less wit, less vivacity, less humor and pathos, and less freshness of imagery in the 1615 *Quijote*. However, the style is more varied, the diction and syntax more eloquent, and the tone more elevated. Sancho becomes tiresome, and Don Quijote runs into extravagances not perfectly in harmony with the prevailing principles of his mind at the time. Ironically, however, we admire Cervantes' ability to make us love the Knight, a man who is little more than a buffoon. He is a man who alternates between folly and calamity, a man of singular variety in his unique character. Sancho is full of moral contrasts: he is a pleasure-loving creature, yet a man of affection, loyalty, and good sense.

451. J. B. P. "*Don Quixote.*" *Notes and Queries* 10 (July-December, 1854): 343.

The *Quijote* figure is an attack on Ignatius of Loyola and the Jesuits, a dominant craze of Cervantes' time; and Dulcinea is a satire on the Virgin Mary. These intentions Cervantes could not afford to state openly.

452. MacCabe, W. B. "*Don Quixote.*" *Notes and Queries* 10 (July-December, 1854): 407-08.

Cervantes was a serious Catholic, not an anticlerical thinker. Cervantes wrote a sonnet to the Virgin Mary and composed verses on the occasion of the beatification of Teresa de Avila. He was a member of the Third Order of Saint Francis, and there is no resemblance between Saint Ignatius of Loyola and Don Quijote (or between Dulcinea and the Virgin Mary). He is too lovable to be a satire of Loyola.

453. Ruskin, John. *Lectures on Architecture and Painting*. In *Works*, XII. London: George Allen, 1903, p. 56. [Delivered at Edinburgh in No-

vember, 1853; published in London: Smith, Elder & Co., 1854.]

The *Quijote* is a book written against the holiest principles of humanity.

454. Ruskin, John. "Letter to Mrs. Hugh Blackburn." March 17 (c. 1855-1856). [As cited in Edward Tyas Cook's *The Life of John Ruskin*, New York: Haskell House, 1968, p. 479.]

If Don Quixote had not been mad, I should have preferred him to Sir Charles Grandison. On the whole I believe I do.

455. Masson, David. *British Novelists and their Styles, Being a Critical Sketch of the History of British Prose Fiction.* Cambridge, England: MacMillan and Co., 1859. 308 pages.

In *Joseph Andrews*, as in Fielding's later novels, the influence of Cervantes is clearly visible, as it is in Smollett as well. The plot of *Sir Launcelot Greaves* is that of the *Quijote*, only slightly changed.

Homer, Shakespeare, and Cervantes are ideal artists, true to nature; not one of their most pronounced characters is exactly as it was to be found, or ever will be found, in nature. They are all the result of some suggestion snatched from nature, in one or other of her uttermost moments, and then carried away and developed in the void. For the ideal artist, the question is, What can be made of this: with what human ends and aspirations can they be imaginatively interwoven, so that the whole, though attached to nature by its origin, shall transcend or overlie nature on the side of the possibly existent?

456. Langford, John Alfred. "Cervantes." In *Prison Books and their Authors.* London: William Tegg, 1861, pp. 58-82.

Cervantes is a writer who knew men and women as they were, not as they were drawn in books. His pages are vital and his characters are of flesh and blood. Even his pastoral and sentimental interpolations have realistic touches which redeem them. Commentaries of the *Quijote* are faulty because what was clear they have made obscure and what was simple they have made difficult. The list of critical follies is long with some critics seeing one design in the romance and others finding in it a whole scheme of metaphysics; one a system of criticism; others a clear,unmistakable satire on all things noble and lofty; one an earnest and sober defense of those all-important parts of our nature; others think it a skeptical and irreligious work, and some a truly pious production, directing its satire only against the abuses of the Church. Critics prone to look beneath the surface of a book can readily dig up theories, but simple readers had very much better take the work as it is.

Every adventure is a source of joy, and Don Quijote is an object of both laughter and respect. Cervantes took care not to make him ridiculous, but a brave, learned, courteous, sensible gentleman, thus keeping his hero from appearing contemptible. This is Cervantes' great art, and even a mark of his genius, for while every adventure in which Don Quijote engages is absurd in the extreme, he never loses our respect. And the genius of Cervantes is even more thoroughly exhibited in the character of Sancho than in that of Don Quijote; in fact, a more thoroughly or better delineated character was never drawn.

457. Lytton, Edward George. *Caxtonia: A Series of Essays on Life, Literature, and Manners.* Part XVI, no. xxii: "On Certain Principles of Art in Works of Imagination." *Blackwood's Edinburgh Magazine* 93, no. 571 (May 1863): 545-60.

Cervantes' hero would have an abnormal and morbid personality subjected to the caricature of a satirist if taken as a realistic portrait, but regarded as a type with certain qualities which are largely diffused throughout human nature, Don Quijote is psychologically true and artistically complete. Hence, the word "quixotic" is used whenever one wants to convey the idea of extravagant enthusiasm for the redress of human wrongs.

The skillful mechanism of plot is much less a requisite in the novel than in drama, and many of the greatest prose fictions are independent of plot altogether. It is only by straining the word "plot" to a meaning foreign to the sense it generally conveys that we can recognize a plot in *Don Quijote*.

458. M'Carthy, D. F. "Cervantes and Shakespeare." *Athenaeum*, March 26, 1864: 440-41.

Louis Viardot noted in 1836 that because of a difference between the English and the Spanish calendar Shakespeare and Cervantes did not share the same date of death after all; the Englishman survived Cervantes by twelve days.

459. Anonymous. "Don Quixote." *The Westminster and Foreign Quarterly Review*, New Series, 30, no. 2 (April 1, 1868): 299-327.

In literature we have to thank God and Cervantes for an increase in good humor, pleasantness, originality, all that makes human nature lovable, and for bringing fiction to the level of common life. As for Cervantes' intention in writing the novel, the author's repeated assertion that his only purpose was to destroy the popularity of novels of chivalry seems to have been merely intended to quiet the minds of court politicians and professional guardians of the faith.

The *Quijote* is not a study of the spirit-flesh duality of life, but instead the result of Cervantes' power of observation and his desire to teach men through laughter and smiles. Cervantes restored Spain's healthy literary taste and thereby purified the affection of Spaniards.

Cervantes had great genius and courage despite his being regarded an outcast by his learned contemporaries. Especially praiseworthy are the proverbs, the manner in which the author presents the scenery and personalities of Spain, and the chaste, sweet music of Cervantes' style.

Cervantes' novel was the first scientific study of insanity and its cure. The novelist discovered the only method of curing chiromania (sic) and used all his might to bring mankind from under the guidance of those who were its victims. The insanity of the hero is a faithful historical picture of the madness of the times; Charles V and the Duke of Lerma were possible originals for the mad hidalgo; and Loyola was a prototype for Don Quijote, the only difference being that the latter was restored to his senses at the end. However, in pursuing his study of insanity, Cervantes did not mean to condemn heroism and personal prowess in the battle of life, self-denial, and deeds of mercy done to wronged or suffering man. Cervantes sought to teach men to live free—free of all Holy Inquisitions and free of priests. Furthermore, the novel is not bitter; it springs from a large and loving heart, full of generous intentions. Cervantes warns men of the horrors of madness in order to save them from going mad and to guard against the schemes of madmen.

460. Ruskin, John. Letter dated August 9, 1870. In *Letters of John Ruskin to Charles Eliot Norton*, II. Boston-New York: Houghton, Mifflin and Company, 1905, pp. 16-17.

[In a letter to Norton dated July 8, 1870, Ruskin had written that Charles Dickens "was as little understood as Cervantes, and almost as mischievous." In this letter, written the following month, Ruskin states that as far as mischief is concerned he sees no distinction between the 1605 and the 1615 *Quijote*. He also writes of the impact of the novel and of its subject, emphasizing that it always affected him "throughout with tears, not laughter" and that it was "always real chivalry" to him because Cervantes renders valor and tenderness vain by madness, and because they are vain, they are made the subject of laughter to vulgar and shallow persons. All true chivalry is, by implication, madness and shame, he concludes, and for this reason, the book is "deadly."]

461. Thornbury, Walter. "Did Shakespeare Ever Read *Don Quijote?*" *Notes and Queries*, 4th Series, 8 (July-December, 1871): 201.

Shelton's translation of the first part of the *Quijote* was published in 1612, four years prior to Shakespeare's death, and thus the English poet probably read the Spaniard's novel.

462. Shorthouse, J. Henry. "Did Shakespeare Ever Read *Don Quijote?*" *Notes and Queries*, 4th Series, 8 (July-December, 1871): 295.

Thornbury was wrong in using Jarvis' translation of the opening passage of the *Quijote*. He should have used Shelton's version.

463. Watts, H. E. "Did Shakespeare Ever Read *Don Quijote?*" *Notes and Queries*, 4th Series, 8 (July-December, 1871): 295.

There is scarcely a doubt that Shakespeare read the *Quijote*, whether Shelton's version or the Italian translation. That there are no allusions to Cervantes' novel in Shakespeare's works proves nothing, although there is a certain parallelism between Christopher Sly and Sancho Panza as governor of his island.

464. Watts, H. E. "Cervantes and his Translators." *Notes and Queries*, 4th Series, 8 (July-December, 1871): 392.

Shelton's version of the *Quijote* is superior to that of Jarvis (Jervas) because Shelton's version is "the least bad of all the bad ones." Jarvis is a dull, prosy, commonplace fellow, utterly insensible to the humor and deeper meaning of Cervantes' novel. Even so, Jarvis' version is better than those of Smollett, Motteux, and Philips.

465. Frere, John Hookham. *Works*, I. London: Basil Montague Pickering, 1872, p. clix.

There are two kinds of burlesque, both of which are found in the *Quijote*: the burlesque of fantasies (Don Quijote's belief that a wench at a country inn is a princess, for example) and the burlesque of rude common sense (Sancho's plans of how he will deal with the subjects of his island).

466. Brown, Rawdon. "Miguel de Cervantes, of Alcalá de Henares, and Carlo Emmanuele, of Savoy, and his Ass-colts." *Athenaeum*, April 12, 1872: 471-73; April 19, 1873: 503-05; May 3, 1873: 564-66.

[Brown tries to relate certain episodes of the *Quijote* to the occupation of Saluzzo in 1600. He believes that Cervantes resented the persecution of the Infante Philip and his brothers by Lerma. After examining the Andrés episode, the delivery of the bill of exchange for three ass-colts to Sancho, and the Eugenio episode in some detail, Brown discusses the identity of Fernández de Avellaneda and concludes that the true author of the spurious *Quijote* was one Gaspar Schöppe, "a creature and pensioner" of the Duke of Lerma.]

467. Duffield, Alexander J. "Cervantes no fué teólogo." *Crónica de los Cervantistas* 2, no. 1 (January 28, 1873): 7-9.

In addition to degrading the genius of Cervantes, attempts to prove he was a theologian accomplish nothing. Similar efforts were made in the case of Shakespeare.

468. Anonymous. "Don Quixote." *Cornhill Magazine* 30 (November, 1874): 595-616.

The object of Cervantes' satire has been misunderstood. It has been declared that he intended to put an end, not to the absurd romances, but to knight-errantry itself, which, as Mr. Ford said, expired a century before Cervantes' birth. The goal of the novel was doubtless to show that the deeper, truer, and purer a man is, the more he will become the jest and butt of this world of ours. Thus, as Charles Lamb said, readers who see nothing more than burlesque in the *Quijote* have but a shallow appreciation of that immortal work. Other misunderstandings arise when irony is mistaken for truth, or, as is more often the case, from the primitive typography of the earlier editions.

Translators who have endeavored to make Don Quijote witty after their own conception of humor have succeeded only in turning him into a buffoon. They look upon Cervantes' work as a comedy, not perceiving the tragedy beneath the surface. What is worse, by eliminating this element, translators have managed also to rid the work of that contrast between the sadness of language and the ludicrousness of situation, which is perhaps the novel's most enduring charm.

[Other matters discussed include: theories concerning the authorship of the Avellaneda *Quijote*; other adaptations of the *Quijote*; the poor quality of English translations of Cervantes' novel; the pre-Cervantine attacks on chivalric novels; Clemencín's criticism of Cervantes' lack of unity and anachronisms; and the question of whether the principal characters of the *Quijote* were intended to be parodies of Cervantes' contemporaries. The critic answers to this last question with the quip: "Those who indulge in these fantasies are like that beetle which, carefully avoiding rose leaves, feeds on dung."]

469. Stephen, Leslie. "Charlotte Brontë." In *Hours in a Library*, III. London: Smith, Elder, & Co., 1892, pp. 1-30. [First published in London, 1874-1879.]

Don Quijote stands apart as one of the greatest creations of the poetic imagination. Paul Emanuel, on the other hand, has too much of the accidental and too little of the essential. Don Quijote is of perennial interest because he is the most powerful manifestation of the contrast between the ideal and the commonplace, and his figure comes before us whenever we are forced to meditate upon some of the vital and most melancholy truths about life. Uncle Toby, to a lesser extent, is a vital creation because he is the embodiment of one answer to a profound and enduring problem. As has been said, he represents the wisdom of love, while Mr. Shandy represents the love of wisdom.

470. Duffield, Alexander J. "Traducciones inglesas de *El Quijote*." *Crónica de los Cervantistas* 2, no. 4 (September 19, 1875): 142-44.

Shelton's translation of the *Quijote* (1612 and 1620) is still considered the best by many, even though a large number of the words are antiquated. Stevens' translation of 1705 contains few changes, and Philips' version of 1687 is obscene. Motteux's translation of 1700 is of some merit, despite its licentious and coarse phrases, while Jarvis' version should be faulted for copying that of Shelton, even its errors. Smollett's translation is more faithful than Motteux's, although it, too, occasionally violates decorum, while the Ozell and Kelly translations, 1725 and 1745 respectively, are only reproductions of the Motteux rendition. The Wilmot translation omits many passages.

471. Burke, Ulick Ralph. *Sancho Panza's Proverbs, and Others Which Occur in Don Quixote, with a Literal English Translation, and an Introduction*. London: Pickering and Chatto, 1892. 116 pages. [The first edition of this work, *Sancho Panza's Proverbs*, was published in 1872; the second edition, under the title *Spanish Salt*, was published in 1877.]

[This collection includes proverbs not only from the *Quijote* but from other Cervantine works as well, although Burke admits that he has stretched the word "proverb" to include pithy sayings which are not technically proverbs. Burke points out that there are more proverbs in the 1615 *Quijote* than in the 1605 *Quijote*, and that Don Quijote himself is also prone to their use. The sayings are arranged alphabetically by key word, and reference is made to the place each is found in Cervantes' works. Four hundred and ten sayings are listed, translated into English (and at times into other languages), and explained. In some cases the origin of the proverb is given.]

472. Meredith, George. "On the Idea of Comedy, and of the Uses of the Comic Spirit." *New Quarterly Magazine* 8 (January-June, 1877): 1-40.

The juxtaposition of Don Quijote and Sancho is a comic conception and the opposition of their natures most humorous. They are as different as the two hemispheres in the time of Columbus, yet they touch and are bound in one by laughter. Moreover, the Knight's great aims and constant mishaps, his chivalric valiantness exercized on absurd objects, his good sense along the high road of the maddest of expeditions, the compassion he plucks out of derision, and the admirable figure he preserves while stalking through the fanatically grotesque and burlesque, assailing them in the loftiest moods of humor, fuse the tragic sentiment with the comic narrative.

The humor of Cervantes and Shakespeare, a humor of heart and mind, contains both the robustness of Aristophanes and the delicacy of Molière.

473. Swinburne, Algernon Charles. "A Note on Charlotte Brontë." In *Complete Works*, XIV: *Prose Works*, IV. New york: Russell & Russell, 1968, pp. 3-42. [First published in London: Chatto & Windus, 1877.]

We smile at Uncle Toby, but never have to wince at anything that is incongruous with the qualities that evoke our affectionate regard, while our sense of Colonel Newcome's intellectual infirmity and imperfection is never quite overcome by our sense of his moral or chivalrous excellence, a feeling which impairs Thackeray's *The Newcomes*. On the other hand, with Cervantes' Knight and Charlotte Brontë's Paul Emanuel, we need make no such allowance. Both Cervantes and Charlotte Brontë are to be praised for their moral insight and dramatic imagination in their creation.

474. Duffield, Alexander J. "*Don Quixote.*" *Notes and Queries*, 6th Series, 1 (January-June, 1880): 22.

How it ever happened that a book so pure in spirit and so chaste in words, so lofty in style and yet so full of human sympathy and love as *Don Quijote* came to be regarded by English men of letters as a book of lowly buffoonery is a question that I trust at no distant day will be satisfactorily answered by those who pretend to know something of the history of English and Spanish humor.

475. Duffield, Alexander J. "*Don Quixote.*" *Notes and Queries*, 6th Series, 1 (January-June, 1880): 158-59.

Byron is wrong to state that the *Quijote* is one of the saddest works ever written. There are thousands of things to laugh at in this book which require no special knowledge, though to understand the work as a satire on *literary* chivalry (not true chivalry) requires an intimate knowledge of such works as the *Amadís*.

476. Oliphant, Margaret. *Cervantes*. Philadelphia: J. B. Lippincott, 1881. 212 pages. [First published in Edinburgh and London: W. Blackwood & Sons, 1880.]

While most people vent disappointment, the sense of having made themselves ridiculous, and the consciousness that their best intended enterprises and boldest efforts for the good of others have turned out foolish, in bitterness, rather than laughter, Cervantes had the heart, with his cheerful genius and vision of ridicule, to turn it all into laughter, with no complaint of injury received and not even a sigh for the follies. This is the secret of *Don Quijote*.

477. Swinburne, Algernon Charles. *A Study of Shakespeare*. London: Chatto & Windus, 1880, pp. 107-09.

Victor Hugo's assertion that Falstaff is inferior to Sancho but superior to Rabelais' Panurge is mistaken. Falstaff is as superior to Sancho as Sancho is superior to Panurge. In Sancho we come upon a creature capable of love—but not a love that can kill or help kill, or a love that may end or even seem to end in anything like heartbreak.

478. Duffield, Alexander J. *Don Quixote, His Critics and Commentators.* London: C. Kegan Paul & Co., 1881. 155 pages.

Cervantes was primarily a social reformer. In the *Quijote* there are sly hits and asides, general satire, and tolerant scorn aimed at the secret vices of the times. The chivalric romances Cervantes ridiculed were used by the Church to tighten its grip on men, for such books were escapist literature that kept the mind of the people in a tropical atmosphere. The Inquisition clearly saw Cervantes' meaning, but kept silent for fear of calling attention to the novelist's true meaning. In contrasting Rabelais and Cervantes, one finds that the principal differences between the two is that Cervantes does not laugh at men; he makes men laugh at themselves.

Cervantes purpose was threefold: first, that it is easy for even the best of men to go insane; second, that it is easy to aggravate the disease by the application of inappropriate remedies; and third, that even for those who are wilfully mad, healing is possible if the right remedy is applied with knowledge and skill.

One should read the 1615 *Quijote* before going on to the earlier edition, because it contains fewer obscure allusions to chivalric literature.

479. Gibson, James Y. "Preface" to translation of *Journey to Parnassus* composed by Miguel de Cervantes Saavedra. London: Kegan Paul, Trench and Co. 1883. pp. ix-lxv.

Behind the visor of the immortal Knight, who seems born for no other reason than to banish loathed Melancholy from the world and replace it with heart-easing Mirth and Laughter holding both his sides, we are confronted with the face of a man whose eyes betray no spark of insanity but a glowing enthusiasm tempered with all sorts of humorous gleamings.

Duffield is wrong for overemphasizing the humor of the book and for his sensational estimate of Cervantes' purpose in writing the *Quijote*. Thanks to Duffield one can no longer look upon it as a book of pleasant pastime, as the *Viaje del Parnaso* says it is, nor merely as a book designed to replace and exterminate certain evil, corrupting books as Cervantes himself maintained, but as one of those peculiar books, whose real contents must be read between the lines.

One would not have to prove that Cervantes was a good Catholic, because it is enough to know that Cervantes was an upright and honest man, whose religion was simply the creed of his country and his comrades, a part of his second nature, never obtrusive, never bigoted, but always sincere. Furthermore, the great avocation of Cervantes was that of letters. His chief pride was to be ranked among the divine order of poets from which lofty elevation he was free to use his brilliant wit to strike at folly, vice, and ignorance, whenever he met them, in Church or State, or in the world of literature. Through Cervantes' laughter the world has grown merrier and wiser.

480. Ormsby, John. "Introduction" to *The Ingenious Gentleman Don Quixote of La Mancha*, I. London: Smith, Elder & Co., 1885, pp. 1-77.

The cause of the *Quijote*'s popularity lies in the catholic nature of the novel: there is something in it for every sort of reader, young or old, sage or simple, while the element of farce insures it success among the multitude.

At first, critics said that the *Quijote* was a droll book, full of laughable incidents and absurd situations, very amusing, but not entitled to much consideration or care. England was the first country to recognize that the *Quijote* deserved better treatment, and a number of admirers now claim that it is a crime to view Cervantes' novel as a humorous book.

Perhaps German philosophy never evolved a more ungainly or unlikely camel out of the depths of its inner consciousness than the allegorical interpretation. And although something of this antagonism between the ideal and real may be found in the *Quijote*, it is because this is found everywhere in life. To suppose that Cervantes deliberately set out to expound such an allegory is something not only very unlike the age in which Cervantes lived, but altogether unlike Cervantes himself. There are those who seek deep political meanings lying under the drolleries of the novel, a kind of pastime for literary idlers who hunt for occult meanings in the various episodes of the work.

Cervantes did not satirize the Church, dogma, or the Inquisition; he was a faithful son of the Church, who was sincere in his support of the expulsion of the *moriscos*. However, Cervantes was a philosopher in the best sense of the word, for he knew how to endure the ills of life philosophically.

None of these elaborate theories and ingenious speculations is really necessary to explain the meaning of the *Quijote*, for the extraordinary influence of chivalric romances in Cervantes' day is quite enough to account for the genius of the book. Cervantes did not attack chivalry itself, as Byron said, but only the degrading mockery of it. Thus the *Quijote* is not a sad and pessimistic book; instead, it is a condemnation of spurious enthusiasm born of vanity and self-conceit.

Cervantes originally intended to write a short story. He first became aware of the possibilities of changing his novel from a string of farcical misadventures to a burlesque of books of chivalry, mocking their style, incidents, and spirit, as he wrote the episode of the examination of Don Quijote's library. At this point, the author hastily and somewhat clumsily divided his work into chapters and introduced Cide Hamete Benengeli. He also found Sancho could work as an unconscious Mephistopheles, always unwittingly making fun of his master's aspirations. In addition, Cervantes was a writer who mistrusted his own powers of extracting from the Don Quijote-Sancho Panza dialogue enough to fill a book and found sustained effort and the limitations of a main plot painful. Since the author felt doubtful of his venture, he sought insurance against total failure by introducing the interpolated tales, which are not only out of place, but are definite blemishes with uninteresting characters and, even worse, a prolix style.

The 1615 *Quijote* possesses the more natural style as the work of a man finally sure of himself and his audience. The Knight of Part I had no character or individuality whatever; he was nothing more than a representative of the sentiments of the chivalric romances. (Byron was absurd in saying that it was Don Quijote's virtue that made him mad, for it was his madness in imitating romances of chivalry that made him virtuous.) On the other hand, in Part II Cervantes invests his hero with a dignity wholly lacking in Part I, making him speak with an exceptionally clear mind as a mouthpiece for his author's own reflections. Sancho is also different in Part II; no longer a caricature, the Squire becomes more important, and more imaginative, in his lies.

While Part I is richer in laughable incidents, Part II is richer in character. And while Part I may be the favorite of those who prefer farce, Part II is the favorite of those who enjoy comedy.

481. Dawson, George. "Don Quixote." In *Shakespeare and Other Lectures.* London: Kegan Paul, Trench & Co., 1888, pp. 128-38.

Why do people like the *Quijote* so much? It is for the individuality and universality of the characters as well as the accurate imitation of men, manners, and the condition of society. The author keeps Don Quijote a poor but upright gentleman in all his troubles. This is just what makes the work so admirable and so wonderful; the hero never once becomes contemptible.

Don Quijote's ascendancy over Sancho shows that his brain, though a little twisted, is born to rule over the thickheads of common sense. Common sense is always gullible, and through credulity Sancho becomes a knight-errant, a lay brother of the order, who acquires a taste for adventure in his own way.

The Barataria episode is the deepest, wisest, most satirical, and most profitable part of the book, for here the work becomes a manual of politics, a satire upon royalty, and a quiz on etiquette; it puts the nonsense of man into the pillory. Don Quijote and Sancho are educated by the events in which they are engaged. The Knight progresses in all, except that he retains his obsession. Sancho graduates, so that when he nears the island of Barataria, he is no longer a simple clown. Cervantes always looks further than the amusement of his readers, though he never forgets it. And in this part of the book he teaches that the science of government is not the secret of a family, cannot be monopolized by a caste, and cannot be communicated in universities, but instead that the chief requirements are a sound mind and good intentions.

Very few books have been debated as much. To those who find the *Quijote* to be a mischievous and melancholy work, let it be said that a great book must always be a melancholy (though not a mischievous) one. Lord Byron's view that Cervantes' novel delivered a mortal blow to chivalry is faulty; chivalry was already dead. While Byron's lines are witty and brilliant, they are false. Cervantes' purpose was to make a clean sweep of all chivalric novels and to teach men that though literary forms may pass away, righteousness, truth, and beauty are eternal; indifferent to literary forms, these values are ready to adopt the highest or lowest manifestations.

482. Forster, Joseph. "Lope de Vega and Cervantes." In *Some French and Spanish Men of Genius*. London: Ellis and Elvey, 1891, pp. 271-310.

Lope's work deals merely with the external, while Cervantes' immortal novel searches into the depths of life and passion. In the *Quijote* are the broad humanity, rich humor, and genial tolerance of human weakness and folly that made Shakespeare the never-failing delight of the whole world. While Lope's genius was ripe at once, the *Quijote* did not spring up like a reed; it contains the hoarded experience of a life, which no young man could have written.

Don Quijote represents the fatal result of romantic feeling and enthusiasm without common sense to guide and control them. On the other hand (and this is the priceless lesson of the book), Sancho Panza shows to what extent the mere worship of ease and the vulgar will degrade men. If enthusiasm could have been combined with a little of the vulgar self-love of the Squire, one extreme might have corrected the other, and we would have had a wise gentlemen instead of a maniac and a brute.

483. Watts, H. E. *Life of Miguel de Cervantes*. London: Walter Scott, 1891. 185 pages.

Because the *Quijote* is a reflection of the author's life, there is no need to speculate about any mysteries regarding its purpose. Only those who ignore Cervantes' declaration (that he meant only to write a book of entertainment) will continue to hug their theories of recondite inner meanings.

It was not until a century and a half after Cervantes' death that Spain recognized the *Quijote* as anything more than passing entertainment. People thought of it as little more than a chapbook, a collection of drolleries which even some Spaniards regarded as a scandalous caricature of prominent vices of their national character. Certain Spaniards thought Cervantes laughed at his own country, and the critic Zavaleta attacked him furiously, in 1750, for his betrayal of Spain.

Laudable is the clarity of Cervantes' style, although he can be the target of critics, such as Clemencín. It is true that his language is loose, irregular, and incorrect, and sometimes a sentence is left in the air with the predicate wanting. Other times, the parts do not join, or there is a confusion of relatives, or a discord of antecedents. But never is the writer false, affected, or vain, except in the way of burlesque and to suit the character speaking or the situation.

484. Fitzmaurice-Kelly, James. *The Life of Miguel de Cervantes Saavedra. A Biographical, Literary, and Historical Study with a Tentative Bibliography from 1585 to 1892, and An Annotated Appendix on the Canto de Calíope*. London: Chapman and Hall, 1892. 396 pages.

The *Quijote* struck a fresh vein by exposing the painful and necessary contrast between the ideal and the actual, the true and the false.

While Cervantes lacks Shakespeare's vast sweep, power, and universality, Cervantes' vision, if not wide, is deep; his grasp, if restricted, is intense; his observation, if narrow, is profound. Also noteworthy are the *Quijote*'s lofty, sustained enthusiasm, its dash of exaggeration, its dignity of sentiment, and its tenacious vigor, which is characteristic of the Spaniard.

485. Ruskin, John. Letter to Mr. F. S. Ellis. [As cited by Edward Tyas Cook in *The Life of John Ruskin*, I. New York: Haskell House, 1968, p. 371. No date given.]

[Cook refers to a letter by Ruskin to F. S. Ellis in which Ruskin states that Sir Thomas More's *Utopia* is "perhaps the most truly mischievous book ever written—except for *Don Quixote*." However, the reference could not be found in *Stray Letters from Professor Ruskin to a London Bibliopole*, London: Privately Printed (for Mr. F. S. Ellis), 1892.]

486. Watts, H. E. "Translations of Don *Quijote*." *Notes and Queries*, 8th Series, 4 (July-December, 1893): 402-03.

[This is a critical review of nine English versions of the *Quijote* (not including abridgments and revised and mutilated editions) that had been published as of 1893. They include those of Shelton, 1612; John Philips, 1687 ("without point or grace"); Peter Motteux, 1712 ("overpraised"); Charles Jarvis (or Jervas), 1742; Smollett, 1755 ("careless and inaccurate"); Miss Mary Smirke, 1818; A. J. Duffield, 1881; J. Ormsby, 1885; and H. E. Watts, 1888-1889. More translations of the *Quijote* exist in English than in any other language, the critic notes, and he adds that the first critical Spanish edition was done in England in 1738 under the auspices of Lord Carteret. He finds that the best annotated Spanish edition was done in 1781 by the Englishman John Bowle. He also praises Cervantes as the purest of writers.]

North American Criticism

487. Dennie, Joseph. "The Life of Miguel de Cervantes Saavedra."
New England Quarterly Magazine, No. 3 (December 1802): 105-07.
[Signed version published earlier in *The Portfolio* 2 (1802): 44-45.]

The *Quijote* most probably was intended as a satire against extravagant tales of chivalry and the public taste they corrupted, not against knight-errantry itself. Most opinions concerning the purpose of the novel have been formed probably with more fancy and sublety than truth. But remember that the chivalric romances that overran Cervantes' age prejudiced the taste and perhaps the manners of his country and did not necessarily corrupt the society at large. The state of society itself does not warrant such a supposition, and Cervantes, a soldier and patriot, could not wish to quell the gallant spirit of martial enterprise. The idea that the novel also lowered the adventurous spirit of Spain is overstrained.

When it comes to evaluating the novel, a critic of the present day may not find in the *Quijote* all those signs of genius which it has been supposed to possess. But a work that has become a classic throughout all Europe, has obscured the fame of all other literature of its country, and has enriched every modern language with words and phrases to express new ideas cannot but rank with the capital productions of the human invention.

488. Wigglesworth, Edward. Review of *Vida de Miguel de Cervantes Saavedra*, by D. Martín Fernández de Navarrete. *North American Review* 38, no. 83 (April, 1834): 277-307.

In addition to ridiculing the fables of knight-errantry, the *Quijote*, with its ample range of adventures, episodes, and incidents, also attacked the vices and prejudices most common in society at the same time it alluded to contemporary personages and events as well as its literary predecessors. Playing upon Voltaire's conviction that the *Quijote* was modeled on the *Orlando* of Ariosto, Señor Ríos' contention that it was an imitation of the *Iliad*, and Pellicer's argument that it resembled the *Golden Ass* of Apuleius, two scholars in Italy, one under the pretense of criticizing and the other of defending Cervantes, put together an ironical exhibition of parallel passages from the *Quijote* and other works. Thus, for example, the adventure of Mambrino's helmet was compared to the bringing of the divine arms to Achilles by Thetis; the wedding of Camacho to the funeral games in honor of Patroculus and of Anchises; the wooden horse, on which Don Quijote achieved the adventure of the afflicted duenna, to the griffin steed of Ariosto; and the disenchantment of Dulcinea to the enchanted wood of Tasso.

The great spirit and humor of the novel, along with its persistently chivalrous air, have obscured many of Cervantes' allusions. Thus far-fetched attempts to pin down definitive allusions are fittingly criticized.

489. Anonymous. "Cervantes and his Writings." *American Monthly Magazine*, New Series, 1 (April, 1836): 342-54.

Ridiculous is Bowle's opinion that the *Quijote* was an attack on Loyola and the Jesuits. Also without merit is the (Ruidíaz) *Buscapié* legend to the effect that Cervantes wrote a work in which he implied that his novel was a satire on certain historical figures of his times. In addition, Cervantes' masterpiece is not an attack on the institutions and manners of chivalry, but a satire on the literary taste of the Spaniards of the time. Cervantes expanded the novel when he saw a rich field for humor and satire and added such elements as Sancho's proverbs. The style of the *Quijote* is a model of language as it extends from intense pathos to fun, while remaining pure and classical. Regrettably, much humor is lost in translation.

Certain shortcomings of the *Quijote* are: anachronisms, false chronology, and inconsistencies (variations in the Housekeeper's age, for instance). Cervantes, in spite of these shortcomings, is particularly to be praised because he is the only writer who has written a book whose second part is equal to the first.

490. Prescott, William H. "Cervantes." In *Biographical and Critical Miscellanies*. Philadelphia: J. B. Lippincott & Co., 1878, pp. 114-62. [Essay dated July, 1837.]

Cervantes brings forward a character who embodies all the generous virtues of chivalry: disinterestedness, contempt of danger, unblemished honor, knightly courtesy, and the longing for ideal excellence, which, if empty, is still the dream of a magnanimous spirit. These virtues are featured by Cervantes as too ethereal for this world, and are successively dispelled as they come in contact with the coarse realities of life. It is this progression of events that has led critics such as Simonde de Sismondi to conclude that the principal end of the author was, as Sismondi put it, "the ridicule of enthusiasm—the contrast of the heroic with the vulgar," the implication of which was profound sadness. However, this sort of criticism is excessively refined; it resembles the efforts of commentators to allegorize the epics of Homer and Virgil, which only works to throw a disagreeable mistiness over the *Quijote* by converting mere shadows into substances, and substances into shadows.

Cervantes' purpose was, doubtless, what he said it was, namely, to correct the popular taste for romances of chivalry. It is unnecessary to look for any other in so plain a tale, although it is true that the effect of the story is, as said, sad. But the melancholy tendency is counteracted to a great degree by the ludicrous character of the episodes, and perhaps the moral is that one must proportion his understanding to his capacities.

Cervantes maintains the dignity of Don Quijote in the midst of whimsical distresses with effort because his infirmity leads us to absolve him of responsibility. Cervantes was equally artful in regard to Sancho, who, with the most contemptible qualities, holds our interest by both his kindness and his shrewd understanding. The subordinate portraits in the romance, though not wrought with the same care, are admirable studies of character. In this view, the *Quijote* may be said to be the original Novel of Character, which is one of the distinguishing characteristics of modern literature. Cervantes has given a far more distinct and richer portrait of life in Spain than can be gathered from a library of monkish chronicles.

Earlier editions of the *Quijote* include that of Lord Carteret (1738), the Real Academia Española (1780), the Bowle edition (1781), those of Pellicer and Clemencín, and praiseworthy English translations, like those of Motteux, Jarvis, and Smollett.

The *Quijote* is a satire against the false taste of the author's times, especially as it was manifested in literature, superstition, and torture. While most satires usually lose their sting, Cervantes' is exceptional.

491. Ticknor, George. *History of Spanish Literature*, II. Fifth edition. Boston: Houghton, Mifflin and Company, 1882, pp. 107-79. [First published in London: John Murray, 1849, and in New York: Harper & Brothers, 1849.]

Cervantes' intention has sometimes been extended by the ingenuity of criticism until it resembles the contrast between the poetic and the prosaic in our natures—between heroism and generosity on one side, and a cold selfishness on the other, as if they were the truth and reality of life. Bouterwek's and Simonde de Sismondi's metaphysical positions are drawn from views of the work at once imperfect and exaggerated and, what is more, contrary to the spirit of an age that was not given to philosophical satire and was contrary to the character of Cervantes himself. Cervantes' spirit seems to have been filled with a cheerful confidence in human virtue, and his whole bearing in life seems to contradict the scorn for whatever is elevated and generous that such interpretations necessarily imply. Cervantes himself does not permit us to give to his romance any such secret meaning, for, at the very beginning of the work, he announces that his sole purpose is to break down the vogue and authority of books of chivalry. Then, at the end, he declares anew, in his own person, that "he had no other desire than to render abhorred of men the false and absurd stories contained in the books of chivalry."

The work of Gregorio Garcés (*Fundamento del vigor y elegancia de la lengua castellana*, 1791) unduly praises Cervantes' style, while Clemencín is too hard on Cervantes' occasional defects. Laudable are the power of Cervantes' character development and the humor of contrasting figures in both parts of the novel. Don Quijote is a gradually independent personage (no longer an imitation of Amadís) infused with generosity, gentleness, and delicacy, a pure sense of honor, and a warm love of whatever is noble and good. We almost feel the same attachment to him that the Barber and the Curate did, and are almost as ready as his family was to mourn over his death.

The case of Sancho is very similar, and perhaps in some respects stronger. At first, he is introduced as the opposite of Don Quijote and used merely to bring out his master's peculiarities. It is not until we have gone through nearly half of Part I that he utters one of those proverbs which afterwards forms the basis of his conversation and humor. And it is not until the opening of Part II that his character is completely developed to the full measure of its grotesque, yet congruous, proportions.

Certain passages in Cervantes' work reveal carelessness, blemishes, and contradictions which seem to show the author to have been almost indifferent to contemporary or posthumous success, while other passages indicate that the author was quite conscious of his own genius. The plot of the novel is sometimes disjointed, and the style, though rich in idiomatic language, possesses numerous inaccuracies and anachronisms.

Cervantes' novel was more than a bold attempt to criticize the absurd taste of the times, for Cervantes wrote his work with unquenchable and irresistible humor, with its bright views of the world at the conclusion of a life marked with disappointed expectations, disheartening struggles, and calamities.

492. Cordova, R. J. de. "The *Don Quixote* of Cervantes." *The Knickerbocker* 38, no. 3 (September, 1851): 189-203.

The *Quijote* is an attack on hypocrisy, false pride, and lesser failings executed delicately yet firmly, and with wise moderation. Cervantes sought to uphold the "Infant Giant Democracy" by attacking the prejudices of the aristocracy. Yet Cervantes did not seek in his attack on chivalry to deprecate moral courage properly directed, or devotion to country even to the extreme.

Don Quijote is a farcical figure, described throughout in ridiculous modes, while Sancho Panza is one of the most truthful sketches of original character which ever fell from the pen of a gifted writer. The Squire has little pride (only a certain respect for his station in life) and no interest in glory. But he is a plain, honest laborer, who, notwithstanding his lack of the world's learning and his ignorance of even the first law of letters, sees through the flimsiness of vainglory and knows fame to be above his capacity.

493. Giles, Henry. *Illustrations of Genius*. Boston: Ticknor and Fields, 1854, pp. 7-65.

Cervantes' passion gave him vast intellection and emotion while his idealism gave them elevation. Cervantes interpreted actual character with a faculty akin to inspiration, separating inherent traits from the accidental, the generic from the specific, and the specific from the individual. To this he added the still more wonderful peculiarity (without which a man may be a genius, but not a creative genius) that enabled him to combine these traits into different forms and which, though ideal in origin and existence, were always true to the laws of unity and fitness, types of unchangeable and indestructible reality. Genius alone can thus interpret and create because only genius can think and work securely beyond the individual sphere of habit.

The kind and measure of Cervantes' humor entitle him to be ranked in the same class with Shakespeare. Ironical or literal, suggestive or droll, no species of humor is wanting in the genius of Cervantes. He is master of the ludicrous in all its varieties, but, as is the case with generous souls, his humor is cordial—emanating from love and joy. Cosmopolitan as Cervantes' humor is, it is also distinctly Spanish and at the same time unmistakably individual. And the most distinctive characteristic of Cervantes' humor is *sweetness*. There is not one leer of scorn, not one wrinkle of derision, not one sneer of sarcasm, and not one air of taunt in all Cervantes' ludicrousness.

What marks the supreme manifestation of Cervantes' imaginative genius is his creation of character, which all criticism without hesitation and without division awards to Cervantes. To create a character is to introduce into men's fancies someone new to them. This first demands novelty, a distinct individual without artificial manners, much less with the exceptional or monstrous. This novelty must be natural, founded on the reality of character, and accordant with the general laws of reason and experience. But since art deals only with the apprehensible, it also demands mainly what is agreeable. And if the ugly has any place in art, it must be as subordinate as possible, since whatever should cause disgust or pain would be fatal to all the true purposes of art. To occupy our attention, a character must move our admiration or win our liking; for, on the whole, we can bear to remain long only with the noble, the grand, the good, or the amusing. No one has been as successful as Cervantes in creating characters that have all four traits: novelty, individuality, naturalness, and interest to the reader.

Cervantes' comic sense is so elevated by the serious and the serious so enlivened by the comic, that the *Quijote* cannot but live. Regarding intent, the *Quijote* was initially written to satirize romances of chivalry, but the author did not attack chivalry itself, with its idealism, generous dreams, and lofty enthusiasm. Purpose is seldom more than an occasion: genius, unlike talent, does not anticipate its end, especially in works of imagination. Genius reverses the original intention and always goes beyond it. Therefore, while Cervantes, on setting out, may have proposed only to laugh absurd romances out of existence, the laughter was soon combined with noble harmonies and was eventually lost in them.

The incidents of the story are not only wonderful in their variety, but wonderful in the means by which they are created. While deriding romances, Cervantes becomes in the highest degree romantic; and while forcing laughter into extravagance, he renders the possible almost as wild and strange as the supernatural machinery it ridicules. If magic changes the heroic into the vulgar to vex Don Quijote, it also changes for our delight the vulgar into the heroic.

There is a miraculous variety in the narrative—the surprising range of feelings and activities, the range of persons from every class and every profession, and the numerous oddities and individualities of character. Moreover, there is abstract thought in union with practical sense, satirical sagacity tempered with gentle wisdom, and learning that mellows diction and enriches the composition. Although the outward form of the story is burlesque and satirical, within it is the soul of grief and pity. Although it treats of life on one side in a spirit of criticism—pushing the idealism to absurdity and the criticism to irony—, the irony does not merely flatter the cynical, nor absurdity merely amuse the idle; both the irony and the absurdity suggest lessons of wholesome moderation and of generosity.

Don Quijote has the continuity that constitutes artistic identity in both parts. In view of Sancho's increased importance in Part II, Cervantes was perhaps tempted by his popularity to give him larger scope as the work advanced. It is also possible that the Squire was a favorite with Cervantes. Cervantes was not callous in his description of the treatment of Don Quijote at the palace of the Duke and Duchess, however. This episode had a moral purpose: to show with melancholy force the inward hardness covered with outward pomp. Cervantes was demonstrating how cruel epicureans seeking amusement in unsuspecting innocence and in misfortune could be. Justice demanded this situation, for Cervantes had shown the barbarism of the unwashed. Therefore, he also had to show the barbarism of the dainty in an episode which might even have come from some latent experience of Cervantes himself.

494. Thompson, Emma. *Wit and Wisdom of Don Quixote*. Boston: Roberts Brothers, 1882. 288 pages.

[The main portion of this work is an abbreviated text of Parts I and II of the *Quijote*, with emphasis on those passages containing proverbs. The introductory portion consists of a general index, an index to the proverbs, and a biographical sketch of Cervantes.]

495. Twain, Mark. "Enchantments and Enchanters." *Life on the Mississippi*. In *The Complete Travel Books of Mark Twain*. New York: Doubleday & Company, 1967, pp. 575-78. [First published in Boston: J. R. Osgood & Co., 1883.]

Sir Walter Scott is mistaken for restoring the enchantments of chivalry and thus checking the wave of modern progress (if not turning it back). Scott sets the world in love with dreams and phantoms, with decayed and degraded systems of government, with decayed and swinish forms of religion, and with the emptiness of a brainless and long-vanished society. Finally, the contrast between the effects wrought by Cervantes' *Don Quijote* and those wrought by Scott's *Ivanhoe* exemplifies the power of a single book for good or harm. The first swept the world's admiration for medieval chivalry out of existence; the other restored it.

496. Warner, Charles Dudley. "Modern Fiction." *Atlantic Monthly*, April, 1883: 464-74.

By overthrowing the absurd romances of chivalry Cervantes created a new school of fiction called the modern novel, characterized by its faithful description of the lower classes and by its intermingling of the phases of popular life. Cervantes had no one-sided tendency to portray the vulgar only; instead, he brought together the high and low in society to serve as light and shade. Although the aristocratic element was as popular as the common in Cervantes' day, this noble element disappeared in the novels of English writers who imitated Cervantes until Sir Walter Scott restored the harmony between the aristocratic and the democratic elements, which is part of the symmetry we admire in the *Quijote*. How Cervantes and Scott represented the higher and the lower is more important than why. Introducing common people into fiction is only one part of Cervantes' achievement; his higher glory is that he idealized them.

497. Lowell, James Russell. "Don Quixote." *Literary and Political Addresses*. In *The Complete Writings of James Russell Lowell*, VII. New York: AMS Press, 1966, pp. 139-64. [From the year 1887.]

As for the moral of the *Quijote*, there are two: first, the moral that whoever quarrels with the Nature of Things, wittingly or unwittingly, is certain to get the worst of it; and second, the deeper moral that arises from the pathos beneath the seemingly farcical turmoil, the tears which sometimes tremble under our lids after its most poignant touches of humor, the sympathy with its hero which survives all his ludicrous defeats and humiliations and is deepened by them, and the feeling that he is, after all, the one noble and heroic figure in a world incapable of comprehending him, because he is distorted by the crooked panes in those windows of custom and convention through which others see him. The second moral, then, is that only he who has the imagination to conceive and the courage to attempt a trial of strength with what we perceive as Nature can achieve great results or kindle support from his fellow men. The Don Quijote of one generation may live to hear himself called the savior of the next.

He reads most wisely who thinks everything into a book that it is capable of holding, and it is the stamp and token of a great book so to incorporate itself with our own being, so to quicken our insight and stimulate our thought, as to make us feel as if we helped to create it while we read. Whatever we can find in a book that aids us in the conduct of life, or to a truer interpretation of it, or to a franker reconciliation with it, we may with a good conscience believe is not there by accident, but that the author meant that we should find it there.

Cervantes clearly intended something more than a mere parody of romances of chivalry, for as far as he is concerned, they had already ceased to have vitality as motives of human conduct. The *Quijote* was intended to be good-humored criticism of doctrinaire reformers, and the work is a satire on attempts to remake the world by the means and methods of the past. Don Quijote quarrels with society, and only by degrees finds out just how strong it is, nay, how strong it must be in order that the world go smoothly and the course of events not be broken by a series of cataclysms.

Cervantes' characters were the first to be drawn from real life with such minuteness, and yet with such careful elimination of whatever was unessential, that they are more than mere actuality. In other words, the Knight and the Squire are real not because they are portraits drawn from actual people, but because of their abstraction and generalization; they are not so much taken from life as informed with it; they are conceptions, not copies from any mold. I do not ask that characters should be real; I need but go out into the street to find such in abundance. I ask only that they should be possible, that they should be typical, because these I find in myself, and with these I can sympathize. Thus, Don Quijote and Sancho are true inhabitants of the world of the imagination because they are symbolical representations of the two great springs of human character and action—the imagination and the understanding.

Cervantes' never-failing but never-obtrusive humor is infinitely varied yet always in harmony with the characters and with the purpose of the story. This does not refer to the *fun* of the novel but to that deeper and more delicate quality, suggestive of remote analogies and essential incongruities, which alone deserves the name of humor.

I do not believe that a character like Don Quijote, so absolutely perfect in conception and delineation, so psychologically true, so full of whimsical inconsistencies, all combining to produce an impression of perfect coherence, is to be found in fiction. He is a monomaniac, all of whose faculties, his very senses themselves, are subjected by one overmastering prepossession, and at last conspire with it, almost against their will, in spite of daily disillusion and of the uniform testimony of facts and events to the contrary. The key to Don Quijote's personality is to be found in his failure to test his helmet the second time; he always sees what he wishes to see, and yet always sees things as they are unless his hallucination compels him to see them otherwise, as it does of course, with ingenuity, even when he is never perfectly convinced himself, except in moments of exaltation. Sancho Panza, on the other hand, sees everything in the dry light of common sense, except when beguiled by cupidity or when under the immediate spell of his master's imagination. But Cervantes was too great an artist to make Sancho wholly vulgar and greedy and selfish. Though he is all of these, the Squire is also witty and wise as well as affectionate and faithful.

The structure of Cervantes' masterpiece, the ingenuity of the story, the probability of its adventures, and above all, Cervantes' unwearied fecundity of invention in devising and interlacing them, in giving variety to a single theme and to a plot so simple in its conception, are especially wonderful. However, the interpolated material in the 1605 *Quijote* is unprofitable digression and there is an excess of jokes in the episode of the ducal palace in Part II, which the reader resents because the tormentors are vulgar.

Cervantes slowly became aware, as he went on, of how rich was the vein he had hit upon, how full of various and profound suggestions were the two characters he had conceived and who together make a complete man. There is no doubt Cervantes at first proposed to himself a parody on the romances of chivalry, but his genius soon broke away from the leading-strings of the plot that denied free reign to his deeper conception of life and men.

498. Matthews, Brander. "Cervantes, Zola, Kipling & Co." *Cosmopolitan* 14 (November, 1892-April, 1893): 609-14.

One's mind does not come squarely in contact with Cervantes' work; it is warded off by the cloud of commentators surrounding every book. Knowing what one ought to think about the *Quijote* makes it almost impossible to think for oneself.

Cervantes was like all other great writers of fiction in that he wrote first to amuse and comfort himself and only second to amuse or even instruct his readers. "There is no mighty purpose in this book" is a proper motto for most masterpieces, which despite the myriad of mighty purposes philosophical criticism sees, were written easily and carelessly and with scarcely a thought to the message that might be deciphered between the lines. But Cervantes built better than he knew. That *Hamlet* and *Don Quijote* yield up to us today meanings and morals their straightforward authors never intended is perhaps the best possible evidence that they are masterpieces.

This is not to say that the *Quijote* is flawless. In fact, the art of fiction has improved since Cervantes: writers today are scrupulous where Cervantes was reckless. Merely in the mechanism of plot and in the craftmanship of storytelling the *Quijote* is indisputably less skillful than Emile Zola's *Débâcle* or the Kipling-Balestier *Naulahka*, however inferior these may be in more vital aspects. Glaring faults in the *Quijote* are the fictitious historian device, the inclusion of irrelevant tales merely because they happened to be on hand, the anachronisms and inconsistencies, and the extraordinary coincidences and improbabilities. It is in its character-drawing and its humanity that the *Quijote* excels even the better-plotted stories of Boccaccio, Chaucer, and Rabelais. Cervantes catches mankind in the act, revealing the secrets of character and displaying the variety, richness, and intensity of human existence. And to do these things with unfailing good humor and goodwill toward all men—this is what no writer of fiction had done before *Don Quijote,* and what no writer of fiction has done better since.

Russian Criticism

499. Belinski, Vissarion. "Tarantas, putevia, vpechatlenia, soch. Grafa V. A. Solloguba." *Sochinenia*, IV. Kiev: 1908, pp. 5-50. [As summarized in Turkevich, *Cervantes in Russia*, pp. 24-27. Dated c. 1845-1848.]

Don Quijote, despite cruel disappointments, remains faithful to Dulcinea and to his vow to protect the weak against the powerful. If only this bravery and magnanimity had been used at an appropriate time and in a proper way, Don Quijote would have been truly a great man.

His nature has another side, however, for frequently the Knight behaves as a clown—or even a madman. Notwithstanding moments of lucidity and wisdom, he becomes a public laughingstock at times.

Such paradoxical characters are numerous. They are wise, but vulnerable to illusion, when everything is comprehensible to them except reality. They are gifted with an extraordinary capacity for conceiving a nonsensical idea and finding it affirmed by the most contradictory manifestations of reality. The more nonsensical the idea, the more intoxicated they become by it and regard all sober individuals as mad, even immoral, malicious, and dangerous. Don Quijote is a highly generic character who will never grow old; he is the creation of a genius.

500. Turgenev, Ivan. "Hamlet i Don Kikhot." *Sovremennik* 79 (1860): 239-58. [As translated by William A. Drake in *The Anatomy of Don Quixote*, ed. M. J. Benardete and A. Flores, Ithaca, New York: Dragon Press, 1932.]

Don Quijote is much more than a parody of chivalric romance. His character has breadth and depth. Beyond his comic qualities, springing from a deranged imagination, he is humble, generous, and selfless. He is confident without being vain. Despite his apparent imbecility, he courageously seeks the extermination of evil. If he is slow to enjoy or to feel compassion, still he conveys faith in something eternal.

Don Quijote's idealism remains untarnished after privation and grotesque humiliation. The strength of his moral composition adds life and grandeur to his ideas and infuses his comic misadventures with the possibility of redemption. Laughing at the Knight, the reader may come to love him. The reader may also come to appreciate the profound significance of Don Quijote's uncalculated sacrifices. What is important is sincerity and strength of conviction; as to results—that is in the hands of destiny.

Various critics have missed the significance of the Don Quijote figure. Many commentators, for example, are offended at the beatings with which Cervantes afflicts his hero. Without the drubbings, however, his true spirit would not come through; he would seem cold and arrogant. Some critics particularly condemn Cervantes for having his hero trampled by pigs after his final defeat. Nevertheless, the scene is important: it shows the world's indifference and lack of understanding.

Don Quijote and Hamlet represent opposite qualities of human nature. All of humanity belongs to one or the other of the two types: the Quijotes stick to their ideals without challenging them; the Hamlets constantly ponder their ideals.

Hamlet's inability to connect with the masses can be seen in his relationship with Polonius, who regards the Prince as more childish than insane. If Hamlet were not a prince, Polonius would despise him for his resignation to futility. Sancho, unlike the obsequious Polonius, makes fun of his master and knows that he is mad. Nevertheless, three times the Squire abandons everything to follow this lunatic. His devotion cannot be explained by the expectation of reward or of any personal advantage. His devotion originates in what is perhaps the finest characteristic of the masses: their capacity for abandoning themselves to a happy and honest blindness in their devotion to a cause, their capacity for disinterested enthusiasm, and their contempt of personal gain. The people always end by following those whom previously they have mocked.

As for women, Don Quijote loves Dulcinea, an ideal figure created by his imagination, and he is prepared to die for her. He loves ideally and purely. When such men disappear, let the books of history be closed, for then there will be nothing more in them worth reading. There is not a trace of sensuality in Don Quijote: he scarcely hopes to possess Dulcinea and almost seems to stand in fear of such a consummation. Can Hamlet ever really love? He is sensual and even secretly voluptuous; but he only pretends to love. Hamlet incarnates the spirit of negation; he is a Mephistopheles.

The deaths of Don Quijote and Hamlet reveal their essential natures. While Hamlet's dying words are beautiful, and while he becomes humble and reticent, his eyes do not search the way ahead: "The rest is silence," the dying skeptic says. Don Quijote's death overwhelms us with an unspeakably poignant emotion. Here the full grandeur and significance of his personality becomes manifest to all. "All things must pass," he says, "save good works, save love."

There are no Hamlets or Don Quijotes in the absolute sense; these figures are extreme expressions of two tendencies. The principle of analysis is carried to the extreme of tragedy in the character of Hamlet, while the principle of enthusiasm is advanced to that of comedy in Don Quijote. However, neither the wholly tragic nor the wholly comic is ever encountered in actual life.

501. Lvov, A. "Hamlet i Don Kikhot." St. Petersburg, 1862. [As summarized by Turkevich, pp. 111-12, and by Const. Derjavin in "La crítica cervantina en Rusia."]

Turgenev grossly oversimplifies human types in his *Hamlet i Don-Kikhot*. Don Quijote is simply a madman; he is not altruistic but egoistic; he does not love a real woman but an abstraction.

502. Karelin, V. "Don Kikhotizm i Demonizm." In *Don Kikhot Lamanchski*, I. Translated by V. Karelin. St. Petersburg: 1893. [As summarized by Turkevich, pp. 85-89, and by Const. Derjavin in "La crítica cervantina en Rusia." Derjavin gives 1866 as the date of publication.]

The tragedy of greatness lies in its proximity to ridiculousness. Don Quijote's noble qualities are inherent, while his environment produces his comical and pitiful aspects. The environment works to submerge and kill the hero instead of permitting his high qualities to benefit society.

A number of economic, social, and historical factors converge to induce Don Quijote's insanity. Books of chivalry, for example, the pathological product of a diseased society, cannot help but make Don Quijote mad. Similarly, social conditions shut off normal outlets for Don Quijote's inclinations and force him to seek self-expression elsewhere.

Quijotismo is a psychological fact not only in isolated men but also in society at certain moments of its political life. Don Quijote would have been a Socrates or a Rousseau if he had lived in another age.

503. Dostoyevsky, Fyodor. *Letters of Fyodor Michailovitch Dostoyevsky*. Translated by Ethel Colburn Mayne. New York-Toronto-London: McGraw-Hill Book Company, 1964. [Letter dated January 13, 1868.]

I will say that of all the noble figures in Christian literature, I reckon Don Quijote as the most perfect. But Don Quijote is noble only by being at the same time comic.

504. Dostoyevsky, Fyodor. *The Diary of a Writer*. Translated and annotated by Boris Brasol. 2 vols. New York: Octagon Books, 1973, I, p. 260. [First published in *Dvevnik Pisatelya*, 1876-1881.]

In the whole world there is no deeper, no mightier literary work than the *Quijote*. This is, so far, the last and greatest expression of human thought; it is the bitterest irony which man was capable of conceiving. And if the world were to come to an end, and people were asked, "Did you understand your life on earth, and what conclusion have you drawn from it?," man could silently hand over *Don Quijote*: "Such is my inference from life—can you condemn me for it?" I am not asserting that man would be right, but...

In the scene where Don Quijote is suddenly concerned about the possibility of a single warrior being able to kill an entire army, he decides that the armies are not humans but evil spirits—illusions, creations of magic. Their bodies are soft, like those of worms, mollusks, and spiders, and thus the knight-errant of *true* books of chivalry is able to destroy as many as ten at a time. Here the great poet and heart-reader Cervantes discerns one of the deepest and most mysterious traits of the human spirit, and such books as the *Quijote* are bequeathed to mankind only once in several hundred years. The passage shows man's paradoxical ability to satisfy an inner need for realism through the creation of multiple fantasies. When one absurd mental construct is threatened, man will create a second fantasy, even more absurd than the first, in order to resolve contradictions.

Such revelations of human nature appear on every page of Cervantes' masterpiece. Sancho is an especially rich source of insights. The personification of common sense, prudence, cunning, and the golden mean chances to become a friend and fellow traveler of the most insane man on earth; precisely he, and no other! Sancho deceives Don Quijote, and cheats him like a child. At the same time, he fully believes him; he gives full credence to the Knight's fantastic dreams.

The *Quijote* is the grandest and saddest book conceived by the genius of man. This work would unquestionably ennoble the souls of the young with great thought and would plant in their hearts momentous queries, helping to divert their minds from the worship of eternal mediocrity, self-complacent conceit, and trivial prudence. This saddest of all books will be taken by man to the Lord's last judgment. He will point to the very deep and fatal mystery of mankind revealed in it. He will show that man's noblest gifts, his most sublime beauty, his loftiest purity, chastity, naïveté, gentleness, and courage, are often reduced to naught, solely because they lack the one gift needed to give them coherence: namely, genius. Only genius can administer such gifts and lead them along a truthful path of action for the benefit of the human race! The cruel irony of fate often dooms the labors of the noblest and most ardent friends of mankind to ridicule.

505. Avseyenko, V. G. "Proiskhozhdenie romana." *Russki Vestnik* (1877), CXXXI, part 9, pp. 95-124; and CXXXII, part 2, pp. 442-62. [As summarized by Turkevich, pp. 91-94.]

The *Quijote* perfectly expresses both its era and its prospects for disintegration. Cervantes' original purpose in writing his masterpiece was to laugh books of chivalry out of existence, but the idea outgrew its plan. The initial concept assumed tremendous proportions and developed a remarkable flexibility. Similarly, the finished book lent itself to countless interpretations, limited only by the reader's keenness and imagination. For example, the *Quijote* can be viewed as a novel of manners or as a political and social satire on Spain. A variety of themes also can be found, including the conflict between the real and the ideal and the impersonation of faith.

The *Quijote* was the product of Cervantes' old age, a time when he was sick, crippled, and degraded, when he felt that his own life, full of suffering, was being reincarnated in this image of the half-mad hidalgo—so severely punished for excessive faith and desire. Between Cervantes' life and his novel there is a bond which must be explained before one can understand his work fully.

506. Vyazemski, P. A. "Staraya zapisnaya knizhka." In *Poloyne sobranie sochinenii kn. P. A. Vayazemskago*, VIII. Saint Petersburg, 1883, pp. 223. [As summarized by Turkevich, p. 20.]

[Vyazemski praises unaffected originality as a sign of manliness and independence of character. For Vyazemski, though Don Quijote is comical, he is first and foremost noble.]

507. Storozhenko, N. I. "Filosofia Don Kikhota." *Vestnik Yevropy* 5 (1885): 307-24. [As summarized by Turkevich, pp. 94-96.]

There are pitfalls in the philosophical interpretation of the *Quijote*. It is proper to evaluate from different angles the types created by an author, to uncover the general meaning of a work, and to draw morals from it, but to abuse this right and to ascribe to a given work ideas or symbols, such as a conflict between realism and idealism, poetry and prose, etc., is absolutely wrong.

Cervantes does not choose a stupid person as his protagonist, but an intelligent, well-read man, who, however, has a vulnerable spot—a pathologically developed fantasy and a passionate interest in human sorrow. This, of course, leads to many conflicts between the hero and society, and Cervantes shows that Don Quijote's knightly ideals are just as out of date as his weapons, that bravery and valor are absolutely unnecessary in the sixteenth century, especially in the form that he offers them to the world, and that as a result of this, at every step he commits injustices and even harms those whom he wishes to help.

Don Quijote invites laughter as well as pity, since he is not only a fool and a knight-errant, but also an intelligent, humane, and, at times, noble person. Does Don Quijote's misrepresentation of reality give him a claim to heroism as philosophical criticism suggests? No! In stressing the Knight's self-sacrifice and altruism, the philosophical critics neglect two points. First, in life, heroism is recognized not only by its moral and spiritual force but also by its conscious, rational instrumentation for the benefit of mankind.

Second, Don Quijote is really a reflection of the novels of chivalry. As a knight-errant, he is motivated in his exploits not only by altruistic ideas but also by a thirst for fame and a desire to distinguish himself for his lady, and sometimes the latter motive takes precedence.

However, Cervantes does not ridicule enthusiasm for goodness and truth per se, but the extravagant form of its manifestation, its caricature, induced by the novels of chivalry, which was not at all suitable to the spirit of the times.

508. Merezhkovski, D. S. "Vechnie sputniki, Servantes." In *Polnoye sobranie sochinenii*, XVII [Moscow, 1914], pp. 101-35. [As summarized by Turkevich, pp. 182-83, and by Const. Derjavin in "La crítica cervantina en Rusia." Derjavin lists the article as appearing in *Severny Viesnik* in 1889.]

A universal work, with time, displays for the perceptive reader significance far exceeding that consciously given to it by its author. *Don Quijote* is a satire on mental inactivity, and he himself symbolically illustrates the deficiencies of medievalism: a blind faith in place of critical examination; imitative qualities instead of originality; a subjection to "higher" thought; a pessimistic outlook on the fate of man; a love of simplicity; an idealization of simple folk and a scorn for civilization. Cervantes is somewhat of a forerunner of Rousseau in that he regards civilized society as a principal cause of contemporary misfortunes.

There are other symbolic values in the book. Don Quijote symbolizes the cold, barren, mystical North, and the Squire the warm, sunny South with its humor and kindliness. Cervantes also is a great religious writer and father of the later mystical symbolism. (Cervantes' allegiance to the Church is revealed by the lack of nature descriptions in his works.) As for the two protagonists, they represent the attraction of opposites, two men who, despite differences, live in complete understanding and love. Don Quijote changes all into fantasy or dream, while the Squire changes all into a joke. Sancho is a ridiculous Mephistopheles at the side of a tragic Faust. As a practical realist, Sancho also is the future bourgeoisie.

509. Korolenko, V. G. *Dnevnik*, I. Giz Ukrainy, 1925-1928, p. 190. [As summarized by Turkevich, pp. 89-91. Dated 1890.]

It is useless to speculate on what Don Quijote would have been if he had lived in another age or if he had known political economics. Don Quijote is an eternal type. Alonso Quijano became Don Quijote not because of his historical context but because he was a Don Quijote by nature, a man born with more imagination and impulse than analysis and restraint. Chivalric romances and the atmosphere of dying feudalism were but secondary features of Don Quijote's madness, features which gave him the coloring of his time and place; they were merely the clothes of an immortal type. Humanity will probably never discover why fictional creations as different as Don Quijote, Hamlet, and Socrates exist also in real life.

510. Veselovski, A. N. "Vityaz pechalnago obraza." In *Etyudy i Kharak-teristiki*, I. Moscow, 1912, pp. 36-45. [As summarized by Turkevich, pp. 97-98. First date of publication is not clear, but an 1894 edition is listed in *The National Union Catalogue*.]

In its happy blending of realism, humor, and comedy Cervantes' portrayal of seventeenth-century Spain is a masterpiece. Also Cervantes' own experiences were key factors in his ability to create his work.

Cervantes first sought to cure and revive contemporary literary taste. As his tale developed, the implications of the initial idea (an attack on books of chivalry) expanded and acquired symbolic twists.

Italian Criticism

511. Mugnoz, Giovacchino. "Biografia di Michele di Cervantes." Estratta dalla Ghirlanda *Fiore di Letteratura* (Bologna, 1844). [From excerpts in Rius, II, pp. 120-21, and III, pp. 274-75.]

The *Quijote* is a satire of vices written in an amusing style. Particularly praiseworthy is the tone in which emotions are described. It is regrettable that translation results in a loss of beauty.

512. Cantù, Cesare. *Storia della letteratura italiana*, V: *Il seicento*. Milan: Garzanti, 1967, pp. 622, 630, and 680. [First published in Turin, 1836-1846.]

The *Quijote* artistically expresses a neofeudal society still containing elements of chivalry. There are similarities between Drusillo and Altobello of Giovanni Ambrosio Marini's later *Calloandro* and the Knight and Squire of the *Quijote*. The heroic-comic poem, exemplified by the *Quijote*, is not merely a satire on a particular genre but a new form of literature that brings a rapport with the real world in a particular way.

513. Gioberti, Vincenzo. *Del bello*. Florence: P. Ducci, 1845, pp. 89-91. [First edition 1844?]

The brutish provides contrast with the beautiful, causing the latter to stand out. Since the deformed excites the sense of the ridiculous it is thus suitable to satire and comedy, and sometimes to the romance and to the epic. However, evil must be used with great moderation and softened with goodness. From the exquisite mixture of these elements is born the perfection of Falstaff and Don Quijote. This cannot be given to Molière's Tartuffe nor to Machiavelli's Timoteo, because the moral brutishness of these two figures exceeds the limits conceded to a poet.

514. Cibrario, Conte Luigi. "Il Don Chisciotte letterario." In *Scritti varii*. Florence-Turin: Tip. Eredi Botta, 1868, pp. 211-13.

[This item does not treat the *Quijote* but does describe a figure dressed as the Knight who complains of the literary tastes of the times.]

515. De Sanctis, Francesco. *Storia della letteratura italiana*. In *Opere*, LVI. Milan-Naples: R. Riccardi, 1961, pp. 456-57 and 463-64. [First published in Milan-Naples: D. Morano, 1870.]

In the *Orlando furioso* the worlds of poetry and prose are not antithetical, whereas they are in the *Quijote*. The *Quijote* is eternally fresh, because the spirit of chivalry melts into the image of a new society, with chivalry rendered comic by the presence of the realistic.

516. Renier, Rodolfo. *Ariosto e Cervantes*. Florence: Tip. della Gazzetta D'Italia, 1878. 199 pages.

One cannot understand Cervantes' masterpiece without appreciating the way in which the conscience gradually prepares for the expulsion of old life and former customs, an attitude found in Italian romances.

One ought to distinguish two aspects in the work: one, more general, that contemplates life; the other, more restricted, that refers to literature.

The old elements in chivalric romance include humiliation, love, and religion, and the new are comprised of classicism, comicity and irony, realism, and adulation. Cervantes consciously pushes naturalism to its ultimate consequences, whereas Ariosto had done so *unconsciously*.

517. Nencioni, Enrico. "Le tre pazzie." In *Saggi critici di letteratura italiana*. Florence: Successori Le Monnier, 1898, pp. 143-93. [From *Fanfulla della Domenica*, Nos. 22, 23, and 24 (1881).]

German and French Cervantists find nonexistent meanings in the *Quijote*, treat the masterpiece as if it were a chapter from the *Apocalypse*, claim the novel conveys revolutionary ideas, and see in the fine humor of Cervantes a key to very arduous problems.

Don Quijote is an anachronistic madman, who is, at times, admirable. In the contrast between his ideals and real conditions, between his lyricism and Sancho's rustic proverbs, one finds Cervantes' ingenious and incomparable humor, a humor without acrimony or declamation.

The *Quijote* belongs with Sterne's *Tristram Shandy* and Jean Paul Richter's *Quintus Fixlein*, works that are truly humorous though lightly skeptical, works that reveal a humor more of the heart than of the mind. Cervantes is the first and the purest of humorists.

Cervantes describes the sympathetic madman from numerous perspectives. In spite of his grotesque aspect, Don Quijote has an air of nobility.

There is an exuberant imagination and a deep Renaissance poetic feeling in Cervantes' novel, and, in the romantic episodes, there is an air of noble elegance. Yet one notes a certain sadness in the story. Such is the wisdom, humanity, and goodness of the *Quijote*.

518. Gubernatis, Angelo. *Storia universale della letteratura*, IX: *Storia del romanzo*. Milan: Hoepli, 1883, pp. 250-67, 276-77, and 455-56.

The *Quijote* is the perfect model of the comic romance, the most vivacious and gayest book in the Spanish language, a work that has lost none of its freshness in spite of passing years. Cervantes' masterpiece is a humorous treatment of the Icarus theme: man's attempt to fly too high. But the *Quijote* does not destroy the ideal, for it points out the true way, the golden mean, as something midway between the attitude of Don Quijote and that of his Squire. The fault of Don Quijote's idealism is that it is rooted in a past that cannot return.

Comparing and contrasting the 1605 *Quijote* with the 1615 sequel, one finds the latter to be less lively and less comic, but to be richer in incidents, in observation, and in critical force. It also displays more maturity, more good sense, and a deeper knowledge of human nature.

Regarding the relationships of various writers to their protagonists, Voltaire loves as an artist his Doctor Pangloss, Gogol his Chichikoff, and Manzoni his Don Abbondio; however, they are not noble types but rather comic figures. There is a more personal note in Cervantes' treatment of his central characters: Cervantes' personal feeling often enlivens the artistic creation; he treats his protagonists as if they were almost real, making them respectable and likeable.

519. Nencioni, Enrico. "L'umorismo e gli umoristi." In *Saggi critici di letteratura italiana*. Florence: Successori Le Monnier, 1898, pp. 175-202. [From *Nuova Antologia*, January 16, 1884.]

The *Quijote* is a truly humorous work, that is, a work that reveals a natural disposition of heart and mind to view sympathetically the contradictions and the absurdity of life. A chapter of Cervantes' masterpiece or of Sterne's *Tristram Shandy* defines humor better than a whole volume of criticism, and clearly distinguishes humor from satire, jest, and caricature.

520. D'Ovidio, Francesco. "Manzoni e Cervantes." In *Opere complete*, VI: *Studi manzoniani*. Caserta: Casa Editrice Moderna, 1928, pp. 73-90. [Memoria letta alla R. Accademia di Scienze Morali e Politiche di Napoli, nella Seduta dell' 8 Marzo 1885, ristampata nelle *Discussioni manzoniane*.]

There are similarities between the *Quijote* and Manzoni's *I promessi sposi*, such as the omission of the name of the place of action, the festive tone, and the use of the fictitious manuscript device. Laudable is Manzoni's humor, but Cervantes' humor is base at times. The work of the Italian contains the totality of life; the *Quijote* is merely a satirical novel.

521. Scherillo, Michele. "Manzoni e Sanciu Panza." *L'Illustrazione Italiana* 11, no. 5 (1885): 67 and 70.

Praiseworthy is Sancho's view (II, 19) that a person should be expected to speak the language he learned as a child and not the polished language of the court. Sancho's idea contradicts in spirit that of Manzoni, who contended that the only true Italian was that of the Florentines.

522. Spera, Giuseppe. "Ariosto e Cervantes." In *Saggio di letteratura comparata*. Cava dei Tirreni, Badia Benedetinna, 1886, pp. 53-90; also in *Letteratura comparata*. Second edition. Naples: Chiurazzi, 1896. [As cited in Joseph G. Fucilla's "Bibliografía italiana de Cervantes," p. 61.]

   The idea of chivalry differs in Ariosto and Cervantes. The irony of the former should be contrasted with the lively humor of the latter regarding the chivalric ideal.

523. Lo Forte Randi, Andrea. "Michele Cervantes." *Pensiero Italiano* 3 (1891): 198-224.

   The *Quijote* has misery as its muse, yet it is a poem that is serenely honest and filled with the sense of perfect justice. The *Quijote* was born because the author was a noble spirit in a world of poverty, and his mind necessarily turned to the desires of dreams. The result is a powerful allegory in which the two strange protagonists are symbols of dualistic factors comprising human life: reality and dream, the palpable and the elusive, the precariousness of existence and the insatiable need for eternity. Don Quijote's ideals are of the heart and not of the mind.

524. Tancredi, Giovanni. *Il poema maccheronico di Teofilo Folengo corredato di riscontri con le produzioni straniere di F. Rabelais e M. Cervantes*. Consenza: Tip. Municipale di F. Principe, 1895, pp. 100-01. [First edition Naples, 1891.]

   Cervantes' open mockery of the artificial passions of knight-errantry may have been drawn from the *Maccheronee* of Folengo, but is not necessarily an imitation of that work. It is beyond doubt that the works of Folengo are, in some manner, precursors of the *Quijote*.

525. Farinelli, Arturo. "Spanien und die spanische Literatur im Lichte der deutschen Kritik und Poesie." *Zeitschrift für Vergleichende Litteraturgeschichte* 5 (1892): 135-206, 276-332; 8 (1895): 318-407.

   [Farinelli concludes that the *Quijote* was not of great influence in Germany prior to the mid-eighteenth century. He finds some allusions to the *Quijote* by Gotthard Heidegger in 1698 and by Postel in 1724. The critic notes a 1682 German translation of Cervantes' novel from an unknown Swiss. A 1690 opera by Heinrich Hinsch and another by J. Samuel Müller in 1722 are said to be based on the *Quijote*, as is a play by Koenig in 1727.

   The critic notes the comments of Lessing on the *Quijote* and discusses adaptations of Cervantes' novel by Wieland (*Don Sylvio von Rosalva*, 1764), Musäus (*Grandison der Zweite*, 1760), and Schiebeler (a dramatic poem "Basilio und Quiteria"). He cites various translations of the *Quijote* and particularly praises that of Ludwig Tieck. Farinelli briefly notes the influence of the Roque Guinart episode on Schiller's *Die Räuber*. Also favorable comments on the *Quijote* by Herder, Böttiger, and Bertuch are set forth.]

526. Scherillo, Michele. "Don Chisciotte poeta." *La Tavola Rotunda* 2, no. 11 (March 13, 1892): 1-3.

[Parallels between certain scenes in the *Quijote* and passages from Italian poetry are pointed out, and the influence of such writers as Ariosto, Petrarch, and Boiardo on Cervantes is suggested.]

527. D'Ovidio, Francesco. "Il *Furioso* e il *Don Chisciotte* (Frammento)." *Varietà critiche*. In *Opere complete di F. D'Ovidio*, XIII. Naples: Alfredo Guida, 1929, pp. 115-19. [1894.]

Ariosto's irony concerning romance is subtler than Cervantes'.

528. Zumbini, Bonaventura. "Il Folengo precursore del Cervantes." In *Studi di letteratura italiana*. Florence: Successori Le Monnier, 1906, pp. 163-77. [First edition is Florence, 1894. Listed by Louis Paul Betz, *La Littérature comparée: Essai bibliographique*, 2nd ed., p. 217, as appearing in 1885 in "Napoli Letter."]

Folengo's *Maccheronee* had important influence on Rabelais' *Pantagruel* and Cervantes' *Don Quijote*. Folengo's poem combines a heroic form with a satirical attitude towards beliefs, institutions, customs, and religious and social practices. There are definite similarities between Folengo's mock-hero Baldus and Cervantes' hidalgo: both exhibit extravagant behavior brought on by the reading of chivalric literature.

Latin-American Criticism

529. Bello, Andrés. *Gramática de la lengua castellana, destinada al uso de los americanos.* Valparaíso-Santiago: S. Tornero, 1845. 278 pages. [As reprinted with notes in Rufino José Cuervo's *Obras*, I, Botogá: Instituto Caro y Cuervo, 1954, pp. 907-1157. See also the 1945 Sopena edition of Bello's grammar with notes by Cuervo and Niceto Alcalá-Zamora y Torres.]

[Bello's Castilian grammar is regarded as a classic and has been reprinted on various occasions. In this edition, each passage is followed by a lengthy comment by Cuervo, and the index lists numerous allusions to Cervantes' grammar.]

530. Barros Arana, Diego. *Elementos de literatura (historia literaria).* Santiago de Chile: A. Raymond, 1869, pp. 410-18. [Briefly summarized by Juan Uribe-Echevarría in *Cervantes en las letras hispanoamericanas*, pp. 162-63.]

The *Quijote* is an original inspiration, not a work influenced by classical models. Cervantes' masterpiece is a perfectly clear, pleasant book of common sense to which most of the ideas of speculative criticism probably do not apply.

531. Varona, Enrique José. *Los estudios cervantinos de Enrique José Varona.* Edited by Elio Alba-Buffill. New York: Senda Nueva de Ediciones, 1979. 107 pages. [From 1872-74.]

[In addition to a sonnet by Varona entitled "A Cervantes ayer y hoy" (dated December 8, 1872) in general praise of Cervantes, this work includes the editor's own "Estudio preliminar," a discussion of Cuban criticism on Cervantes and Varona's critical works in particular, a rather lengthy bibliography of Latin American Cervantine criticism, several short studies by Varona, and a summary of Varona's lecture (April 23, 1883). Also included are two letters, one to Mariano Pardo de Figueroa (October 7, 1872), concerning various critics' praise of Cervantes, and another to Ramón León Máinez (June 9, 1874), noting Cuban celebrations in honor of Cervantes and discussing contemporary works on Cervantes.]

532. Varona, Enrique José de. "Epístola cervántica." *Crónica de los Cervantistas* 2, no. 1 (January 28, 1873): 9-11.

[In this brief discussion of non-Spanish Cervantists, Varona takes special note of Roque Barcia's *La filosofía de la lengua española* (1870), commenting particularly on Barcia's analysis of Cervantes' use of the words *desatino* and *disparate* and of how the novelist gave color to words.]

533. Caro, Miguel Antonio. "*El Quijote.*" *Anuario de la Academia Colombiana de la Lengua* (1874-1910): 33-50. [Reprinted in 1935. Found in *Obras completas*, II: *Estudios literarios, primera serie*, Bogotá: Imp. Nacional, 1920, pp. 143-65. Originally dated April 23, 1874, this essay also appears in *Cervantes en Colombia*, edited by E. Caballero Calderón, Madrid: Patronato del IV Centenario de Cervantes, 1948, pp. 151-88.]

A poem is a book which belongs morally to mankind, historically to one nation, and literarily to one writer. Thus, the *Quijote* bears the three chief characteristics of a great poem: (1) a theme that interests humanity; (2) the peculiar attributes of a people; and (3) an original style.

The basic theme involves a perpetual contrast between the poetic spirit and the prosaic, as Simonde de Sismondi stated, or, as Cantù expressed it, the depiction of types symbolizing the soul and the body. But Cervantes does not present the two tendencies in pure forms: he adds madness to the spiritual-poetic and discretion to the bodily-prosaic. One of the charms of the *Quijote* is the perpetual vacillation which the reader undergoes while waiting to see which characteristic will dominate in a given episode: the Knight's madness or his bravery and the Squire's foolishness or his prudence. The adventures in the novel would be merely a series of events if it were not for the unifying feature of the two protagonists.

The many surprises in the novel lend a comic tone to the story, even though the *Quijote* is a serious work. Furthermore, if one considers only the ridiculous parts of the novel, one would believe that its only intent was to destroy the popularity of books of chivalry. However, Cervantes sought to inflict sorrow on himself in a more festive than bitter way because of the bad fortune which fell to his lot in his own chivalric enterprises.

Sometimes genius is not a competent judge of itself, and Cervantes is a good example. Most of the beauty in a work arises without study or deliberate effort, and God seldom gives to creative genius the ability to analyze. Genius produces through instinct rather than through conscious awareness. Therefore, it is impertinent for the critic to attribute to the author any particular intention.

The inspiration for the genesis of the *Quijote* is equally difficult to identify, but several things fertilized it, without any being necessarily the generating principle of the theme: Cervantes' reading of chivalric novels, his travels, and the adventures that he had. But the story of Don Quijote is much more than an autobiography: the author speaks through several characters, not just through the hero, and all his creatures have something of the author in them. In this respect, the *Quijote* of 1615 is more Cervantine than the *Quijote* of 1605.

There is a change in the method of character description in the 1615 *Quijote* and a progression toward religion which can be explained in two ways: first, because Cervantes was preparing for the Christian death of his hero or for his abandonment of knight-errantry in favor of a pastoral life; and second, because Cervantes, speaking for himself through his hero, created a contradiction between deeds and words.

While some lyrical writers (Byron, for example) are egotistical and cannot produce characters because they reproduce themselves in all they attempt, and others, like Shakespeare, are highly dramatic without letting themselves be seen, Cervantes, in the *Quijote*, is eminently dramatic in his actions, but lyrical in his discourses. For that reason the actions of his characters may form an overall biography of the author, while the fragments of the discourses may form a spiritual biography.

The *Quijote* is comparable to an opera buffa in which the sublime music of its noble style and wonderful language gives to the whole composition a tone which drama alone could not achieve.

534. Ferrer de Couto, José. *Relación de los primeros festejos religiosos y literarios que se hicieron en la ciudad de Nueva York el día 23 abril de 1875.* New York: Imp. de El Cronista, 1875. 62 pages.

[Couto discusses the circumstances that led to the *velada literaria* for Cervantes on April 23, 1875, the first such celebration staged in New York and, in fact, the first *velada* including representatives from all the New World countries. The aim of this homage to Cervantes, states Couto, was to unite the peoples of the Spanish-speaking world under the banner of Cervantes. The volume includes a long list of artists and diplomats as well as the foreign ministers from Spain, who joined those from all countries in the Spanish-speaking world.]

535. Uribe Angel, Manuel. "Discurso pronunciado en Nueva York el día 23 de abril de 1875." In *Escritos varios*. Reproducido en *Elocuencia colombiana* por Roberto Ramírez, Bogotá, 1929, pp. 154 et seq. [As summarized by Rafael Torres Quintero in *Boletín del Instituto Caro y Cuervo* 4 (1948): 86-87.]

Cervantes' novels are the synthetic expression of all that is beautiful, all that is good, and all that is useful in literary matters. Don Quijote is the "pequeño Evangelio de la humanidad" and Cervantes a man seeking to regenerate his people. Sancho is the picture of sensuality.

536. Urdaneta, Amenodoro. *Cervantes y la crítica.* Second edition. Caracas: Dirección Civil y Política, Gobernación del Dto. Federal, 1975. 400

pages. ["Plan Caracas para la Cultura," No. 4. First published in Caracas: Imp. a vapor de La Opinión Nacional, 1877.]

The *Quijote* is not a sterile critique of human vices and passions, but a work that fulfills the true and elevated goal of poetry by guiding rational beings along the path of honor, nobility, and liberty. In other words, it improves on reality by showing the world not as it is but as it ought to be and rehabilitates humanity by returning its primordial splendor and dignity. In order to do this Cervantes uses the tragic and the comic.

The *Quijote* is an attack on the irrational preoccupations of society and on the negative aspects of the thought and the literature of the times. It was Cervantes' mission to remove knight-errantry from the Christian spirit and imagination, and thus it was necessary to return Don Quijote to sanity after a dream: he had to face the reader under the natural and inherent misfortune of our existence; he also came to condemn all the lies and extravagances which had seduced him and ruined his mind. Thus Cervantes ingeniously uses a dream to condemn the madness of his era and then has Don Quijote symbolically confess the dreams of the world.

The hero's mad efforts and his continual anxiety are the image of the human heart in this vale of tears, while Dulcinea, platonic love, always invisible, is the shadow of our hopes and dreams, the truth of human perfection, always yearned for but never achieved.

The *Quijote's* superiority is attributable to four factors: first, it belongs to all ages; second, its very lack of plan; third, its spontaneous episodes and natural outcomes; and fourth, its style and language.

Salvá, who found that Cervantes attacked spiritualism, was mistaken. Cervantes' barbs were directed at the evil influences of chivalric novels which led to rash behavior. Ríos and Pellicer, who argued that Cervantes imitated the classics, and Voltaire, who said that the *Quijote* was an imitation of Ariosto's *Orlando furioso*, were inaccurate.

Five episodes that critics have attacked as not believable are: Grisóstomo-Marcela, the departure of the Priest and the Barber, the intervention of Sansón Carrasco, Sancho's government, and the *Curioso impertinente*. These episodes are largely based on scenes from chivalric novels, which Cervantes was avowedly parodying. Salvá, who attacks Part II as inferior, and Clemencín, who criticizes the lack of unity, the unrelated episodes, the defective language, and the lack of proper chronology in the novel, were overzealous. In addition, Martínez López' unfavorable remarks about the discourse on arms and letters are unpardonable.

In the *Quijote*, Cervantes gave Spanish a true, frank, and simple native style. Salvá is censurable for stating that Cervantes was affected; the so-called affected passages are clear imitations of the language of chivalric novels.

537. *Aniversario CCLXII de la muerte de Cervantes*. Santiago de Chile: Imp. de La Estrella de Chile, 1878. 159 pages. [Libro compuesto para honrar la memoria del príncipe de los ingenios por sus admiradores de Chile.]

[This work begins with a sketch of Cervantes' life punctuated by copies of the author's baptismal documents. It then includes Crescente Errázuriz' argument that Cervantes sought to purify the literary tastes of the times by introducing realism into his works, B. Vicuna Macknenna's discussion of his own trips to La Mancha, Antonio Espineira's imaginary description of Cervantes' encounter with other great literary figures on Mount Parnassus, a fictional account of Cervantes' burial, and poems by J. A. Soffia and Francisco Concha Castillo, among others.

Of particular interest is E. Nercasseau Morán's selection, "Sobre este libro," which praises the universality of Cervantes' work and examines various theories concerning the identity of the author of the spurious *Quijote*. This piece also discusses the purpose of the *Quijote* and critics who have regarded Cervantes as a theologian, moralist, philosopher, geographer, legislator, navigator, doctor, and political economist. In addition, Morán reviews various editions and translations, noting that as of January 1, 1878 there were a total of 1,385 editions of Cervantes' novel, and briefly discusses illustrations of the *Quijote* as well as imitations.]

538. Arboleda, Sergio. "Cervantes y *El Quijote.*" *Universidad* (Panamá) 22 (1943): 103-42. [Originally published in *Repertorio Colombiano* 2 (1879).]

While Cervantes indeed reflects Spain and his times, this is not the greatest of his claims to glory. He is the only man since Homer to shake off the heavy yoke of imitation and create entirely on his own.

The *Quijote* is a true epic, though in prose, and what is more, a creation devoid of those fictions and exaggerations that clash with the Christian spirit of modern civilization. For instance, Cervantes, unlike Quevedo, is not sarcastic toward society and seeks to correct and moralize, not to injure and scorn, as do Voltaire and Molière, or to be vindictive, as is Dante. Cervantes has a lofty opinion of human dignity, and there is no unsympathetic figure in his novel.

Cervantes took his characters from the world at large, and they are not caricatures. We continue to be persuaded that Don Quijote and Sancho not only lived but continue to live. We are friendly with them and we know them better than we know many of our intimate acquaintances.

Also admirable is the collective truth of the *Quijote*, that is, Cervantes' ability to eschew character *types* which exaggerate or diminish real people, and to personify, instead, all of humanity in his two protagonists while offering in his minor personages all of sixteenth-century Spanish society.

Regarding the political ramifications of the novel, an inherent aspect of every literary work, it is not enough that it reflects the ideas of its era; a work must also satisfy some social necessity. And what the society of Cervantes' time, a society of censorship and religious intolerance and one that lacked science, industry, and arts, needed above all was laughter. Cervantes' life—his lack of education, his poverty, his imprisonment, and his menial jobs—was also influential. And yet, while his very imprisonment gave him the idea for the *Quijote*, his noble-hearted nature enabled him to create a sympathetic hero.

Cervantes had a gift for transmitting his own spirit and feelings to the figures he created. Thus, underlying the madness of Don Quijote is a moral sketch of his author, a man of greatness of soul, a love of virtue, good sense, and loyalty and honor, all accompanied by exquisite taste and an intimate feeling for both moral and literary beauty. Surrounded by a society of utilitarianism, greed, passion, and idleness, Cervantes could only observe, meditate, remain silent, and suffer. A successful Cervantes in a free and open society would have had neither the occasion nor the time to produce his masterpiece.

539. Martínez Silva, Carlos. "La política del *Quijote*." In *Escritos varios*. Bogotá: Editorial Kelly, 1954, pp. 37-68. [Discurso de recepción en la Academia Colombiana, el 23 de abril de 1879. First published in *Repertorio Colombiano* 2 (May, 1879).]

For many years the *Quijote* was regarded as either an amusing book or as an attack on novels of chivalry, but there is growing interest in this and other works as a compendium of the customs, vices, preoccupations, and dominant ideas of their times.

Interest in political activity was not great in the era of Cervantes, since democracy was not then an important element in society. However, we cannot therefore assume that people did not notice the evils of bad government or desire reform. Nor can we assume that a man of Cervantes' intelligence, imagination, and genius ignored politics. Various passages from the *Quijote*, including the visit of the Priest and the Barber to Don Quijote's home and his advice to Sancho on being a successful governor, demonstrate Cervantes' interest in government. Cervantes' decision to allow Sancho to be a governor (the opposite of the ideal recommended) shows the novelist's awareness of the danger of suddenly lifting the lowly to power. The Squire further symbolizes the struggle between duty and self-interest, as well as bestial instinct versus ecstatic flight of the angel.

The utilitarian Sancho is a caricature of the political figures of the reign of Philip III, such as Olivares, Lerma, Uceda, and Villalonga, who were, in essence, greedy men whom Cervantes would have liked to attack vehemently. But because of the restraints of his society, he could only indirectly criticize them through irony. There are also inconsistencies in the character of Sancho, who is by turns selfish and unselfish. After the Squire has viewed the earth from the heavens in the Clavileño episode, his passion for power is diminished and he sees human matters in a broader and deeper way.

As for the role of the military in society, Cervantes viewed the institution basically as a peace-keeping force designed to preserve order and eliminate confusion. The reason for this was that Cervantes saw the evil inclinations of man as a perpetual threat to society and found great wisdom in maintaining order.

540. Montalvo, Juan. "El *buscapié* (prólogo)." In *Capítulos que se le olvidaron a Cervantes. Ensayo de imitación de un libro inimitable.* Barcelona: Montaner y Simón, 1898. 340 pages. [First published in Besançon: J. Jacquin, 1882.]

Cervantes' novel serves two purposes. The first is the obvious desire to debunk the books of chivalry; the second is visible to only a few: to embody truth and virtue in the form of a caricature. While Cervantes stated only one purpose in writing his masterpiece he built a statue with two faces, one looking at the real world, the other looking at the ideal.

Don Quijote is a disciple of Plato with a cape of folly; he is the noble, virtuous, and imaginative man in opposition to the ordinary real man, Sancho. Together they represent the two natures of mankind—spirit versus senses—, and although Cervantes criticizes the baser side with a smile, he also demonstrates that the lower one is just as necessary to life.

The special knowledge of music, cuisine, law, astrology, insanity, medicine, theology, and poetry that many critics have attributed to Cervantes was not necessary to a great novelist; he simply knew the human heart.

Various writers have imitated Cervantes, such as Calderón, Guillén de Castro, Meléndez Valdés, and Gómez Labrador, and many philosophical conclusions can be drawn from the *Quijote*. Especially important are the contrasts of Don Quijote's folly and Sancho's rascality, and the work's ability to move even melancholic temperaments.

541. Varona, Enrique José. "Cervantes." In *Los estudios cervantinos de Enrique José Varona.* New York: Senda Nueva de Ediciones, 1979, pp. 37-65. [An editorial note states that this item was a lecture delivered at the Nuevo Liceo de La Habana on April 23, 1883 and that it was also published that same year by Soler. Alba-Buffill states that this lecture can be found in Varona's *Seis conferencias,* Barcelona: Gorjas Y Cia, 1887, in *Revista de Cuba* 13 (1883), in the 1936 "edición oficial" of Varona's works, and in *Revista Cubana* 22 (1947), p. 7 et seq.]

Personal elements always enter into a novel like the *Quijote*. But more important than this and the faithful picture of the Spain it presents is the human problem that Cervantes develops: Don Quijote and Sancho are always fighting yet always united, contradicting each other yet always in agreement, seeing at the same time the double aspect of things. The adventures of the Knight and the Squire are a transparent symbol of human life, showing the lofty passions of the human spirit and raising the question, what does failure matter if a man struggles for the truth?

542. Armas y Cárdenas, José de. *El Quijote de Avellaneda y sus críticos.* Havana: M. de Villa, 1884. 90 pages. [As summarized by Rius II, p. 264, and by Manuel Pérez Beato, p. 26.]

Avellaneda's *Quijote* is one of the best novels of the seventeenth century but wretched when compared to Cervantes' original.

543. Nercasseau y Morán, Enrique. "Estudio de un capítulo del *Quijote.*" *Revista de Artes y Letras* (Santiago de Chile) 6 (1884): 333-51. [As summarized by Juan Uribe-Echevarría, p. 168.]

[Nercasseau examines the adventure of the lions, pointing out sources for this episode and observing that many chivalric heroes had the name "Caballero de los Leones."]

544. Sarmiento, Domingo Faustino. *Obras*, I, pp. 223, 255, 337; II, pp. 48, 302; X, p. 64. Vols. I and II were published in Santiago de Chile: Imp. Gutenberg, 1885-1887; vol. X in Buenos Aires: Imp. Mariano Moreno, 1896. [As noted by Emilio Carilla in "Cervantes en la Argentina," *Revista de Educación* (La Plata, Arg.) 3 (1958): 479-81.]

While Cervantes' language is admirable, it should not always be followed as an exclusive model.

545. Piñeyro, Enrique. "Entre mis libros—Carta al Director de la *Revista Cubana.*" *Revista Cubana* 3 (February 28, 1886). [As briefly summarized by Manuel Pérez Beato, p. 25.]

[Piñeyro refers to documents about Cervantes published by J. M. Asensio, as well as to the supposed portrait of Cervantes and to Cervantes' petition to Philip III, seeking a position in the New World. He also criticizes the corrections made by Hartzenbusch.]

546. Sanhueza Lizardi, Rafael. *Viaje de España.* Santiago de Chile: Imp. Victoria, 1886, pp. 118-21. [As summarized by Juan Uribe-Echevarría, pp. 173-74.]

Cervantes conceived the figure Don Quijote while he was imprisoned at Argamasilla de Alba and wrote the *Quijote* to avenge the slights he had received. Sismondi is correct in finding the *Quijote* the saddest of the manifestations of the human spirit.

547. Caicedo Rojas, José. "El 23 de abril." *La Caridad* (Botogá) 3, no. 37 (April 26, 1887): 579. [An article briefly summarized by Rafael Torres

Quintero in *Boletín del Instituto Caro y Cuervo* 4 (1948): 47.]
[The article generally praises Cervantes and Shakespeare, comparing
their lives and work.]

548. Nolasco Cruz, Pedro. [Article concerning Quevedo in *Revista de
Artes y Letras* (Santiago de Chile) 9 (1887): 603. As briefly noted by Juan
Uribe-Echevarría, p. 175.]
    What separates Quevedo from Cervantes is a lack of creative genius.

549. Barros Grez, Daniel. "Apuntes para escribir la historia del
apólogo." [A manuscript of 1888 briefly summarized by Juan Uribe-
Echevarría, p. 173.]
    [Pages 402 to 423 contain a biography of Cervantes and an attack on
    Avellaneda's *Quijote*. Pages 424 to 438 analyze various apologues in Cervan-
    tes' *Quijote* and in his *Novelas ejemplares*.]

550. Sánchez de Fuentes y Paláez, Eugenio. *Determinación del género
literario en que aparece El Quijote y significación artística, científica y crítica de esta
obra*. Havana: La Propaganda Literaria, 1888. 27 pages. [Dated August
20, 1885.]
    Books of chivalry offended Cervantes' tastes because of their false
idealism, which clashed with the social and political organization of the
contemporary state based on the Renaissance sense of realism. Cervantes
objected to such works because instead of uplifting feelings and teaching
men, they encouraged credulity and superstition, confused rational bravery
with capricious temerity, inspired false ideas about man's duties, and gave
way to chimera and to a pitiful corruption of customs. And yet the *Quijote* is
neither an epic nor essentially a satire. It is primarily a novel in which the
author is a poet, moralist, and philosopher, a work of art in which many
elements are molded into a mirror of life, including virtue, vice, bravery,
illusion, and the great and the small. Although instinctively concentrating
in his novel on the character of the Spanish people, Cervantes is a universal
writer.
    The novel was a genre first cultivated in Spain in such works as *Cárcel de
amor, La Celestina*, and *Guzmán de Alfarache*, and with subject matter, plot,
characters, dialogue, and style the *Quijote* has all the standard elements of a
novel. Yet it is neither a book of ideas in advance of the author's time nor an
allegory of idealism and realism. Merely because Cervantes, as a superior
man, condemns the abuses of his era, we cannot assume that he was a
learned man or, as some assert, a freethinker or revolutionary. What we do
know from a literary point of view is that the *Quijote* destroyed the
corrupting books of chivalry, contributed to wholesome reading habits, and
encouraged the use of intelligence, the primary element of civilization.

551. Saldías, Adolfo. *Cervantes y el Quijote*. Buenos Aires: Félix Lajouane, 1893. 277 pages.

The *Quijote* is a condemnation of political absolutism, and Cervantes is a champion of liberty. The work is a protest against tyranny, and Sancho the representative of pure democracy in conflict with conservative aristocracy (Don Quijote).

Sancho represents the salutary common sense of the people and their capacity to govern themselves, while Don Quijote embodies authoritarian preoccupations, incongruent and even monstrous from the point of view of good government. Important is Sancho's mockery of the nobility and its privileges, but Sancho is also guilty of plebeian impatience, the urge to reach the top in one leap. With Sancho's increased maturity and dominance, he becomes a synthesis of pure democracy and authoritarian aristocracy. In support of this argument is the implication of the cave of Montesinos episode: Disenchantment with the absolutism of nobility is inevitable and hence becomes a necessary force in favor of democracy.

Concerning the influence of the *Quijote* in the Americas, especially in Argentina, the *Quijote* and the works of Paley, Paine, and Moreno were the books most cited during the movement of independence (c. 1810). The men most involved in the movement of 1810 were the very same men as those who reread the *Quijote* with the most fervor, men such as Moreno, Funes, and Padre Castañeda, to whom Cervantes was a friendly echo of liberty. The thread has not been broken since 1810, for men such as Vélez Sarsfield and General Mitre have continued to read Cervantes' novel as a political tract affirming personal liberty.

Other Criticism

552. Palmblad, Vilhelm Fredrik. "Sobre la novela." *Phosphorus*, 1812. [As cited and discussed by Gustaf Fredèn in *Don Quijote en Suecia*, Madrid: Insula, 1965, pp. 31-33.]

The *Quijote* is the perfection of the medieval romance. Those who see Cervantes' novel as merely a trivial pastime, an ingenious satire of books of chivalry, are sadly mistaken.

553. Stiernstolpe, Jonas Magnus. "Preface" to his Swedish translation of *Don Quijote*, 1818-1819. [As cited and discussed by Gustaf Fredèn in *Don Quijote en Suecia*, Madrid: Insula, 1965, pp. 33-37.]

The *Quijote* is a lively and far-reaching satire directed against all types of fools, including educated and learned people, priests, judges, unreasoning readers and bad orators. Cervantes' aim was in part to correct the evil influence of chivalric novels on the customs and thought of Spain. Don Quijote is a good-hearted fanatic who is reasonable when chivalry is not involved. His advice to Sancho on governing is useful. Sancho himself is a perfect example of the lower classes: credulous, superstitious, cowardly, restless, ignorant, and gluttonous.

554. Hagberg, Carl August. *Cervantès et Sir Walter Scott, parallèle littéraire.* Lund: C. F. Berling, 1838. 16 pages.

There are great differences in the works of Scott and Cervantes, but each writer is deserving of praise. Scott's greatness is seen in the light of realism and the technical achievements of the Cervantine novel. Cervantes ridicules the romanticism of the Middle Ages, the glory of chivalry, and the cult of the woman, but there is a profound gravity beneath his work's apparent satire. This makes it a book of supreme irony. By introducing realism into the novel, Cervantes destroys the chivalric novel. Also, Cervantes makes way for the historical novel, of which Scott is the best exponent.

Scott looks back to the Middle Ages, but not as Cervantes does, for all the perversity of that time disappears in Scott. Like Cervantes, he introduces realism into his novels, but it is a reality of the highest form, couched in idealism. Scott gives the reader a historical tableau of living characters drawn naturally and reaching the interior truth of man and events. His historical characters are unique, even undefinable, but the reader becomes acquainted with them intimately. Mary Stuart, Charles I, and Richard the Lion-Hearted are three of Scott's most brilliant figures.

Love is a central theme in Scott's works. There is also a guarded sacredness about societal institutions. Scott knows and respects all human passions. His creations, furthermore, are profound and conceived with new life and fresh intelligence, not with the blind romanticism of which he has been accused. Thus, while there are many contrasts between Scott and Cervantes, one finds in both the conceptual genius common to great artists.

555. Latino Coelho, José Maria. *Cervantes*. Second edition. Lisbon: Santos & Vieira, 1925, pp. 35-148. [First edition, 1919, Lisbon: Emprêsa Fluminense. From articles in *O Panoramo* 10 (1853).]

The *Quijote* was begun at Argamasilla. Cervantes did not write merely to attack and destroy ridiculous books of chivalry. He had a more elevated and philosophical purpose: to satirize the vices of his times and the corruption of the society that so humiliated him.

Both the Antonio Ruidíaz *Buscapié* as well as the later Adolfo de Castro version are pertinent. The former regarded the lost pamphlet as an attack on certain contemporaries of Cervantes; the latter is largely a literary commentary. Castro's hoax has been exposed by Bartolomé José Gallardo, who condemned Castro's prank. But it is not advisable to abandon the *Buscapié* tradition altogether.

556. Oliveira Martins, Joaquim Pedro. *Historia de civilização ibérica*. Lisbon: Livraria Bertrand, 1879. [Translated into English by Aubrey F. G. Bell as *A History of Iberian Civilization*, New York: Cooper Square Publishers, Inc., 1969. Passage excerpted and discussed in Alberto Xavier's *Dom Quixote (Análise crítica)*, Lisbon: Portugalia, 1942, pp. 236-46.]

Cervantes announced the decline of Spain to an audience that would not listen. Spain had rejected Europe and withdrawn into the intimate recesses of its now decadent genius. The country had grown rigid and stale following the days of its expansion. Spain's gallant spirit had been perverted; it was a country ravaged by Jesuitism and intolerance. The gold of the New World had filled the people with corruption. Nevertheless the country applauded its own suicide.

Gil Vicente and Cervantes are historical analysts who were not heeded. Spaniards of Cervantes' time saw the Don Quijote figure as a satire on the knights of old; the book was merely a learned trifle. But Cervantes' target was the obstinacy of a heroism no longer significant. Cervantes himself had been attacked by this mania, and now, old and disillusioned, he revived the old humor of the clowns of Spanish drama and produced a work of genius.

The dualism of Spain, stated Cervantes, was reflected in his own life as he went from hero to clown, and he ended by condemning utterly the Spanish character, which he saw in himself.

Author Index

Subject Index